COUNCIL
OF EUROPE

CONSEIL
DE L'EUROPE

INTERCULTURAL LEARNING IN THE CLASSROOM

CASSELL COUNCIL OF EUROPE SERIES

This series is the result of a collaboration between the Council of Europe and Cassell. It comprises books on a wide range of educational material, drawn largely from seminars and research which have been initiated and sponsored by the Council of Europe.

TITLES IN THE SERIES

Intercultural Learning in the Classroom

Crossing Borders

Helmut Fennes and Karen Hapgood

CASSELL

London and Washington

Cassell
Wellington House   PO Box 605
125 Strand   Herndon
London WC2R 0BB   VA 20172

The authors and publisher wish to thank EFIL, the Intercultural Centre, Vienna, and the Council of Europe, Strasbourg, for permission to reprint material from their workshops and publications.

British Library Cataloguing-in-Publication Data
A catalogue record for this book is available from the British Library.

ISBN 0-304-32685-2

Typeset by Action Typesetting Ltd, Gloucester
Printed and bound in Great Britain by Redwood Books, Trowbridge, Wiltshire

Contents

List of Exercises

Preface

The European Federation for Intercultural Learning (EFIL) is the umbrella body for AFS organizations in more than twenty European countries. The European AFS organizations have a long history of organizing exchanges for young people at secondary school level through the AFS Year Programme and other school-based activities. This relationship with schools and young people served as the impetus for establishing a study group to research the development of intercultural learning materials.

During the research period of the study group, EFIL held a number of seminars with the support of the European Youth Foundation and the European Youth Centre of the Council of Europe. These meetings, which drew on the expertise of teachers and AFS staff and volunteers from all over Europe, as well as the Council of Europe's own Department of Education, Culture and Sport and the European Youth Centre, enabled EFIL to test its ideas and to assemble the creativity and experience of a wider intercultural network. The research and subsequent findings resulted in the document *Intercultural Learning Materials: A Tool for School Curricula* (1987).

Europe has changed in the meantime, and schools throughout the broader European region show an increased interest in exploring other cultures. EFIL has continued its collaboration with the Council of Europe and with schools and has further refined its training tools and methods. It now offers a number of services to schools interested in intercultural learning and global education, providing teacher and headteacher seminars and various intercultural training modules.

EFIL welcomes the opportunity to share its intercultural learning materials with teachers and students and wishes to acknowledge the work and vision of the study group whose research helped form the basis of this book. Both authors were part of the original group and, although Helmut Fennes left the organization in 1991 to pursue other opportunities in the intercultural field, Karen Hapgood remains actively involved with AFS.

The Federation of AFS Organisations in Europe

CHAPTER 1

A Rationale

'The real voyage of discovery is not in seeing new lands but in seeing with new eyes.'

Marcel Proust

This book addresses the need and opportunity to prepare pupils for living in a wider Europe. Pupils at school today are likely to take part of their further education in another European country tomorrow. Living and working throughout Europe will be the norm, not the exception, and to do this requires preparation. Guided experiential learning is the key to what follows, not facts. Knowing historical dates, being able to cite the names and significance of national figures, appreciating the periods of art which span European history and geography – these are important. They will not, however, wholly serve young people today when they wish to further their studies, understand the news, apply for a job, be transferred to another country for their work, or simply live in another part of Europe.

The activities mentioned above – higher education, jobs, living – are deemed to be 'adult' by nature. We prepare for these activities, primarily at school. This preparation has to date taken place in the context of a single national culture and environment. The facts of history, important personages, periods of art, have been presented in the confines of a national framework. The process of preparing young people for study, work and life has been integrated into the mainstream of national education systems.

The original title of this book was *Crossing Borders*, but this phrase does not adequately describe its contents. Crossing physical borders is increasingly easy. Between some member states of the European Union there are no border controls; a passport is no longer required to move between the Netherlands, Belgium and Germany. Crossing cultural borders is something else. Is it possible to go from Leiden to Ludwigshaven for a meeting and to understand the outcome of a day's deliberations? Is it enough that countless school classes spend a week in a school and community in another country? Both situations are a beginning but more is

1

required than the ease of physically crossing borders to achieve a successful meeting outcome or understanding and appreciation of another school environment.

Now, in the 1990s, young people are confronted with differences as well as opportunities when they contemplate a wider market-place or living environment across borders. These differences may be backed up by stereotypes and prejudices. These, in turn, are compounded by the lack of ways to communicate – not only because the language may be unknown to the young person but also because the cultural factors involved must be translated and understood if response is to be effective.

Confronting differences, understanding our prejudices, recognizing stereotypes as what they are, finding ways to communicate – this learning is done through process, practice and reflection. There are no 'right' answers; an examination would not tell us that a pupil passed or failed. There are ways to find out about differences, to learn more about prejudices and stereotypes, to learn how to communicate effectively with others who communicate differently, to know oneself as others do. These are known as intercultural learning.

THE EUROPEAN ENVIRONMENT

The Europe in which teachers and parents (and the authors) have grown up has changed dramatically in a very short time. From 1 January 1993, a single market has become a reality for European Union member states, but few people can articulate what that means. The European Free Trade Association (EFTA) members – Austria, Sweden, Norway, Iceland, Liechtenstein and Finland – entered that common trade market on 1 January 1994 as part of the European Economic Area (EEA). Finland, Austria and Sweden entered the EU in January 1995. In the aftermath of border openings throughout Eastern Europe, the EU is taking tentative but firm steps to recognize and involve all parts of the new Europe. The Council of Europe already counts 40 countries as members, an increase from 25 members seven years ago, with a waiting list to be considered. European institutions, then, have forged a greater economic interdependence. The networking required to make this happen has meant increased interaction between people from different cultural backgrounds.

Concurrent with the official movements are actions of a more pragmatic nature. Students in European Union member states may elect to take part of their tertiary studies in another member state under the aegis of the ERASMUS programme. Vocational training qualifications are recognized among member states, so that an apprentice with a set of qualifications from one member state is able to seek professional experience in another member state.

Additionally, when we speak of litres of liquid or metres of material, safety standards or copyright regulations, these are being harmonized throughout Europe. This means, in the short term, adjustment and new learning for all Europeans; in the long term it will mean greater ease for living and working in all of Europe. This harmonization or 'Europeanization' is not a new idea.

Umberto Eco has referred to the quest for the perfect language in the history of Europe, the search for the Holy Grail, the utopian ideal of harmony or peace. Whether trying to resolve conflicts between Catholic and Protestant or among Jew, Muslim and Christian, the effort to bring political and religious harmony in Europe has been a persistent theme in its history. The European Union and the Council of Europe are twentieth-century institutional manifestations of this quest – a concern to find a European identity, to make European citizens, to belong to Europe.

The reader can well appreciate that *all* is not yet harmony in *all* of Europe. At the same time as movements towards integration are taking place, other contradictory or fragmenting activity is occurring. Xenophobia, racism and nationalism continue to exist side by side with movements of harmony. Homes which accommodate migrants are burned, parliaments act to limit immigration. Political boundaries fixed after World War II become unfixed; atmospheres of racist violence are perpetrated and sustained by prejudice; nationalism is used to define and defend narrower or new-found identities; barriers with respect to migrants and refugees continue to be built and hamper the development of multicultural communities throughout Europe.

Pupils will study today, and will work and live tomorrow, in a Europe which simultaneously experiences integration and fragmentation. Mobility has created enlarged opportunities to study and work abroad while people fear the loss of their cultural and national identities in a larger Europe governed by the European Union. In Germany, change has been very rapid; the old borders and all that those borders encompassed have been torn down; a new order is not yet fully realized. The vision of 'building a European house' conflicts with the charge that what this amounts to is 'fortress Europe'. Both trends exist. There is an imperative to support integration, the quest for the holy grail, and the positive aspects of fragmentation.

APPROACHES TO BORDERS

There are a number of approaches to crossing borders. The common market has established and enabled, indeed encourages, the free flow of capital, goods, services and labour. At one level this is understandable, as the transnational lifestyle, whether it be regarding music, fashion, food and drink or furnishings, has become nearly indistinguishable from one country to another. Advertising agencies talk about 'global ads', which appeal in the same manner in Leeds, Caen, Gøteborg or Oporto, as well as Osaka, São Paolo, Chicago or Lagos.

Linked to European integration and the subsequent increasing interdependence of European economies is the need for politicians and bureaucrats to meet frequently to negotiate and agree common policies and standards, whether these negotiations are concerned with a common currency, a common agriculture policy, training equivalents or standards for electric plugs.

The media – the evening news, the latest film, this week's soap opera episode or sporting event – all enter the immediacy and intimacy of our homes. The news brings first-hand reporting from towns and villages in Bosnia. It enables a view of daily parliamentary democracy at work. The cinema offers many films from Hollywood but also from France, India, Latin America and Africa. The soaps, be they Spanish, Australian, French or British, depict another view of our cultures. Sporting events – a grand prix at Monaco, tennis at Wimbledon, the Tour de France, the World Cup – come live to our screens at breakfast, dinner or Sunday lunch. With satellite technology the British can tune in to French broadcasting, the Belgians have a choice of Dutch, French, German or Luxembourg stations. Borders are crossed simply by turning on the television. The intensity of intercultural viewing means that our daily lives are touched and influenced by events and entertainment in other countries and cultures. The geopolitical borders have little import to the media.

Tourism represents yet another approach. See a superficial Europe, eat at restaurants which promote a *menu touristique*, stay in an enclave of sand, sea and sun, but don't meet the inhabitants, tour monuments and galleries to view the relics of a past culture, emphasize the past. Tourism rarely permits contact with the living culture of today.

ANOTHER APPROACH

The recitation of some realities in the Europe of today suggests that borders are being crossed permanently as if they were non-existent, that people communicate and cooperate across cultural and national borders without difficulty, that there is a sense of European unity. We know that this is not the case. We know there is resistance to giving up national symbols like national currencies. We are confronted with a lack of understanding of people and their situation in other countries, as can be seen from discussions concerning agriculture. Respect for lifestyles other than one's own is still the exception.

Intercultural competence does not occur incidentally or by accident. One does not become interculturally literate by wearing Italian or French clothes (if you live in Austria or England), driving a VW (if you live in Portugal), reading a French book (if you live in Scotland), or listening to British music (if you live in Denmark). Nor is it enough to learn about other cultures. There is another way to experience a wider Europe, indeed a wider world; a more natural and intensive way which integrates learning about differences, understanding of prejudice and stereotyping, the attainment of skills to communicate effectively and appropriately.

If pupils are to be prepared to live and work in a wider Europe, they need more than holidays in the sun or soap operas that perpetuate stereotypes. Pupils need to be interculturally competent: to cross borders with confidence; to be socially at ease in different cultural environments; to understand differences both in others and as others see them; to gain in communication skills, both verbal and non-verbal. The classroom is identified as the environment in which such learning should take place. The resources available – the grouping of youth in one place, the parallel and potential networks of education systems within Europe – conspire to make school the key focus for intercultural learning.

We will argue for intercultural learning to be integrated into school curricula. It is practical and experiential by nature, a part of social learning. The school is the principal environment outside home and family where children are prepared for adulthood. As adulthood will increasingly require intercultural competence so that advantage can be taken of opportunities for living and working, it is logical and appropriate that this part of social learning be integrated into the school and class-room. Intercultural learning is long-term. One cannot swot for three hours and change stereotypes and prejudices. Acquiring non-verbal language skills can be just as time-consuming as learning to speak another language.

Intercultural learning does not happen by accident. A chance encounter between two individuals from different cultural groups, or between two groups from differ-ent cultures, does not imply or guarantee that the individuals or groups will be able to understand each other, be able to communicate effectively. Intercultural learning requires a structure; it means planning and preparation; it needs monitoring and guiding; and it necessitates evaluation to realize what has been learned and what change has occurred. It demands the resources and expertise to be found in the educational environment. Today's pupils will live and work tomorrow in a world that demands very different social skills and attitudes from those promulgated and taught yesterday. This approach argues for intercultural learning as an opportunity for educational development and growth in the European multicultural society.

This book enables the reader to be more effective at planning, integrating, implementing and, most of all, facilitating intercultural learning in the school en-vironment. It will be useful for anyone who is confronted with intercultural encounters, who is concerned with a multicultural society or who is interested in intercultural issues.

CHAPTER 2

The Fear of the Foreign

In recent years the media throughout Europe have reported events and actions which discriminate against foreigners and examples which promulgate a fear of the foreign – residency requirements for migrants that are not applied to natives, discriminatory treatment of seasonal workers, illegal and destructive acts against refugees. These news stories, as well as the experiences of individuals, demonstrate an increase in both xenophobia and ethnocentrism.

Fear of the foreign seems to be a universal phenomenon. Usually this fear has little to do with an actual threat from the foreign, but relates to a fantasy that such a threat exists, an attitude not based in reality. Dietmar Larcher describes fear of the foreign as a historic heritage.[1] It is in us like a piece of nature while not being natural. Although the fear of the foreign and, subsequently, xenophobia and ethnocentrism have been a tradition for thousands of years, they cannot be explained as natural phenomena.

Fear of the foreign is not a fate or destiny that cannot be changed. Unlike animals, human beings are able to suppress and cultivate fear and subsequent aggression. The commandment 'you shall love your neighbour as yourself' (as well as the admonishment 'you shall love your enemies') has raised a demand which has strongly influenced the cultural evolution of the occident. In his cultural theories, Freud refers to this commandment as the greatest challenge for culture to overcome the barrier that is the constitutional disposition of human beings for aggression towards each other.[2] According to Freud, the fateful issue of humankind is if and to what degree it succeeds in its cultural evolution in controlling the disturbance of coexistence through the human instinct for aggression and self-destruction. It seems that a modern society based on freedom, justice and democracy can only be created if it is possible to overcome fear and rejection of the foreign.

Julia Kristeva goes a step further.[3] Referring to Freud, she writes that what we are afraid of when confronted with the foreign is in us. Our fear and rejection of the foreign is in fact caused by a fear of what is in ourselves, what has been suppressed so far as part of our cultural effort. Fear of the foreign is a projection of

6

fear of the 'dark' areas in ourselves. When rejecting the foreign we are rejecting what is threatening us within ourselves.

Along the same lines, Mario Erdheim writes that fear of the foreign can also be caused by experiences during separation from one's mother.[4] The fact that the foreign always implies separation continues to be a source of feelings of fear and guilt, which can be avoided by rejection of the foreign – by xenophobia. The foreign occupied with fear becomes a scapegoat. Everything I dislike about myself and the people next to me – the evil parts of myself, the evil parts of my relationships to my mother, father, brothers, sisters, friends, foreigners – is projected on to the foreign. The foreign outside is the same as the foreign inside, which I do not want to perceive consciously.

Fear of the foreign can result in two different and contradictory reactions. One is the aversion to persons who represent the foreign – xenophobia. From this point of view, everything that is outside one's own culture is considered to be foreign – foreigners, cultural or ethnic minorities, and possibly homosexuals, persons with mental or physical disabilities, people with extreme political positions, men or women. Consequently, the relationship towards the foreign becomes one of defence against the threat attached to it.

The other possible reaction is referred to as exoticism, which is a specific form of xenophilia (love and adoration of the foreign). Exoticism is an idealistic glorification of the foreign. Typical examples of exoticism in Europe are the glorification of Native Americans or of other indigenous cultural groups in Africa, Asia or America. But the increasing tourism to exotic [sic] places in Asia, Africa and Latin America can also be interpreted as exoticism. The adoration of the foreign far away has no consequences for one's own life. One is not confronted with these foreigners in one's living environment or in one's workplace. Exoticism can be interpreted as idealistic glorification of the foreign sufficiently far away to compensate for the fear caused by the foreign or social change in the immediate environment and, thus, can be interpreted as escape from one's personal situation into idealism.[5] Xenophilia, though, becomes credible when it is applied not only to foreigners far away but also to those in one's own environment: refugees, migrants, cultural minority groups.

Nevertheless, the latent fear of the foreign does not automatically surface when the individual is confronted with the foreign. It depends on the socio–economic and psycho–social condition of the person. A teacher in secure employment does not feel as threatened by migrant workers as the industrial worker who is in danger of losing his/her job owing to recession.

It can be assumed that much of the xenophobia in Europe in recent years has resulted from instability caused by either recession in the Western European countries or the dramatic political, social and economic changes in Central and Eastern Europe. Stable (though disliked) systems that had lasted for more than forty years were abolished more or less overnight while the anticipated new systems were not yet in place and functioning. Industries and small businesses were closed down, and agricultural and food production was reduced to a minimum, resulting in severe unemployment. People perceive and experience the economic dominance of

Western Europe, where many companies consider Eastern and Central Europe as an economic investment region. The self-confidence and feeling of self-esteem of a whole generation has been shaken because what it worked for, for over forty years, is now considered to be worthless.

What is even more significant is that in those forty years of separation into different societies, different cultures evolved. Although there might be a common language, the separation resulted in different symbols, values, norms, patterns of behaviour and lifestyles, which could not be changed overnight. A longer process will be required to enable the culture to adapt and become compatible with the new situation. The result of all this is a high degree of economic and social instability and insecurity, which serves as a prerequisite for xenophobia.

For example, in the two states of former Czechoslovakia, the feelings of dislike towards language minorities, as well as towards the Gypsies,[6] have increased visibly during the course of the political, social and economic transformation. While the size of the cultural and ethnic groups involved is relevant, the threat is not. The language minorities have neither the intention nor the ability to influence the country in a dominant way. The Roma and Sinti have little intention to integrate into the majority culture. (Possibly there are elements in their lifestyle which are secretly or unconsciously perceived to be very attractive by members of the majority culture but are rejected because they do not comply with the norms of the majority culture. In a certain way, of course, this is a threat.)

Another aspect of the fear of the foreign occurs in wealthy countries in Western Europe, where people assume that they have a right to their wealth. The confrontation with foreigners who are not as wealthy, e.g. refugees and migrants, threatens the myth that their wealth is deserved, owing only to hard work, and that everyone has the same chance to achieve it. The destruction of that myth results in fear of the foreign and xenophobia. The fear is very simply that, if they acted according to their conscience (or feeling of guilt), they would not be able to maintain their level of wealth.

It is not only the collapse of the old order of Europe that has resulted in an increased appearance of fear of the foreign. It is also the structure and development of modern society. Modern technologies and their political organization lead to rapid social change. People have to adapt constantly to a changing environment: new working conditions, new mobility, new consumer behaviours, new lifestyles. Once they have adapted, innovation has changed the environment again. This is a permanent challenge for one's individual identity. Individual judgements and decisions are relinquished in favour of adaptation to the constraints of production processes and of changing society in general. This causes fear that individual identity is threatened; fear of becoming an outsider in society. Again, this fear is projected on to the foreign rather than dealt with in society, by engagement in its socio-political evolution.[7]

Another reason for the increased appearance of fear of the foreign is the fact that it is being misused to maintain and increase political power. This follows a very simple pattern. First, foreigners (migrants, refugees, ethnic and cultural minorities) are described as a threat to jobs, income, living conditions, cultural identity. This is not difficult since this fear is latent. An extreme view of the future, possibly contradicting known facts, can be drawn (e.g. a frequent argument used is that migrant workers are a burden on the economy, though in many countries the opposite is true). In a second step, a political solution is presented that 'rescues' the 'natives'[8] from the envisaged catastrophe and gains sympathy and allegiance from those people whose fear of the foreign has been nourished.[9] Since the 'problem' has actually not been caused by those it is projected on to, subsequent actions (e.g. legislative restrictions) have little or no effect. The fear remains and the politicians – at least for a while – can continue to act as saviours of the 'natives'. Political power is maintained, as is the dependency of the 'natives' on the politicians.

CONSEQUENCES OF XENOPHOBIA

As history tells us, there are many possible consequences of xenophobia. They depend on the specific setting of the cultural or ethnic groups involved as well as on socio-economic and political conditions.

The most drastic consequence is the *extermination* of the foreign represented. The best-known example of this is the genocide undertaken by the Nazis, which was directed not only at cultural and ethnic groups such as the Jews and gypsies but also at homosexuals, persons with disabilities and the political opposition. A very recent example is the genocide in former Yugoslavia, where in a number of villages and even in some regions one ethnic group exterminated another. Another recent example is the genocide of the Kurds in Iraq. There are numerous other examples: the genocide carried out by Stalin (mostly of his political enemies), the extermination of Native Americans in North and South America in the past as well as the ongoing massacres of Indians in Brazil, the whole history of colonization, the crusades and the Inquisition aimed at destroying the heathens, etc. In some instances, the (dominant) minority exterminated the (suppressed) majority.

Another result of xenophobia can be *expulsion* or *resettlement* of the minority group, or the *emigration* of the minority group owing to ongoing discrimination or threat – possibly the threat of being destroyed. Again, there are many examples of this, the most recent being the ethnic cleansing in former Yugoslavia, where people have been forced to leave under the threat of being killed, the result of which is more than two million refugees and displaced persons. After World War II the German population was banished from Central and Eastern Europe. Examples of forced resettlements include those of the Tatars under Stalin or Slovene-speaking Austrians expelled by the Nazis to provide living space for German-speaking people from Südtirol. During the Nazi regime, many people in Germany and Austria decided to emigrate to escape discrimination or threat from those in power – not only Jews, but also artists and members of the political opposition who were marked as enemies of the national culture.

Another result of xenophobia can be *segregation*, where the dominant group forces all those it perceives to be foreigners to live as a separate society. In extreme cases, the separation can be geographic, as with the reservations for Native

Americans in North America, but it implies a structural separation where interaction between the two societies is kept to a minimum and limited to formal and specific economic relations, while social interaction happens only within each society. Usually, the socio-economic structure of the suppressed society is incomplete and consists of farmers or workers and a few academics like teachers, while the resources are controlled by the dominant society.[10] A specific form of segregation is referred to as ethnopluralism, where the majority group allows the minority group to live according to its (cultural) values and traditions but separately and in a way that does not affect the majority group. Ethnopluralism can also be reciprocal, in that two or more groups agree to organize themselves as separately as possible. In many cases, the underlying belief seems to be that the more the groups live separately, the better they will understand each other.

An obvious example of segregation was the apartheid system in South Africa. But there are many examples from Europe where segregation is practised as ethnopluralism. In Südtirol many public institutions (such as schools) are separate for the German- and Italian-speaking populations. In Switzerland, four language groups live autonomously in relatively separate societies. In Belgium, the separation between the Flemish-, French- and German-speaking groups is reflected in different public administrations.

The strategy of segregation or ethnopluralism has been pursued by many governments with regard to smaller cultural or ethnic groups (including migrants) all over Europe. The smaller or more dispersed the minority group, the more its members travel between two worlds, e.g. they might have their job within the majority group but withdraw to the minority group for their social life.

Segregation can be chosen as a strategy of the minority to maintain its language, values and lifestyle and thus to prevent assimilation by the majority (though this decision is always interdependent with the way the majority relates to the minority, so it is not a really free choice). This could be said about gypsies, and most travellers, who all over Europe live in separate societies. In many cities (especially in the USA), ethnic groups such as the Chinese or the Italians have established their own 'town in town', Chinatown or Little Italy.

The most common result of xenophobia is *assimilation*. From the point of view of the suppressed group, this is the only way in which 'individuals may abolish the basis of their allegiance to the group which offends the hostile majority, in this way solving the problem by destroying the group in order to ensure the survival of the members of the group.'[11] From the point of view of the dominant majority, assimilation is another strategy for eliminating the foreign, forcing the minority to adopt its values, norms, patterns of behaviour, language and lifestyle. The foreign is absorbed and, thus, eliminated.

Strategies to implement assimilation can be anything from positive incentives in the areas of education, housing, employment, etc., to sanctions for non-conformity with the dominant group, the most drastic being extermination or expulsion. Only in the more recent past have some of these assimilation strategies been given up in favour of more cultural autonomy. Nevertheless, the outcome is mostly ethnopluralism rather than truly intercultural societies.

Although it is less drastic than extermination or expulsion, assimilation is still a painful process for those being assimilated. Enormous energy is required to suppress an old identity and to forget the language learned from childhood. This can also be seen in high rates of alcoholism and suicide in assimilated groups.[12]

DESIRABLE SOLUTIONS TO FEAR OF THE FOREIGN

The strategies of xenophobia as described are not desirable. Either they are aimed at the abolition of the foreign by killing or banishing those who represent it, or they are aimed at conquering the foreign through assimilation, or the strategy of segregation keeps the foreign at a secure distance with as little contact as possible.

Instead of trying to organize the existing multicultural societies in Europe in a democratic way, most states act as if they were national states with culturally homogeneous populations. They reintroduce mechanisms of discrimination, whose abolition had been an achievement of modern democratic societies. The physical violence applied against the foreign in the past has been replaced by the more subtle tool of structural force: restricted access to the labour market, restricted access to housing, residential permits required for 'foreigners' even if they were born in the country, etc. If discrimination against and rejection of foreigners and the reduction of human rights continue and if the relationship between 'natives' and 'foreigners' is increasingly polarized, the situation might escalate even more than it has done recently. The consequence could be that protecting the majority results in a reduction of democratic rights for the whole population.[13]

It is, therefore, necessary to find an approach where 'natives' and 'foreigners' peacefully develop situations on the basis of consensus and where they negotiate a means of coexistence. These solutions would have to ensure equal rights for all members of society, regardless of their being part of any ethnic, cultural or language group. A first step towards this would be intercultural education: an education aimed at a constructive encounter with the foreign, resulting in less racism and xenophobia; an education aimed at a critical view of ideologies and at an understanding of structural discrimination; an education aimed at the ability to empathize with, relate to and interact with the foreign; an education aimed at engagement in the process of developing a democratic multicultural society.

Notes and references

1   Dietmar Larcher, *Fremde in der Nähe*. Klagenfurt: Drava, 1991, p. 15.
2   Sigmund Freud, *Das Unbehagen in der Kultur* (1930). In *Kulturtheoretische Schriften*, Frankfurt/Main: S. Fischer Verlag, 1984, p. 267.
3   Julia Kristeva, *Fremde sind wir uns selbst*. Frankfurt/Main: Suhrkamp, 1990, p. 208.
4   Mario Erdheim, *Psychoanalyse und Unbewußtheit in der Kultur*. Frankfurt/Main: Suhrkamp, 1988, p. 259.
5   *Ibid.*, p. 260.

6   It should be noted that the gypsies call themselves 'Roma' or 'Sinti' depending on which tribe they belong to. In fact, in some countries the equivalent term to Gypsies is not appreciated by the Roma or Sinti.

7   Dietmar Larcher, *Fremde in der Nähe*, p. 24, p. 27.

8   The term is written in quotation marks because those referred to as 'foreigners' could be members of an indigenous minority or second-generation migrants. Instead, one could use the term 'members of the dominant national culture'.

9   Dietmar Larcher, *Fremde in der Nähe*, p. 16.

10   Dietmar Larcher, *Fremde in der Nähe*, p. 33.

11   Orlando Patterson, 'Context and choice in ethnic allegiance: a theoretical framework and Caribbean case study', in Nathan Glazer and Daniel P. Moynihan (eds), *Ethnicity: Theory and Experience*, Cambridge, MA: Harvard University Press, 1975, p. 313.

12   Dietmar Larcher, *Fremde in der Nähe*, p. 32.

13   *Ibid.*, p. 36.

CHAPTER 3

Culture

'And when I say form, I mean both what is seen and what isn't seen, namely, all her way of being Priscilla, the fact that fuchsia or orange is becoming to her, the scent emanating from her skin ... because she was born with a glandular constitution suited to giving off that scent ... because of everything she has eaten in her life, because of what is called culture, and also her way of walking and sitting down which comes ... from the way she has moved among those who move in the cities and streets where she's lived ... but also the things she has in her memory and also the forgotten things which still remain recorded somewhere in the back of the neurons ...'

Italo Calvino, *Time and the Hunter*, pp. 77–8

There are many ways of defining the concept of culture, all of which face the same dilemma: we are trying to reflect on something we are part of. Such a reflection will never be absolute. It will always be limited by the restricted view of our consciousness and our understanding. While it is difficult to reflect on the traits of the specific culture we are part of, it is even more difficult to comprehend the concept and essence of culture in a general sense.

An analogy can be drawn that to understand culture is like a fish trying to understand water – the water is something that a fish is surrounded by at all times, that it is part of and cannot get away from. Culture surrounds us at all times and, therefore, it is not possible to perceive one's own culture objectively. The way we think, the way we approach the understanding of the concept of culture, is affected by culture – by the water that surrounds us (as is the way this chapter as well as the whole book is written).

The existence of culture is to a large degree not noticed by those who are part of it – like the existence of water for fish (if one can speak of a 'consciousness' of fish). The existence of culture is only realized when we are confronted with the presence of something different. For the fish, this might be fresh water instead of sea water, or a different fauna or flora; for a human being this might be different norms or

13

lifestyles. In extreme cases, it is possible that one is not able to cope with this 'other' surrounding (culture/water). While for the fish the consequence might be death, for a human being this can result in 'culture shock'.

The analogy, though, only applies to a limited extent. A fish does not shape the water in which it swims, whereas culture is shaped by those who are part of it. Culture is not static but dynamic. It is in the process of permanent change, as is society. This change is determined not only internally but also by external influences, such as nature or other cultures.

THE ICEBERG CONCEPT OF CULTURE

A frequent approach to describing the concept of culture is the analogy to an iceberg, in that only a small part of it is visible (see Figure 1). A large portion of what constitutes culture is beyond or below our conscious awareness. This does not mean that it has less influence on our daily lives. We know how to act and behave according to it but we are not aware of it and subsequently cannot control it. We take culture as self-evident, like nature, and not as if it were a construction of our society. It is obvious for many cultures to nod for agreement and not to belch in

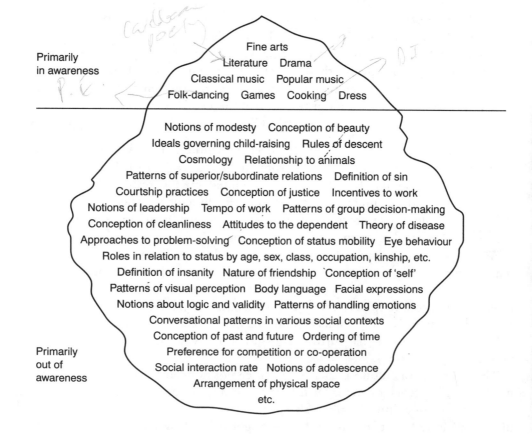

Figure 1 The iceberg concept of culture

14

public, but this is not the case in all cultures. We do not know that what is obvious could be different and that what seems to be obvious to us is not necessarily so to representatives of other cultures.

SOME ATTEMPTS TO DEFINE THE CONCEPT OF CULTURE

Georg Auernheimer describes the culture of a society as its means of communication and representation repertoire.[1] This includes the symbolic way of using objects in everyday life, the rituals of communication, the style of housing, etc. Culture enables the interpretation of social life and thus provides orientation for actions and behaviour. Auernheimer also describes culture as being dynamic and in the process of change. Since the elements of culture are symbolic, they allow ambiguous interpretations which can result in confusion or conflict when encountering representatives of different cultures.

According to Patterson, culture is an identifiable complex of meanings, symbols, values and norms that are shared consciously or unconsciously by a group of people.[2] Patterson makes a point that for members of a cultural group there need not be a conscious awareness of belonging to it, and that the meanings, symbols, values and norms shared by a cultural group can objectively be verified. Cultural groups are clearly distinct from an ethnic group for which a conscious sense of belonging to it is critical.

A more refined approach is taken by the Centre for Contemporary Cultural Studies at the University of Birmingham.

The 'culture' of a group or class includes the special and distinct lifestyle of this group or class, the meanings, the values and ideas as they are reflected in the institutions, in the social relationships, in systems of beliefs, in customs and traditions, in the use of objects, and in material life. Culture is the specific shape in which this material and this social organisation is expressed. Culture includes 'maps of meanings' which make these things understandable for its members. These 'maps of meanings' are not carried in one's brain. They are represented in the forms of the social organisation and relationships through which the individual becomes a 'social individual'. Culture is the way through which the relationships of a group are structured and shaped; but it is also the way they are experienced, understood, and interpreted. Therefore, men and women are shaped by society, culture, and history and by themselves. Existing cultural patterns constitute a kind of historical reservoir − a previously constructed 'field of possibilities' − which groups adopt, transform, and develop further. Each group does something with these initial conditions and, through this 'doing', culture is reproduced and conveyed. This practice, though, is taking place within the given field of possibilities and constraints.'[3]

The concept of culture referred to in these definitions is related to everyday culture. It is this culture of daily life which is the focus of this book about intercultural learning, not the fine art or permanent monuments that are too frequently referred to as the sum total of 'culture'. This culture includes everything that determines daily life: the way we eat and what we eat, the way we dress, maintain body hygiene, behave, take decisions, solve problems, greet and relate to others, the physical distance we keep from others, whether we show feelings or not, how we make love. Culture determines basic forms of social behaviour and actions. This includes everything from gestures (such as those to indicate agreement or disagreement) and more complex actions (such as how to establish contact with another person) to written rules and laws (such as how to run a meeting or an organization). Culture includes everything that determines interaction, relationships and social life within a society.

CULTURE AS A CONTINUUM

Larcher describes culture as a continuum (see Figure 2).[4] At one end are the cultural rules which are considered to be 'natural' and which are instinctively known and adhered to by everyone. They determine 'natural' behaviour, such as covering one's nakedness. But in fact this behaviour is not natural; it is a barrier against nature. It is some kind of 'second nature', which is actually determined by culture. This 'second nature' has been developed over thousands of years and is learned through socialization in early childhood. Usually, it is part of the collective or individual unconscious. For example, the length of time for which one can gaze into the eyes of a person of the other sex is regulated differently in different cultures, although the representatives of each culture perceive their rules as 'natural'. What is considered to be offensive in one culture might not even be registered in another. The distance between persons in an informal conversation is determined by culture. A distance considered to be 'natural' in one culture might be perceived to be threateningly close (or impolitely far) in another.

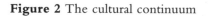

| Unconscious habits | Routine behaviour | Tradition | Custom | Rule | Law |

Figure 2 The cultural continuum

At the other end of the continuum are those rules which societies have consciously formulated to direct and control the relationships between its members, such as laws and religious commandments. These (usually written) rules can be enforced and their non–adherence is sanctioned. They are not considered to be natural, but made by society or revealed by God. They may reflect differences between cultures, such as between the Christian and the Muslim cultures.

Between these two contrasting ends of the continuum are all those cultural rules that seem to be evident but are by no means natural – routine behaviour, tradition, custom. They too have been formed by society and constitute cultural differences.

One of the authors remembers a trip he took to Southern Europe when he a student aged 23. When passing an attractive girl he would now and then look over his shoulder to catch a second view of that girl. He did it casually or secretly since, in his native country, this was the rule – a demonstrative look behind would not have been proper. At home, the girls would never or very rarely have a casual or secret look at boys for the same reason: it was not considered appropriate to look at a man openly. It would have been considered indecent and loose. Hiking through the mountains, he experienced girls turning to look at him. He was embarrassed because he was caught looking at girls, but the girls were not embarrassed – for them this was not improper behaviour.

Another typical example is greeting rituals. In some cultures it is customary that men embrace and kiss each other when greeting and that male friends walk hand in hand in the street. In other cultures, men would be disgusted by being kissed by other men. Even touching the skin of an unfamiliar person (as happens during a handshake) could cause uneasiness. This is an example where a feeling that is considered to be 'natural' has in fact been learned during socialization within a specific culture. Similarly, in some cultures it is common for men and women to kiss each other on the cheek when greeting, while in others this would be considered an affront.

While these habits are considered mostly to be 'natural', other rules, such as rules of politeness, are recognized as artificial. It is a more conscious act to stand up to greet a person, to dress formally for specific occasions, not to belch in public or to eat with the fork in the left hand and the knife in the right hand.

Larcher refers to the iceberg concept of culture in a more refined way. The visible parts of the iceberg are laws, rules, customs and traditions, while routine behaviour and unconscious habits are unconscious and thus not visible (see Figure 3). The line between the conscious and the unconscious is not a rigid one. It varies individually and depending on the respective society. This refers to the idea that culture is dynamic. It changes and evolves, as does society. While seven-eighths of

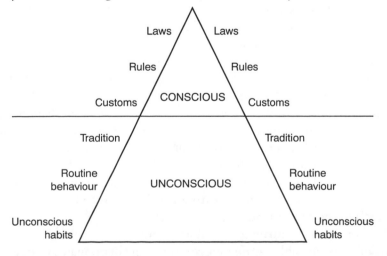

Figure 3 A refined iceberg of culture

the iceberg always remains invisible, this is not necessarily true for culture. New experiences (such as encounters with the foreign) and reflection can increase the conscious part of culture, while suppression can decrease it.

Larcher goes even further, saying that culture not only is changeable but has to be changed if it limits the freedom and justice of some of its members for the benefit of others. He rejects a concept of culture that considers it as a destiny which is attached to the individual as collective identity, and which determines his or her value and dignity.[5] Such a concept underlies the notion of 'national cultures', which aim at preservation and segregation of cultures, thus undermining the perspective of a society based on equality and individual freedom.

CULTURE AS MENTAL PROGRAMMING

Another approach is taken by Geert Hofstede, who refers to the patterns of thinking, feeling and potential acting learned through a lifetime as 'mental programs' and, in analogy to the way computers work, as 'software of the mind'.[6] Unlike a computer, however, a person can deviate from her or his mental programs and act in new and different ways. The programming only indicates which actions are likely and understandable, given one's past. According to Hofstede, most of the programming takes place in early childhood within the family, but it continues in one's social environment, in school and in the workplace. Since the programming is at least partly shared with people who live or lived within the same environment, culture is a collective phenomenon. In this sense, Hofstede defines culture as 'the collective programming of the mind which distinguishes the members of one group or category of people from another'.

Hofstede refers to three levels of mental programming. The first level is human nature, which is inherited and common to all human beings (in the computer analogy, it is the 'operating system', which determines one's physical and basic psychological functioning). The second level is culture, which is learned and is specific to a group or category. The third level is personality, which is inherited as well as learned and which one does not share with any other human being.

On this basis, Hofstede searched for ways to compare cultures and came up with the following areas in which cultural differences basically manifest themselves: symbols, heroes, rituals and values (see Figure 4). According to Hofstede, symbols are the most superficial manifestations of culture. Symbols can change – as culture changes – and their meaning is only recognized by those who share the culture. The next, deeper, level is heroes: persons, alive or dead, real or imaginary, who are glorified within a culture and who thus serve as models of behaviour. The next level is rituals, which are described as collective and socially essential activities within a culture – such as greeting or eating rituals, social and religious ceremonies, but also rituals in the political and business world.

Symbols, heroes and rituals are visible manifestations of cultures, and their cultural meaning is invisible (again, suggesting an iceberg analogy) but recognized and interpreted by members of the respective cultures. They are based on the

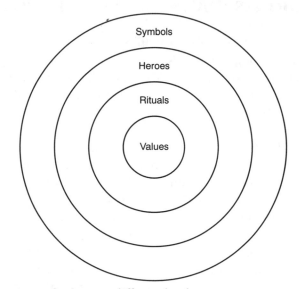

Figure 4 Manifestations of culture at different levels

deepest level of cultural manifestations, represented by values, which Hofstede describes as 'broad tendencies to prefer certain states of affairs over others'. Values are learned unconsciously and implicitly, mostly during childhood. Since, to a large degree, they remain unconscious to those who hold them, they cannot be directly observed by outsiders.

In order to identify actual differences in value systems, Hofstede has defined four areas of comparison: social inequality, including the relationship with authority; the relationship between the individual and the group; the concepts of masculinity and femininity (the social implications of having been born male or female); ways of dealing with uncertainty, relating to the control of aggression and the expression of emotions. These areas refer to basic problems of human society: the relation to authority, the concept of self, and ways of dealing with conflict. (These 'dimensions of cultures', as Hofstede calls them, are referred to in more detail in Chapter 7 and in the exercises later in this book.)

On this basis, Hofstede carried out a large research project involving more than 100,000 people in fifty countries around the world (see also exercises CU/CD 1 and CU/CD 2 in Chapter 10, pages 186–97). Although the concept outlined above seems to be quite useful for such research, the outcome of the specific research can be questioned, since the data were collected on the basis of national culture, which, according to Hofstede, is the only feasible criterion for classification. Thus the statistical data do not reflect possible differences between French- and Flemish-speaking Belgians or between different cultural groups represented in many countries included in the research.

CULTURE AS 'DARK AREAS OF BECOMING'

Another approach is taken by Roberto Ruffino, who compares culture to a building that makes sense as long as it stands, but if torn apart is no longer a building. It is thus not possible to have culture and knowledge about it at the same time. Ruffino views human life as a continuum between nature, culture (small c) and Culture (capital C).[7]

Nature refers to everything beyond human control, such as one's biological condition (being male or female, short or tall) or the geopolitical environment into which one is born (in which year, in which town, under which kind of government). One is aware of such conditions of nature but is unable to make significant changes. It is possible to know that one is tall but it is not possible to do much about 'tallness'. Where and when one is born is not a matter of choice, but it is possible to be aware of being 14 years old and living in Scotland. Realizing such conditions of nature, a human being begins to adapt and react to them. In doing so, the human being begins to develop certain internal rules, which then determine behaviour and action. These rules could be referred to as 'functional values'. This process of reaction and adaptation does not seem to be a conscious process.

At the other end of the continuum, Ruffino sees Culture, representing the permanence of human effort and endeavour. The fact that human beings create something of permanence – material or immaterial – that will survive beyond death is caused by a vision of the world which reaches beyond the life of the individual. These visions become ideologies, whether they are religious or political. In Culture these ideologies are represented by religious institutions, states and other institutions where the ideologies are passed on from generation to generation. Science is another kind of ideology, which also attempts to give description to the world, to nature.

Ruffino suggests that this striving for permanence, Culture, implies 'the realization of death'. The realization of death prompts a human being 'to reflect on the sense of suffering and the presence of evil in the world'. This perception of death, then, enables one's visions and explanations for the existence of the world.

Ruffino suggests that human life moves along a pendulum path between these two extremes – nature and Culture – and that in between them is culture – 'the dark area of becoming' (see Figure 5). This is daily life: behaviour, relationships, ideas that are shaped day-by-day in this pendulum situation between functional values and the realization of death. The assumption underlying this scheme suggests that human history moves from the unconscious to the conscious; that the area which is growing is Culture; that human beings react to whatever Nature is received, produce their own visions of the world and translate those reactions or visions into situations of permanence.

When human life is understood as a continuum, culture can be seen as a 'dark area of becoming'. It is an ungraspable, indefinable area that swings between what is received from nature, the reactions and adaptations, and what remains in the form of permanence. It is the area of becoming, of transformation and evolution, between two areas of being. But culture can only exist as long as it is unconscious.

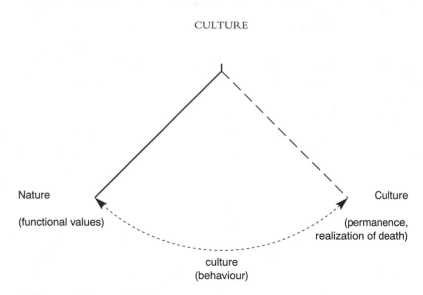

Figure 5 The pendulum of the human continuum

For intercultural learning, this means that the only thing which can be enlarged or learned is that of which one is aware. Nature cannot be enlarged: it is as it is. Culture (capital C) can be enlarged by acceptance of the existence of Cultures different from one's own. What can be attempted is to become transcultural, to reach out for an awareness of other cultures in ways that are different depending upon the respective unconscious backgrounds.

This process is very intellectual, but there is a role for emotions. The reassurance of the arts, sciences, institutions and ideologies is a means to get a sense of the richness of the interactions that are happening in culture which can never be grasped.

A PSYCHO-ANALYTIC APPROACH TO CULTURE

According to Freud, human culture – which he did not want to separate from civilization and which he described as everything in human life that is different from the life of animals – has two sides. It includes all the knowledge and skill that human beings have acquired to control natural forces and to obtain and produce goods which satisfy human needs. It also includes all the institutions that are necessary to regulate the relationship between people as well as the distribution of attainable goods.[8] If relationships between human beings are not regulated, they would be left to the arbitrary actions of the individual, which implies that the physically stronger person would determine any relationship according to his or her interests and instincts – even if he or she was later confronted by an even stronger person. According to Freud, the coexistence of human beings is only possible if there is a majority that is stronger than any individual and holds together against the individual. The power of the community, referred to as 'law', confronts the power of the individual, which is judged as 'raw violence'. The essential cultural step is thus the replacement of the power of the individual by the power of the community.[9] The advantage of the individual being subordinated under the dominion of its culture is that, as a community, human beings can accomplish more than as individuals. They can defend themselves better against the forces of nature, they can make better use of nature, they can produce more.

According to Freud, culture is to a large degree based on the renunciation, the suppression, the non-satisfaction, the sublimation of powerful instincts. This determines the large area of social relationships and causes the hostility against which all cultures have to fight. One cultural demand is the suppression of the instinct of aggression by the renunciation of the use of force against other members of the same culture. The fact that the stronger renounces the use of force against the weaker reveals the possibility of cooperation between people.

Another cultural demand is equity, which implies that, once a system of rules and laws has been established, it is not given up in favour of an individual. If such a system of rules were limited to a small group or community, this group would be likely to act towards a larger group or society like a violent individual. It seems, therefore, that the development of culture aims at a system of rules to which every-one – excluding those who are asocial – has contributed through suppression of instincts, which protects everyone – again excluding those who are asocial – against raw violence.

According to Freud, individual freedom is not a cultural value. Through cultural development, individual freedom is limited and equity requires that no one is excluded from this restriction. What is perceived as a craving for freedom within a human community can well be the opposition to an existing inequity and thus can result in a further cultural development. But this could be a remnant of original personality which has not been controlled by culture and thus results in hostility against culture.

CULTURE AND LANGUAGE

Language is a strange phenomenon that can be seen from different points of view. Some view language as something that is separate from culture but goes along with it. Some view language as a tool of culture. Others see language as totally separate from culture.

Language and its use are both part of the conscious as well as of the unconscious. In the evolution of most cultures, it moved from the less conscious to the more conscious, the key event bringing it to the conscious level being the invention of writing. Referring to the iceberg concepts of culture, language is partly visible and partly invisible. Visible (and graspable on a cognitive level) are the grammar, the spelling, the rules, according to which it is spoken and written. What are not visible are the structure of a language and the underlying values and beliefs. Even the use of language happens on a conscious as well as on an unconscious level. While the words are usually expressed and perceived consciously, the intonation and the way the words are expressed are mostly unconscious. This also applies to gestures and non-verbal expressions attached to the use of language.

There is a strong interdependence between language and thinking. On the one hand, language is a tool for expressing thoughts and mental structures in such a way that they become stable and independent from a given situation. On the other hand, not only does language express a thought, but the thinking is shaped by the language through which it is expressed. Similarly, the structure of a language is interdependent with patterns of thinking and, consequently, culture. Considering this, it is not only culture that shapes language but also language that shapes culture.

The interdependence between language and culture is strong. Language is an essential tool for organizing the relationships between the members of a culture. It is a tool for negotiating the rules according to which these relationships are regulated. It is a tool for conveying ideologies and visions of the world and it has, therefore, an influence on the evolution of a culture. At the same time, language reflects culture as it reflects how perception is organized and how, therefore, experience is sorted, interpreted and memorized. Language reflects culture as it transmits beliefs, values and norms that are determined by culture. Furthermore, language reflects the history, experience and wisdom of a culture. It is possible to assert that the structure of a language serves as a cultural memory and that language is a perceivable manifestation of culture.

A minority forced to give up an original language in favour of the language of a majority culture will consequently be assimilated. It is, therefore, obvious that a threat against one's language is perceived as a threat against one's culture.

Notes and references

1   Georg Auernheimer, *Einführung in die interkulturelle Erziehung*. Darmstadt: Wissenschaftliche Buchgesellschaft, 1990, p. 112.

2   Orlando Patterson, 'Context and choice in ethnic allegiance: a theoretical framework and Caribbean case study', in Nathan Glazer and Daniel P. Moynihan (eds), *Ethnicity: Theory and Experience*. Cambridge, MA: Harvard University Press, 1975, p. 309.

3   J. Clark, S. Hall, T. Jefferson and B. Roberts, 'Subcultures, cultures and class', in S. Hall and T. Jefferson (eds), *Resistance through Rituals. Youth Subcultures in Post-war Britain*. London: Hutchinson, 1976, p. 10.

4   D. Larcher, 'Das Kulturschockkonzept, ein Rehabilitierungsversuch'. Institut für Interdisziplinäre Forschung und Fortbildung der Universitäten Innsbruck, Klagenfurt, 1993, p. 4.

5   *Ibid.*, p. 9.

6   Geert Hofstede, *Cultures and Organizations, Software of the Mind*. Maidenhead: McGraw-Hill, 1991, p. 4.

7   Roberto Ruffino, 'Culture: human life seen as a continuum', Lecture at a seminar held at the European Youth Centre, Strasbourg, June 1987.

8   Sigmund Freud, 'Die Zukunft einer Illusion'. In *Kulturtheoretische Schriften*. Frankfurt: S. Fischer Verlag, 1974, p. 139.

9   Sigmund Freud, 'Das Unbehagen in der Kultur'. In *Kulturtheoretische Schriften*. Frankfurt: S. Fischer Verlag, 1974, p. 225.

CHAPTER 4

Intercultural Encounters

'The moment you grasp what is foreign, you will lose the urge to explain it. To explain a phenomenon is to distance yourself from it.'
Peter Høeg, *Miss Smilla's Feeling for Snow*, p. 212.

Stories or 'urban folklore' abound about intercultural encounters. For example, a western woman went everywhere with her beloved pet dog on a lead. One day while she was visiting China, she went into a traditional restaurant with her dog. Someone came and pointed to the dog and said, in broken English, 'We take dog?' She thought the restaurant owners didn't want pets in the dining room and assumed that they would put it outside until she finished eating. You can imagine the uproar when the dog returned, cooked, on her plate! Suppose now that this woman was in the Middle East and had been invited to dinner in the home of an Arab family. The chances are that the uproar would occur at the door, before she even entered the house. In Arabic culture dogs are considered to be degrading creatures and people do not want to be directly associated with them.[1]

Different categories

Incidents such as the one described above happen frequently when people with different cultural backgrounds meet. There are a number of possible reasons underlying such 'critical incidents'. In this case, the reason was that in different cultures the same thing might be put into different categories. Although a dog is generally put into the category 'animal' in all cultures, it belongs to the category 'house pets' in some, while in other cultures it might belong to the category 'work animals', 'degrading things' or 'food delicacies'. But knowing that a dog belongs to the category 'food delicacy' in another culture does not really solve the problem. Most Europeans would probably feel sick when confronted with a cooked dog on their plate (even if it was not their own dog) because it is not perceived as 'natural' to eat a dog. Obviously, this has nothing to do with 'nature'. In fact, taste is something like a 'second nature' that is actually determined by culture. We are not just hungry but we are hungry for something we know from our own culture.[2]

The problem of different categorizations also appeared in tests that migrant children had to pass in order to be accepted as regular pupils. They were confronted with pictures of a number of animals, told that all except one had something in common and asked to pick the odd one out. The children were supposed to pick the deer, because it was a wild animal and all the others were domestic animals. A Muslim child, however, picked the pig because it was not supposed to be eaten while all the other animals could be eaten. The result was dramatic: the child was considered to be mentally disabled and was sent to a special school although he/she was completely normal.

Different rules and norms

Another area of frequent misunderstanding is rules and norms. Most of these rules are learned in early childhood and are usually not written down. They are taken as self-evident and are adhered to unconsciously. An adult (or adolescent) who is encountering another culture and does not know its rules feels and behaves like a little child. He or she makes mistakes even a child would not make. He or she does not know rules known by every child and much of what he or she has learned to be 'normal' does not apply in the other culture. On the other hand, his or her behaviour is perceived as that of an adult (or adolescent) who should know all these rules. Consequently, this causes misunderstandings for members of the receiving cultural group. They might perceive such an adult as being rude and may also feel offended. Together with latent fear of the foreign this might result in open conflict.

A teacher in a Western European country reports that during a lesson a recently arrived migrant who was new in the class asked if he could leave the class for a minute. The teacher agreed and the pupil in fact returned shortly after. This happened two or three more times, so the teacher became angry because she thought that the pupil wanted to annoy her on purpose. She advised the pupil that he should not disturb the lesson or otherwise should stay at home. Since the pupil seemed to be embarrassed and apologized the teacher felt sorry about having been so harsh. After the lesson, she enquired why he left the room so often. After some hesitation the pupil said that he had a cold and had to blow his nose. At home it was considered to be impolite to do this in public, so he asked to leave the room. It does not really help to be aware of differences in rules of behaviour. Even knowing that it is OK to blow his nose in the classroom, the pupil would still feel uneasy because his perception of politeness is deeply rooted in his personality. Similarly, most Western Europeans would feel uneasy eating with their bare hands, just as cultures accustomed to this practice would feel uneasy eating with a knife and fork.

There is a good reason not to blow one's nose in public: avoiding the danger of passing on one's cold to others. In fact, the habit of blowing one's nose into a hand-kerchief which is put into one's pocket might well be considered to be unhygienic by members of a culture where one blows one's nose on the ground outside. In other cultures the use of the right or the left hand can be determined by their practices of hygiene.

There can also be reasons of a less practical nature, which are based on religious beliefs. For example, in Buddhist cultures it is a taboo to touch someone else's head because this would interrupt his or her link with God. Since such a belief is rooted deep in the collective memory, it is difficult to accept its being broken: it is a direct threat to one's existence.

Different patterns of thinking

Most cultures that have developed a large and complex set of norms have also developed principles of organizing these norms.[3] A problem arising in intercultural encounters is that different cultures have developed not only different norms but also different organizing principles for their norms. These organizing principles are usually compatible with the way society is organized, and vice versa.

In the Western cultures, these organizing principles are the so-called axioms of logic. They basically say: norms have to be clear and unequivocal; two norms must not contradict each other; norms are ranked; there has to be an understandable link between a norm and the rules it requires. The second axiom referring to the avoidance of contradiction, for example, implies that, if two statements contradict each other, at least one has to be wrong. This is 'either/or' thinking. Asian cultures do not have this axiom of logic. Truth means that, with a given aspect, its opposite is included. If only one side of a matter is known, it is not possible to have the whole truth. Only those who know both sides are approaching truth. While Europeans tend to eliminate the 'wrong' side, Asians try to include it.

This can have a problematic effect on a relationship between a European and an Asian. If something is contradictory, the European will be likely to feel uneasy and try to find out what is right, while the Asian might feel comfortable with the situation. If the situation seems to be clear and unequivocal, the European will be likely to feel comfortable, while the Asian might be searching for the other side of the matter.

Differences in roles and relationships

One of the authors remembers an 18-year-old African pupil who was living with a Western European family as part of a one-year exchange programme. While he developed a very good relationship with the father of that family, there were ongoing conflicts with the mother. One of the reasons was that the mother expected him to help in the household – clear the table, possibly wash the dishes, clean his own room – while he perceived these activities to be humiliating for a man. He was also confused by the relationship between the parents, which was based on partnership and equal rights. The mother was involved in decisions which he perceived to be men's business and the father did things which were to be done by women only. On top of this, he perceived himself to be a grown-up man while the parents treated him as an adolescent.

Another incident was recently reported when a group of business people from an Asian country went shopping in a Western European city. When they wanted to pay for their purchases with credit cards, the shop owner checked by telephone with his bank. Since the bank did not know the specific credit card, the shop owner called the police, who took the whole group into custody on suspicion of fraud. The members of the group were questioned for some hours until it turned out that the credit cards were good but unknown by the bank. The group consisted of employees of a large car company, including the chief executive. The result of this incident was that the chief executive 'lost face' because of being questioned in the presence of his subordinates. All of the group 'lost face' *vis-à-vis* the host country. Only an official excuse by the government could re-establish the condition of dignity.

There are role differences in different cultures. The incidents described above could partly be explained by one of the cultural dimensions which Hofstede refers to as 'power distance'. The example involving the African pupil could also be explained by the cultural dimension referred to by Hofstede as 'masculinity/femininity' which describes the consequences of being born male or female.

In different cultures, there are different perceptions of roles for men and women, for children and parents, for adolescents and adults, for superiors and subordinates. While there might be practical reasons for a specific distribution of roles within a society — such as a nursing mother taking care of raising babies — there are also values attached. A patriarchal society will value physical strength while a matriarchal society will value the ability to give birth and closeness to nature. Some societies value maturity, wisdom, experience, continuity and thus age, while others value physical strength, the power to change something and thus youth. While it is possible to adapt one's behaviour to a different distribution of roles, it is not so easy to change the underlying values.

Different patterns of interaction and behaviour

A famous example for differences in patterns of interaction is described by Paul Watzlawick.[4] Among American soldiers stationed in England during World War II, it was a widespread opinion that English girls were easy to get into a sexual relationship. Strangely enough, English girls claimed that American soldiers were impetuous lovers. Research conducted by Margaret Mead and others came up with an interesting explanation of the phenomenon. They discovered that in England as well as in the USA the courtship pattern — from getting to know the partner until sexual intercourse — covered some thirty steps of behavioural actions, but that the ranking of these actions was different for the two cultural groups. While the kiss happened rather early for the American soldier — approximately at step 5 — it appeared in the typical courtship pattern of English women at approximately step

25. This means not only that an English woman who was kissed by an American soldier felt cheated of most of the courtship pattern she intuitively perceived to be 'normal' (steps 5 to 24), but also that she now had to decide whether she wanted to break off the relationship right there or to give herself to him sexually. If she decided on the latter, the American soldier was confronted with behaviour which did not fit into this early stage of the relationship and which he perceived to be shameless. Both perceived the behaviour of the other to be indecent and 'wrong'.

Incidents such as this happen frequently when someone is confronted with members of another culture. They are caused by differences in routine behaviour and habits, which are mostly unconscious, as are the patterns, rules and values underlying them. Because they are to a large degree unconscious, they are difficult to grasp, to explain, to observe or to describe. While it could be possible to compile a 'dictionary' of the most important rules and norms in another culture − the 'dos and don'ts' − it is impossible to describe all habits and patterns of behaviour and interaction in a given culture. Even if they were brought to a conscious level, they would be too complex and to a large degree not measurable. If and for how long one can look into the eyes of a person of the other sex is not just different in differ-ent cultures but can be different within a culture. It might be determined by the relationship to that person − an unknown person sitting opposite in the bus, a person one has just met at a party or a colleague at the workplace. The same is true for the distance between persons in an informal conversation.

The description of such habits might soon be outdated. Cultures are not static but dynamic and are changing continuously. For example, it is very likely that courtship patterns in England and the USA have changed since 1945 and that the conflicting behaviour described above does not happen any longer.

Visions of the world

Culture also provides answers to the existential questions of human beings: why do we live, why do we live as we live and what is there after life? The perception of life is always linked to the perception of death. The answers cultures give to these questions claim to be exclusive and definitive. Each culture thus contains a dogma which is binding for its members. This common vision of the world provides a sense of belonging together for each culture.

A confrontation with another culture can be threatening because it implies a confrontation with different answers to these existential questions. They might give a different explanation for life and thus for one's very existence. These are perceived to be foreign and cause fear. A common reaction to this fear is rejection and in extreme cases hostility. Many religious wars have been caused by such confrontations of different dogmas.

On the other hand, there is a chance for development in such an intercultural encounter. The other culture bears possibilities and opportunities which one's own culture does not offer. Nevertheless, these opportunities are only accessible and, consequently, the intercultural encounter can only be positive and fruitful if the culture which is stronger in this specific encounter renounces the use of force against or exploitation of the weaker culture.

CULTURE SHOCK

Culture shock can be experienced when we realize that the behaviour we consider to be 'normal' or 'natural' is not perceived as appropriate or is possibly rejected by another culture; when what has always been self-evident does not seem to be so any more; when we do not understand the behaviour of members of another culture; when we get the impression that they do not behave in a 'normal' way. This is the case when, for example, someone is confronted with others who slurp their soup noisily, eat with their bare hands or belch in public without apologizing, and these behaviours are considered to be inappropriate in his/her culture.

JoAnn Craig thought that the term 'shock' was misleading and used instead the term 'culture impact', for which she gave the following definition: 'Culture impact is, in fact, a state of stress and anxiety that results from the disturbing impressions we get and the loss of equilibrium we feel when we lose all our familiar signs and symbols of social intercourse, and when we encounter environmental differences in an alien culture.'[5] Belching in public does not necessarily cause a shock to someone in whose culture it is not considered to be appropriate. But it can be a real shock for a pupil who for religious reasons is accustomed to remain covered to undress completely and to take a shower with other pupils.

Most of the incidents described in the previous pages can cause culture shock as defined here. The question is what effect it has on the people concerned. Generally, the reaction will depend on the socio-economic and psycho-social condition of the person experiencing it. It can be said that a person who is not threatened by culture shocks because he or she is economically independent and psychologically stable is most likely to be able to experience the positive effects of an increased awareness of self and the foreign and a critical reflection of elements of one's own and the foreign culture. Contrary to this, someone who has little or no economic security or someone who is psychologically unstable will suffer from culture shock because he or she will be irritated by experiencing even more insecurity and threat to his or her identity.[6] An intercultural experience will be perceived differently by a pupil whose family is stable middle class and by a pupil whose parents are long-term unemployed. The situation is even worse if a person is confronted with a culture that has little or no ability or willingness to empathize with him/her and help him/her to integrate into society. Under such conditions an individual must not show irritation because he or she could then be recognized as foreign and would risk being excluded. This could be the case for an illegal immigrant.

Craig, who has done a research study on expatriates, describes as primary reactions to culture shock frustration, stress, anxiety, disorientation and psychological instability.[7] These are evidenced through symptoms such as absent-mindedness, desire for familiarity, fear of being cheated, excessive drinking, fits of rage, etc.

Craig finds three general reactions to culture shock and subsequently describes three 'cultural types':

- The 'encapsulator', who either fights and rejects the foreign or runs away from it and withdraws into the community of members of his or her culture in that country. The encapsulator has minimal contact with the receiving culture and maximum contact with members of his or her own culture.
- The 'absconder', who goes 'native', falls in love with the receiving culture, adopts its lifestyle, food, dress, speech etc. The absconder has maximum contact with the receiving culture and minimal contact with members of his or her own culture.
- The 'cosmopolitan' shows optimism, empathy, curiosity, interest, acceptance and intercultural contacts. The cosmopolitan adjusts to both receiving culture and the culture of members of his or her own culture in the receiving country. The cosmopolitan has roots in both these cultures and has about the same contact with both.

Craig points out that, according to her research, the encapsulator is the most common, the absconder is the most rare and the cosmopolitan is the most successful cultural type.

Craig's conclusions are consistent with the outcomes of exposure to the foreign as outlined earlier in this book: The encapsulator cannot survive without social contact in the long-run. He or she will mostly relate to other encapsulators of his or her cultural background, which results in segregation of this cultural or ethnic group from the majority/native culture. The outcome is settings that could be described as Little England, Little France, Little Italy, Little Germany, etc. The absconder as described by Craig relates to xenophobia and exoticism. The absconder gives up the ties with his or her own cultural group and possibly adopts not only the lifestyle and patterns of behaviour of the receiving culture but also its values and vision of the world. It is thus very likely that the absconder will be assimilated into the majority/native culture.

An outcome of an intercultural encounter that Craig has not referred to is that of adaptation, where a person establishes contact with members of the receiving culture and adapts his or her patterns of behaviour in order to function effectively in the new cultural environment, while preserving his or her original cultural identity. Thus the person avoids possible conflicts as well as isolation and loneliness. It seems that such a state is unstable and cannot be maintained by an individual over a long period. One can role-play for a period of some weeks (as is the case for a class exchange) but not for months or years.

There are various possible long-term developments following adaptation. The person can still reject the receiving culture sooner or later and thus become an encapsulator. The person can become an absconder or be assimilated. Or the person can develop a deeper relationship with the receiving culture. The outcome of the last, according to Craig, would be a cosmopolitan who not only has a sympathetic understanding of the receiving culture but who is also able to empathize with its members. As Craig describes it, the cosmopolitan is able to pass back and forth between his or her own and the receiving culture, thus becoming a 'traveller between cultures'. This relates to the 'bicultural' person described by Hoopes,[8] referred to in more detail below.

POSSIBLE OUTCOMES OF INTERCULTURAL ENCOUNTERS

Organizers of exchange programmes observed that pupils and students going abroad for a longer period (e.g. for a term or for a school year) would go through a similar sequence of ups and downs in experiencing the perplexities of the culture they were visiting. This sequence is commonly referred to as the 'adjustment cycle' (see Figure 6).[9]

At the very beginning of their stay abroad they would be very excited and positive because they were experiencing many new and interesting things. After this initial excitement, they would experience culture shock on being permanently confronted with a foreign environment. They would not understand the language or much of the behaviour of the people around them. They would have difficulties making themselves understood in terms of language as well as behaviour. And they would have difficulties in developing personal relationships. In a next step, they would learn survival skills and adjust to their cultural environment. They would learn to communicate and to behave in a way perceived to be 'right' in the receiving culture. But the adjustment would be only superficial in the beginning. The pupil would be role-playing to a certain degree and would suppress his or her actual feelings, which would then cause frustration and possibly depression. To avoid this ambiguity the person would go through a process of learning to explore how he or she could transform the cultural patterns of his or her origin so they became compatible with the receiving culture and the person could 'feel at home'. This step of 'genuine adjustment' could be considered as crucial for intercultural learning. Another crucial phase is that of the return after the stay abroad. The person is again experiencing culture shock because of being confronted with a new and unfamiliar view of his or her culture of origin.

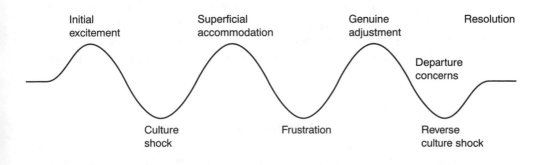

Figure 6 The adjustment cycle

Of course, this model is a simplification of a much more complex process. The ups and downs can have very different qualities and will depend on the psycho-social condition of the exchangee as well as on the willingness of the social environment in the receiving culture to empathize with and support the exchangee. The model also takes a very simplistic view of the nature of adjustment, limiting it to emotional feelings while other aspects of the underlying process are not considered.[10] Nevertheless, the model as outlined here can be quite helpful for a teacher trying to understand similar reactions experienced during an exchange activity. The model can also be applied to any person living in another culture for some time, such as a person going on a work assignment abroad, a teacher partici-pating in an international exchange scheme, a migrant worker or a refugee (for the last the 'departure concerns' and 'reverse culture shock' phases will not apply).

A possible outcome of an intercultural encounter not indicated in this model is isolation. The threat caused by the confrontation with the foreign can be so great that the person reacts with regression and withdraws from the receiving culture. JoAnn Craig referred to such a person as an Encapsulator, who will seek to establish close contact with members of his or her own culture. In the case of a class exchange, such a pupil will seek to stay with the classmates or the teacher. In the case of an individual exchange scheme, it is very likely that the person will interrupt the programme and return home early.

What is referred to as 'adjustment' in this model can be of a very diverse nature. According to David Hoopes there are four possible outcomes for an individual exposed to a different culture.[11] All of them are archetypes and thus of a theoretical nature, since they will not surface in exactly that form.

Assimilation

Assimilation means that a person adopts the language, habits and patterns of behav-iour of a second culture and rejects or refrains from the use of his or her primary language, habits and patterns of behaviour. To give an example, a person brought up in a culture where one would usually eat with knife and fork would be assim-ilated in a culture where one eats with bare hands only when he or she actually felt comfortable doing so and uncomfortable eating with knife and fork. Assimilation can be a very painful process. While seemingly the original cultural identity is replaced by a new cultural identity, this is not the case. In fact, assimilation implies the permanent suppression of one's old cultural identity, which can result in confu-sion and unrootedness.

Adaptation

The individual adapts his or her patterns of behaviour in order to function effec-tively within another culture. However, the person does not absorb and incorporate the new behaviour and thus preserves his or her original cultural identity. The person tries to understand and empathize with the other culture, learns the language, gestures, habits, rules, etc., but does not internalize the underlying values and beliefs. According to the example described above, an adapted person would have learned to eat with bare hands but would feel uncomfortable doing it and still prefer eating with knife and fork. Adaptation implies some kind of role-playing, which means that the person will not really act in a genuine way. This might surface and cause disturbance when the adopted behaviour contradicts actual values and beliefs. It is, therefore, questionable whether cultural adaptation is possible for a longer period without the backing and security of one's original cultural environment. It is likely that without this backing the person will experience an unwanted assimilation.

'Biculturalism'

According to Hoopes, a bicultural person has developed a dual cultural personality. The person has learned the new language, has learned to think in it, has learned the new cultural norms and behaviours and is thus able to pass back and forth between his or her own and the receiving culture. This definition suggests a split cultural identity, which seems to be impossible: one cannot change one's cultural identity like a shirt. A more satisfactory explanation seems to be that a 'bicultural' person has been able to transform his or her values, norms and patterns of behaviour so that they become consistent with those of the receiving culture. In fact, the person has developed a new cultural identity that is compatible with both the original and the receiving culture. Describing it again according to the example outlined above, a 'bicultural' person has learned to eat comfortably with bare hands but would still feel comfortable eating with knife and fork.

'Multiculturalism'

This is a step further, where the skills learned and the mind-sets developed in an intercultural encounter are abstracted and transformed into tools that can be used in any intercultural setting. 'The person learns the framework of intercultural communication and cross-cultural human relations and then applies it successfully to new cultures encountered.'[12] It could be said that such a person has learned how to learn culture and thus has become 'culturally literate'. Referring again to the example mentioned above, a 'multicultural' person has learned to eat comfortably with bare hands as well as with knife and fork but can also adapt comfortably and effectively to other eating habits.

While the authors of this book use the terms bicultural and multicultural to describe the plain presence of more than one culture, Hoopes used the terms 'biculturalism' and 'multiculturalism' differently. To avoid misunderstandings, the terms used according to the definition of Hoopes are set in quotation marks.

POSSIBLE FORMS OF BICULTURAL AND MULTICULTURAL SOCIETY

So far we have dealt with the effect of an intercultural encounter on the individual. The question still to be dealt with is what possible outcomes there are if two (or more) different cultural groups are living together within a region or country. It seems that such settings are determined by two factors. One is the perception of and attitude towards their own culture of the groups involved. This attitude can take any position between preserving one's cultural identity and giving it up, resulting in assimilation. The other factor is the relationship with and the attitude towards the other culture(s), which can be characterized by a position between segregation and integration. Segregation would imply minimal contact and interaction between the different cultural groups and possibly unequal rights and access to resources. Integration would mean convivial coexistence and would imply maximum contact and equal rights and access to resources. While the concept of segregation can be forced unilaterally by one cultural group, any form of integration depends on the agreement of all cultural groups involved, because the majority (or stronger group) might offer integration, while the minority (or weaker group) might reject integration because it feels threatened in its identity.

This model is shown in Figure 7.[13] The extreme position in this model in the upper-right quarter would be a setting where cultural diversity is valued highly. This implies the right to one's own cultural identity as well as the willingness to interact with people of different cultural backgrounds. To some extent, a number of European countries have established such settings, where the minority are integrated socially and economically to a high degree while being very conscious of their cultural identity and preserving their traditions and their language by practising them in everyday life.

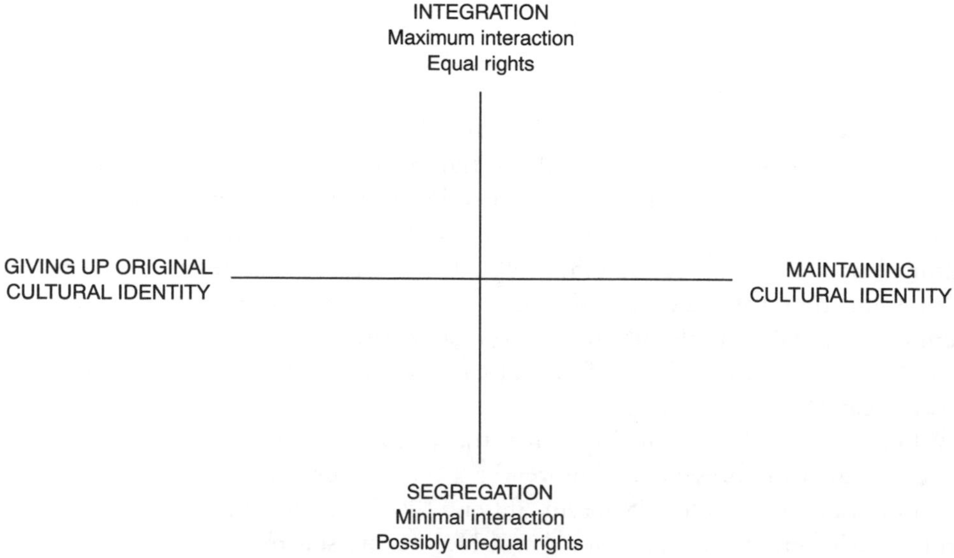

INTEGRATION
Maximum interaction
Equal rights

GIVING UP ORIGINAL
CULTURAL IDENTITY

MAINTAINING
CULTURAL IDENTITY

SEGREGATION
Minimal interaction
Possibly unequal rights

Figure 7 Forms of bicultural and multicultural society

The lower-right quarter of this model represents societies with cultural diversity but segregation between the different cultural groups. An extreme example for this was the apartheid society of South Africa. The situation of the gypsies in most European countries also shows these characteristics. A more subtle form for this setting is the ethnopluralism practised in many countries with ethnic minorities, including migrant workers and their families. This model is frequently characterized by separate schools for the different language groups or by cultural homogeneity within the workplace.

The upper-left quarter of the model represents a setting where integration goes together with assimilation. Owing to the nature of this setting, the original cultural diversity disappears or at least becomes invisible after a relatively short time. Frequently, such a setting is imposed by the majority (dominant) culture, which provides equal rights to the minority (weaker) group at the price of its giving up its cultural identity. It seems that this concept was pursued by the former Soviet Union to a certain degree. It has also been favoured by many European countries with respect to their cultural and ethnic minorities. The Europeans migrating to the USA in the nineteenth century could serve as an example.

It seems that there is no example for the lower-left quarter. It would be ridiculous to give up one's cultural identity to be segregated. Nevertheless, there is the strange phenomenon that members of a cultural minority group who have been assimilated by the majority are among those who are most extreme in segregating the minority cultural group that they (or their ancestors) have been part of.

Many multicultural settings can be found between these four extremes. There are cultural groups that are partly assimilated but maintain their cultural identity in some areas. One could, for example, say that Asians in the United Kingdom have been assimilated in some areas but maintain their cultural identity to a certain degree in social life.

The model does not give an indication as to which outcome is desirable. There does not seem to be a universal answer. While there is no question that equal rights have to be provided for all cultural groups, the demand for maximal interaction between cultural groups can mean a threat to cultural identity and thus a challenge to the individuals and groups involved. While assimilation contradicts the right to one's own cultural identity, preservation of cultural identity is not an end in itself. Interaction with a different culture implies reflection on one's own culture and thus an evolution of cultural identity. It seems that the outcome depends very much on the specific setting and the cultures involved. What is crucial is that it is negotiated and developed in a peaceful and democratic way, the underlying principle being that freedom and justice for one cultural group are not limited for the benefit of another cultural group.

Notes and references

1   Kenneth Cushner, *They Are Talking about Me!* New York: AFS Intercultural Programs, 1990, p. 94.

2   D. Larcher, 'Das Kulturschockkonzept, Ein Rehabilitierungsversuch'. Institut für Interdisziplinäre Forschung und Fortbildung der Universitäten Innsbruck, Klagenfurt, 1993, p. 4.

3   Gerhard Schwarz, 'In verschiedenen Logiken denken'. *Hernsteiner*, **4**, 1991, p. 5.

4   Paul Watzlawick *et al.*, *Menschliche Kommunikation. Formen, Störungen, Paradoxien*. Bern/Stuttgart/Vienna: Verlag Hans Huber, 1974, p. 20.

5   J. Craig, *Culture Shock. Singapore and Malaysia*. Singapore: Times Books International, 1984, p. 159.

6   D. Larcher, 'Das Kulturschockkonzept ...', p. 10.

7   J. Craig, *Culture Shock. Singapore and Malaysia*, p. 169.

8   David Hoopes, 'Intercultural communication concepts and the psychology of inter-cultural experience'. In Margaret Pusch (ed.), *Multicultural Education. A Cross-cultural Training Approach*. Yarmouth, ME: Intercultural Press, 1979, p. 20.

9   Alvino Fantini *et al.*, *Cross-cultural Orientation, a Guide for Leaders and Educators*. Brattleboro, VT: The Experiment in International Living, 1984, p. 43.

10   Cornelius Grove, *Orientation Handbook for Youth Exchange Programs*. New York: Intercultural Press, 1989, p. 188.

11   David Hoopes, 'Intercultural communication concepts ...', p. 19.

12   *Ibid.*, p. 21.

13   Based on an idea presented by Dietmar Larcher at a seminar held in 1992.

CHAPTER 5

Intercultural Learning

'There is one way to understand another culture. Living it. Move into it, ask to be tolerated as a guest, learn the language. At some point understanding may come. It will always be wordless.'

Peter Høeg, *Miss Smilla's Feeling for Snow*, p. 212.

INTERCULTURAL LEARNING AS A NEW DISCIPLINE OF PEDAGOGY

Intercultural learning has become a fashionable term, and has been used in a quite inflated way. It sometimes seems as if intercultural learning could provide solutions for numerous problems in today's world. The term is not very precise in its meaning, and can cover many generalities. We will, therefore, try to discuss the concept of intercultural learning in a more precise way.

Intercultural learning implies the development of a greater openness towards other cultures, the appreciation of cultural diversity, the overcoming of cultural bias and of ethnocentrism. Intercultural learning is necessary in situations where people of different cultural backgrounds and languages live together. The tensions and conflicts caused by coexistence and an inevitable lack of understanding must not result in violence, but have to be resolved in a communicative process. This does not mean that this process must result in mutual understanding. It is a large step to learn to accept that you do not understand each other.[1]

The use of terms about the learning process that relate to the coexistence or interaction of people of different cultural backgrounds has been and still is quite confusing. The terms used not only depend on the context but can have different meanings in different countries and languages. In North America, the attribute words 'intercultural' and 'cross-cultural' were in use shortly after World War II in the context of training Americans to function more effectively during studies or work abroad.[2]

The developments with respect to multicultural societies created by migration seem to have followed similar patterns in most European countries. At first, cultural differences were frequently ignored until it became evident that this could not continue. Later, many countries introduced pedagogic measures aimed at integrating migrant children into the existing education systems by compensating for the lack of language proficiency through 'preparatory/initiation/induction classes', 'special classes' or 'catch-up classes'. These approaches aimed at assimilation or – if this could not be achieved – at segregation. Following this, many countries pursued a two-fold objective: integrating the migrant children into the existing education system while at the same time maintaining links to the country of origin to prepare them for later reintegration after returning 'home'. To achieve the latter, classes were provided in the mother tongue of the migrant children. It has since been recognized that this is also necessary for the personal development of pupils and that it supports their ability to cope with the challenges of a multicultural society. Only recently, in a number of countries, has the multicultural nature of society been accepted as a fact, has it been assumed that the migrant population will not return to its country of origin and that, consequently, the curriculum must reflect the existing cultural diversity. Contrary to earlier pedagogical approaches, intercultural education is not aimed at the development or preservation of cultural identity but at overcoming and transcending cultural barriers. This implies that intercultural education is understood as a multilateral and reciprocal process, where one learns to be open towards and to accept the culture of others. The trend seems to be moving away from assimilation (or segregation) towards the recognition of different cultural identities. Exceptions to these developments are in Sweden and the Netherlands, where this has been the case from very early on. Sweden especially recognized the irreversible nature of migration and established a system of education in the mother tongue of immigrants.

It is obvious that the developments in pedagogy did not happen independently from political and economic developments. The migration from South to North initiated and supported by the highly industrialized countries in Europe in the 1950s and 1960s was reduced and then stopped in the 1970s. Some countries even introduced strategies to encourage or force migrants to return to their countries of origin. Only when it became evident that these strategies could not be implemented – a second- or third-generation migrant usually does not consider the native country of his or her parents or grandparents as 'home' if he or she has never been there – did the strategies move towards accepting the situation as being permanent. In many countries the situation is far from desirable. Although the migrant population can participate actively and passively in community elections in some countries, there is still structural discrimination in many other areas of society. This refers to job opportunities, to housing access, to full participation in political life.

Intercultural teaching is often confronted with problems it cannot resolve. Educational approaches cannot make up for the shortcomings of societies and political structures. There is a danger that delegating the task to education conceals the actual problems.[3] The limitations of education with respect to multicultural societies must be understood in order to avoid disappointment and frustration. The introduction of an intercultural education will not have an immediate influence on the structural and political issues related to multicultural societies.

So far we have mostly referred to intercultural learning with respect to multicultural societies caused by migration during the past few decades. Nevertheless, there have been indigenous cultural and ethnic minorities in many European countries throughout history. There have been waves of migration, particularly in the Middle Ages, resulting in the movement of cultures across Europe. In the nineteenth century, national boundaries were drawn regardless of cultural associations. Rights pertaining to cultural identity and the use of language were suppressed in favour of nation states. It is only in the context of discussions in the 1960s and 1970s related to education in a multicultural society that the right of indigenous cultural and ethnic minorities to education in their mother tongue and the subsequent need for intercultural education have been recognized.

Another stimulus to the discourse about intercultural learning has been provided by pupil and student exchange organizations and by development aid organizations that send personnel on assignments abroad. Since their respective activities were mostly aimed at education and development, they soon recognized the cultural dimension of the relationships their clients or personnel were confronted with. In fact, the objective of most educational exchange organizations founded after World War II was to promote peace and mutual understanding across borders. Exchange organizers from the beginning recognized that intercultural encounters not only were a source of tension and conflict but could also be an enrichment and contribute to personal development. During the 1980s many exchange organizations shifted their objectives towards intercultural education to prepare young people for an increasingly international and intercultural environment. (It has to be mentioned that frequently organizations claim to promote intercultural education for marketing reasons, while their activity has little to do with it.)

The socio-economic and psycho-social conditions of exchange pupils cannot be compared with those of second-generation children. Exchange pupils choose voluntarily to become exposed to another culture, will stay only for a limited period of time and can return home earlier if they cannot cope with the situation faced abroad. They will have access to most aspects of education and social life; the experience abroad is most likely to be perceived as an enrichment. Contrasted to this, migrant children are confronted with individual as well as with structural and institutional discrimination, have limited access to education and social life or to the economic resources of the country, and usually have no social or economic interest in going back to the country of origin of their parents or grandparents.

Nevertheless, there are comparable phenomena when it comes to intercultural encounters. There is the deeply rooted fear of the foreign, there are prejudices, there is misunderstanding and non-understanding, there is culture shock, there is conflict. Some exchange organizers, such as AFS Intercultural Programs and The Experiment in International Living, have dealt with these issues intensively. In the 1970s the European Federation for Intercultural Learning (EFIL) was the first organization to develop a concept of intercultural learning in exchanges. EFIL has since organized numerous seminars and conferences on this topic and has produced publications and educational materials to implement intercultural learning in school curricula.[4] Since the late 1970s research on intercultural learning through exchanges has been carried out, especially in Germany and in the United States, where there was a thirty-year experience to draw on. All this has provided a valuable contribution to the theory and practice of intercultural education.

There are a number of different starting-points for approaching intercultural learning. Coming back to the confusion about the terminology pointed out earlier in this chapter, it seems that this confusion is linked to the different contexts in which the terms are used as well as to the changes in pedagogical approaches taken towards multicultural societies.

The authors of this book have used the terms 'bicultural' or 'multicultural' only to describe the presence of two or more cultures. Thus multicultural describes a situation which has evolved historically or which has been brought about 'artificially', e.g. by an exchange programme. Multicultural does not imply any objectives for such a situation. Contrary to this, the term 'intercultural' is used with respect to the interaction of and relationship between different cultural groups. It implies that there *is* an interaction between the different cultural groups in a multicultural setting. In fact, the term intercultural implies that this interaction is desirable and that it follows specific ideas with respect to pedagogical, political and social objectives. A more detailed description of the terms used can be found in the Glossary.

DIFFERENT CONTEXTS FOR INTERCULTURAL LEARNING

There seem to be five major contexts in which intercultural learning is relevant:[5]

- the coexistence of the indigenous majority population of a country with the migrant population, resulting from migration in the third quarter of this century;[6]
- the coexistence of the majority population with indigenous minorities within a country;
- the moving together of the countries in Europe as well as the expansion of global networks, resulting in increased work mobility and increased interaction between people of different cultural backgrounds;
- the relationship between the highly industrialized countries and the developing countries in Africa, Asia and Latin America;
- modern mass tourism.

In the context of the coexistence of majority and migrant populations, intercultural learning is mostly directed towards a constructive integration of the children of migrants. This is very difficult because the relationship between majority and migrants is characterized by social as well as cultural conflicts. In most European countries migrants belong to the lowest income group, have access only to housing with minimal standards and are held responsible for taking jobs away from the majority population and thus causing unemployment. This situation asks not only for intercultural learning but for social learning, which involves both the majority and the migrant pupils and which is based on the principle that the migrant culture is equivalent to and not less valuable than the majority culture.

It is important to support bilingualism, which means that the migrant children also need education in their native language to avoid 'semi-lingualism'.[7] But it would also be desirable to motivate all pupils to learn the mother tongue of the migrants, thus reinforcing the principle of parity and equality. All this requires special conditions with respect to education systems and schools: team-teaching, special teacher training, possibly bilingual teachers, special curricula, experimental teaching methods and intensive contact between teachers and parents to make such schools equally attractive for both majority and migrant populations. Only then can the encounters between different cultures and languages be constructive and fruitful.

Intercultural learning in the context of the coexistence of the majority population with indigenous minorities within a country is aimed at discovering one's own cultural roots in the other – the 'foreign' – cultural group and seeing that the two cultural groups have much in common owing to a common development. This implies an understanding that the other cultural group is not really foreign, that not only has the majority culture influenced the minority culture but the minority group has influenced the lifestyle, traditions, attitudes and values of the majority group. Again, bilingualism is an essential principle to be achieved: for the minority group because the mother tongue is a crucial element of its cultural identity and for the majority group to be able to understand part of its cultural heritage. Bilingual schools and bilingual education are a prerequisite to this.

In the context of the countries of Europe moving closer to each other, it can be said that current developments in Europe will result in increased mobility and thus in increased interaction between people of different cultural backgrounds. This applies not only to Western Europe, where political and economic integration is moving towards a union of fifteen or more countries, but also to Central and Eastern Europe, where the opening of borders has resulted in an enormously increased mobility and interaction. These developments mean that more people will need to be prepared to work and live in other cultural environments. This implies fluency in two or more foreign languages and an ability to relate constructively to other cultural environments. The emerging cultural realities in Europe will require greater cultural self-awareness, the ability to empathize, an understanding of cultural differences and how they are reflected in values, norms and patterns of behaviour. One of the objectives of intercultural learning is to prepare young people for this new cultural reality.

Intercultural learning in the context of the relationship between the highly industrialized countries and the developing countries in Africa, Asia and Latin America is aimed at creating an understanding of the cultural dimension of this relationship and a realization that differences in attitudes and value systems have been and still are supporting exploitation. Prices for natural resources, for the transfer of services and products, are globally determined by a market system that is inherent to the cultural values of the industrialized countries and that prevents solidarity and equal access to resources and production. It is obvious that intercultural learning cannot provide solutions for the political and economic dimension of this conflict. It can contribute to the solution by enforcing the principle that the cultures of the developing countries are equivalent to and not less valuable than the cultures of industrialized countries; by promoting global solidarity; by enabling an understanding of the patterns of thinking, the approaches, the actions and the decisions of the other culture as a result of different values, norms and traditions; by helping effective communication across these culturally determined differences. Intercultural learning in this context is extremely challenging, since it involves confrontation between cultures which are different from each other in existential areas, whereas the variety of cultures within Europe could be considered to be rather homogeneous.

Intercultural learning in the context of increasing tourism is directed at showing more sensitivity towards the foreign. Intercultural learning could help tourists to cope with the culture shock they are confronted with while travelling abroad. It could create awareness of cultural differences and enable more culturally sensitive behaviour in a foreign environment. While intercultural education can achieve this only in a limited way, it can at least contribute to overcoming ethnocentrism to a certain extent.

DIFFERENT VIEWPOINTS FOR INTERCULTURAL LEARNING

In all the contexts described above, intercultural learning can be seen from two different perspectives. First, intercultural learning can be seen as an approach to addressing cultural conflict, encouraging awareness of conflicts and their cultural dimension as well as an understanding of their cultural origin. From this perspective, the promotion of intercultural learning is a reaction to a given situation. This has especially been the case for intercultural learning with respect to the coexistence of native and migrant populations.

The second perspective is to look at cultural diversity and intercultural encounters as a resource and as a potential enrichment that can be realized by intercultural learning. This perspective has been taken by exchange organizers for many years, but only since the early 1980s has a similar perspective been observed in approaches to education in bicultural or multicultural societies. Educators in multicultural settings often perceived exchanges aiming at intercultural learning as a luxury, because they were not connected to the reality of multicultural societies. Nevertheless, the intercultural competence acquired during an experience abroad, such as greater cultural self-awareness, enlarged perception, increased ability to empathize, etc., will enable the exchangee to function more effectively in a multicultural environment at home.

INTERCULTURAL LEARNING AS A GLOBAL CONCERN

Since the different contexts described apply to most countries in Europe and all over the world, intercultural learning must be considered a global concern. Even more, not only should intercultural learning involve those who are directly confronted with or affected by multicultural settings, but, because of the complexity of modern societies, intercultural learning has to involve everyone. It should not be considered an exclusive hobby or an abstract learning experience for those who are not directly concerned with cultural diversity.

Prejudice is created mostly without concrete personal experience with the group concerned. Nevertheless, prejudice influences attitudes, feelings, thinking and subsequent actions and decisions: which products we buy, where we decide to live, how we raise and educate our children, which schools we or our children choose, which political parties we support. For example, it can be assumed that the development of laws and regulations with respect to foreigners, migrants and minority cultures is strongly influenced by people who have had little or no experience of other cultures or the cultural groups concerned. It is very likely that the decisions would have been taken differently by people with intercultural competence.

This underlines the necessity for a broad approach to intercultural education involving all areas of the community. Many initiatives in intercultural education have evolved since the 1970s at local, national and international level. In many European countries, intercultural education has been integrated into the curriculum in response to multicultural classroom realities. Ministries of education have taken other intercultural education initiatives. In Portugal, the Ministry of Education sponsors domestic exchanges – urban/rural, north/south – involving schools and classes. In Switzerland, domestic exchanges between linguistically different schools and culture groups are supported. In Finland, the Ministry of Education works with a consortium of exchange organizers to ensure that exchange pupils are treated as an intercultural education resource. In Austria, teachers are offered in-service training in intercultural education with respect to teaching in multicultural classes and to organizing international school projects and exchanges. Non-governmental organizations at national and international level, such as EFIL, are promoting intercultural learning. The European Union and the Council of Europe have recommended and implemented actions with respect to migration, multicultural societies, cultural and ethnic minorities, exchanges and the integration of Europe, some of which are listed in Appendix 2.

PRINCIPLES AND OBJECTIVES OF INTERCULTURAL LEARNING

There are two principles for intercultural learning which have been assumed in this discourse so far. The first is cultural relativism, which means that there is no hierarchy of cultures. Intercultural education accepts differences in the thinking and behaviour of people from other cultures. This implies that the values and norms of one culture cannot be applied to judge the activities of another culture.[8] This does not mean that another culture cannot or must not be judged. Yet such a judgement must be based on a complete understanding of its character, traits and complexity and not on the values and norms of one's own culture. The possibility of judging another culture includes the possibility of a critical judgement of one's own culture. Nevertheless, judgement on a culture must not be confused with judgement on members of this culture.[9] Cultural relativism also implies that there is a 'right' to have a culture, whether it be one's own or another. As a logical consequence, cultural diversity is seen as a value itself. It is assumed that cultural diversity enables development and growth. The appreciation of other cultures implies the possibility of understanding one's own culture but also of learning through a different mental filter how to adapt to and benefit from another social environment.

The second principle is reciprocity. Intercultural learning is not a one-way process but – as the prefix 'inter' suggests – a process between cultures. In contrast with earlier approaches where intercultural education in multicultural societies aimed at assimilation, intercultural learning here implies learning from and with each other across cultural boundaries. These two principles require equal status of cultures, shared dependence and interdependence, shared responsibility and cooperation.

Based on these principles, there are a number of objectives for intercultural learning, which can be summarized as follows:

- overcoming ethnocentrism, which implies a consciousness that one's perception is influenced by one's culture and experience;
- acquiring the ability to empathize with other cultures, which implies an openness towards the foreign and unknown;
- acquiring the ability to communicate across cultural boundaries, which implies bilingualism;
- developing a means of cooperation across cultural boundaries and in multicultural societies.

Unlike in the static concept of culture as promoted by an ethnopluralistic ideology, intercultural learning does not focus on preserving cultural identities but on overcoming and transcending cultural barriers. This approach is based on a dynamic concept of culture, which means that cultural values, norms and lifestyles are evolving under the influence of other cultures.

LEARNING FROM DIFFERENCES

Intercultural learning is understood as a process of growth and development emerging from understanding and accepting differences; such learning in a state of homogeneity does not seem to be possible. Only when confronted with another culture and thus realizing cultural differences can I become aware of my own culture. This experience enables me to reflect on what has been unconscious to me so far or what has been perceived to be 'natural' and evident. The notion and understanding of culture is possible only when one has been exposed to a different culture. The second step in this process is not to reject the other culture, which is perceived to be threatening because it gives new and different answers to existential questions of life, but to explore the possibilities it offers that have not yet been discovered in my own culture. Rejection through prejudice must give way to receptiveness to these possibilities, which open new perspectives for human development.

Intercultural learning is more than an encounter with another culture and is more than culture shock. Intercultural learning is based on the assumption that the fear of the foreign is not a natural destiny and that cultural development has always been a result of an encounter of different cultures. The prefix inter suggests that this fear and the historical barriers can be overcome. It also suggests a relationship and exchange between cultures. But, even more, intercultural learning is based on the readiness to make the encounter with other cultures productive, to gain greater awareness of one's own culture, to be able to relativize one's own culture and to explore new ways of coexistence and cooperation with other cultures.[10]

Intercultural learning is not necessarily a harmonious process. The confrontation between different cultures with different value systems results not only in opportunity but also in conflict. The nature of this conflict means that many difficulties cannot be resolved. Different attitudes towards the value of nature, family, age, etc., or different perceptions of destiny and death, can be discussed at length but will not easily change since they are also influenced by culture. The idea is not as much to resolve conflict as to recognize and accept it and to deal with it in a democratic way.

The approach of learning from differences has been pursued by pupil exchange organizations, which have provided valuable contributions to the discourse on intercultural learning. The idea of most exchange organizations is that a pupil or student living in another country is confronted with different values, norms and patterns of behaviour and that he or she will learn from these differences – about his or her own culture, about the other culture, about relating to people of a different cultural background. One of these organizations, EFIL, which has been promoting intercultural learning through exchanges since the beginning of the 1970s, has defined intercultural learning as follows:

A new learning situation where learners are helped to see their differences as strengths and as resources to draw from and to gain a greater awareness rather than as barriers and as deviations from established norms; one where each culture is explained in the context of others through a process that stimulates self-inquiry, curiosity for others and understanding of the interaction between the two. Such a process should involve the learners both intellectually and emotionally.[11]

This approach also refers to the dialectic nature of intercultural learning between the self and the foreign, and thus to cultural diversity as a resource. It underlines again the necessity for interaction across cultural barriers.

Another definition has been developed by Alexander Thomas, who has worked intensively in the area of research into international exchanges.

Intercultural learning takes place if a person seeks to understand the orientation system of perception, thinking, valuing and acting of another culture by interacting with its members and if this person attempts to integrate this orientation system in his or her own culture orientation system and to apply it in his or her thinking and acting in the foreign environment. Intercultural learning implies not only understanding the orientation system of a foreign culture but also a reflection of the orientation system of one's own culture.[12]

This approach includes pedagogic objectives that can be applied to other contexts of intercultural learning. This refers especially to reflection on one's own culture in connection with attempts to understand another culture and with the process of integrating elements of another culture into one's own thinking and behaviour.

PEDAGOGICAL APPROACHES TO INTERCULTURAL LEARNING

From what has been written so far, it is evident that intercultural learning implies a number of complementary educational approaches, which could be summarized as follows:

- Intercultural learning implies what Christian Alix refers to as 'dialogic learning'.[13] Dialogic learning includes confrontation with the foreign, the comparison of own culture with the foreign, the communication and negotiation of conflict with another culture, the comprehension of own and other culture as well as the interrelation between them, and cooperation across cultural boundaries.
- Intercultural learning implies experiential learning and thus practical learning. The learner responds to a given situation – whether it is familiar or not – in a specific way and evaluates the outcome to determine future actions in the same or in a similar situation.
- Intercultural learning is theme-orientated and person-centred, which means that the learning takes place with respect to the real concerns of the persons involved. This learning involves not only the 'me' and 'you' but also a specific theme or issue.

As can be seen, intercultural learning does not represent a single learning theory. Different aspects of intercultural learning can be described. It is usually intentional learning rather than incidental learning. Of course, it is possible to learn incidentally while being exposed to a foreign culture but it is likely that latent fear and the subsequent rejection of the foreign will prevent intercultural learning. Usually, a specific intent and motivation based on specific objectives is necessary to overcome these barriers and to learn interculturally.

Intercultural learning also implies observational and imitative learning, which refers to the way children usually learn. In the case of exposure to a new cultural environment, adolescents and adults have much in common with children in their native environment. To function effectively in a new foreign environment, it is necessary to observe and imitate the behaviour and actions of those who have been socialized in this environment.

Social learning is closely linked. It is important to adapt to the norms, taboos and expectations of a social environment, and thus to learn appropriate behaviour, and to understand the meaning and underlying values of rules, as well as the interdependencies, relationships and structures within this environment. It is not enough for a pupil to know how to address a teacher; it is also necessary for the roles of pupils and teachers and their relationship in a given society to be understood.

Finally, intercultural learning implies cognitive learning. Experience is not an end in itself. It is necessary for the learner to reflect on and analyse an experience, and to integrate the experience into his or her mental frame of reference, enabling appropriate behaviour to take place in future experiences.

THE PROCESS OF INTERCULTURAL LEARNING

The total process of intercultural learning has two facets. The first relates to the degree to which an individual's patterns of behaviour, and what those behaviours are based on (values, norms, beliefs), is deemed to be consistent with behaviour patterns of others. Recently arrived migrant children or exchange students will perceive themselves as having a low degree of behaviour consistency with that of classmates in the 'new' culture, while within their own culture they would have a high degree of behaviour consistency with classmates. During the process of intercultural learning this factor moves from a low degree of behaviour consistency to a high degree and is affected by such things as learning the language, how and when to 'touch', rituals of eating and drinking, etc.

The second facet relates to a mental frame of reference that incorporates the individual's value system and filters any new or different experience. Such a frame of reference – or filter – expands, adapts and changes during the intercultural learning process, from an ethnocentric position where there is a high degree of clarity or a clear response to events and situations based on an individual's value system filter, to a confused state where there is a lack of clarity, where the filter does not work, to a more balanced frame of reference which involves openness and flexibility and which again provides clarity of reaction.

This is not only a body of knowledge and skills (e.g. how to communicate through both verbal and non-verbal language, how to greet, how to eat) but also a state of mind that develops a greater capacity for tolerance and ambiguity, an openness to different values and behaviours. It does not always imply accepting or taking on different values as one's own, but acquiring the flexibility of seeing them as they are in the context of another cultural filter, not through one's own ethnocentred frame.

Hoopes suggests that this process takes place along a continuum from ethnocentrism at one end to some form of adaptation or integration at the other.[14] Hoopes in fact sees four possible outcomes of this process, which were described earlier (see pages 32–3). Since to the authors the desirable outcome of intercultural learning is intercultural competence, we have adapted the model accordingly (Figure 8). However, intercultural competence as meant by the authors is to be seen in accordance with what we have written on the previous pages and thus is set in a broader context than what Hoopes refers to as 'multiculturalism'.

| Ethnocentrism | Awareness | Understanding | Acceptance and respect | Appreciation and valuing | Change | Intercultural competence |

Figure 8 Continuum of intercultural learning

Ethnocentrism seems to be a natural condition as long as one is not confronted directly or indirectly with other cultures. As long as there is no awareness of culture and therefore no awareness of cultural differences, it is an obvious result of socialization that other people's way of life is measured by the standards of this cultural group. It lies in the very nature of culture that it is defended against everything which does not meet these standards and which, therefore, is foreign. For this reason, the development of identification from the family to the community to the cultural or ethnic group to nation stops right there – at ethnocentrism and nationalism. Ethnocentrism and nationalism divide the world into two parts – us and them. While it might be possible to develop something like an identification with humankind as a whole, this is not enough to enable an understanding of people of a different cultural background so as to relate to them.

The first step out of ethnocentrism is to become aware that there is something different from one's own culture. This does not mean that a cultural self-awareness is developed.

Understanding in this model refers to developing a concept of culture and of cultural differences – how and why is another cultural group different and how does this difference affect the relationship between people of different cultural backgrounds? As part of this, a person can become aware of prejudices and stereotypes and develop an understanding about how thinking and behaviour are affected.

The next step is when a person accepts the validity of the cultural differences he or she encounters, when a person accepts another culture without judging it against his or her own and when a person can respect elements of another culture even when they contradict elements of his or her own culture.

Appreciation and valuing refers to the ability to understand cultural diversity as a resource for growth and development. This is possible when opportunities in another culture are recognized but have not been discovered in one's own culture.

Change refers to the development of new attitudes, skills and behaviour when a person consciously or unconsciously reacts to characteristics encountered in another culture. This can mean the adoption of attitudes and behaviour of another culture that are felt to be useful or desirable for effective functioning in another cultural environment. It can also mean the development of new attitudes, skills and behaviour as a result of the intercultural experience, which are inherent to neither one's own nor the other culture.

Although this model emphasizes the cognitive dimension of an intercultural learning process and thus lacks sufficient consideration of its emotional aspects, it can be useful for developing a didactic approach to intercultural learning when an appropriate methodology as described in the following chapters is applied. To summarize, it can be said that intercultural learning:

- is understood to be more than acquisition of knowledge;
- implies a change, a process of behaviour and skills development, the development of a new attitude and openness towards the unknown and foreign, but also a different awareness and response to one's own environment;
- is not just learning about, but learning from and with, other cultures (merely observing and cataloguing lists of differences is not an intercultural learning experience; it is necessary to go beyond the list, to understand the reasons for differences and to cooperate across cultural boundaries);
- is reciprocal and interdependent with learning even within one's own cultural environment (it is not possible to understand other cultures without understanding one's own; it is also not possible to understand fully one's own culture until the encounter with another culture has put it in perspective).

STRATEGIES AND STRUCTURES FOR INTERCULTURAL EDUCATION

We have pointed out the need for intercultural learning in our societies. The question is where to start and how. Given the global conditions in which we live, it is reasonable to say that everyone – from a multicultural society or not – should have the possibility of learning interculturally.

As a consequence, intercultural learning cannot be left to the initiative of individuals, but should be inherent to education and educational institutions, which, in turn, suggests that intercultural education should be integrated in school curricula. Since intercultural education is a relatively new discipline of pedagogy, this has to be reflected in the training of teachers. The Council of Europe has reacted to this need with a specific recommendation and numerous activities.[15] There are already teacher training schemes with respect to intercultural education in a number of European countries, but it seems that a much broader approach is necessary to involve as many teachers as possible who might be interested. Another initiative undertaken by the Council of Europe is the development of a framework for teacher training for school links and exchanges.

Intercultural education can and should take place outside school too. This would require the training of what can be called 'intercultural facilitators': people who are trained to work with multicultural groups, to use their skills to support the resolution of conflicts with a cultural component and to act as facilitators to make use of cultural diversity as a resource. These intercultural facilitators could be active in educational institutions other than schools, in youth and community organizations, in working environments, administration, factories, services, etc.

One approach to promoting intercultural learning is the artificial creation of intercultural or multicultural settings through intercultural exchange programmes, international group meetings, etc. In social environments without a multicultural component, activities such as intercultural exchange programmes are essential for intercultural learning, since they imply personal exposure to representatives of a different culture. There is an enormous need for additional intercultural contacts in exchange programmes within as well as outside a school context, to create and increase awareness and appreciation of cultural diversity.

There are many different types of structured international exchange activities for different target groups and contexts. Although intercultural learning is recognized as a potential element of most exchanges, the emphasis can also be on other objectives. A thorough discussion on the nature of structured exchanges was prepared as part of the working document for a UNESCO meeting on youth exchanges organized in 1987.[16]

It is important to point out that the intercultural learning process within an exchange takes place not only for those who go to a different culture on such programmes, but also for those who receive someone from a different culture – pupils, families, teachers, work colleagues (depending on the type of programme), friends, etc. With this understanding, schools and classes receiving exchange pupils from another country can serve as 'laboratories' for intercultural learning on an experiential and emotional as well as on a cognitive level, while teachers can serve as intercultural facilitators.

One element of many exchange programmes is that the participants live with families in the receiving culture. This has a strong experiential and emotional dimension: learning to live together by living together, learning by experience. This approach has a great impact on the learning process of the family, which encounters a different culture without leaving home.

Exchange organizations have always been concerned that this learning process should be not only incidental but also structured. Thus exchange programmes include a number of pedagogic events before the visit abroad (preparation), during the experience in another country (guidance) and after return to the home country (assessment or reorientation). These events are intended to support and deepen the learning experience and to enable participants – adolescents as well as families – to reflect on their experience in a structured and cognitive way. This concept is referred to as orientation.

While some exchange organizations have developed a pedagogic concept for their activities it seems that the majority of exchanges within as well as outside a school context lack adequate pedagogic preparation, guidance and assessment. The following chapters of this book are intended to support teachers in their efforts to provide such a pedagogic framework as part of intercultural education.

Notes and references

1   Dietmar Larcher, *Fremde in der Nähe*. Klagenfurt: Drava, 1991, p. 62.

2   David Hoopes, 'Intercultural communication concepts and the psychology of inter-cultural experience'. In Margaret Pusch (ed.), *Multicultural Education. A Cross-cultural Training Approach*. Yarmouth, ME: Intercultural Press, 1979, p.10. This discussion refers to the terms 'intercultural', 'multicultural', 'cross-cultural', etc. and the respective national translations.

3   Georg Auernheimer, *Einführung in die Interkulturelle Erziehung*. Darmstadt: Wissenschaftliche Buchgesellschaft, 1990, p. 29.

4   H. Fennes and K. Hapgood (eds), *Intercultural Learning Materials – a Tool for School Curricula*. Brussels: European Federation for Intercultural Learning, 1987.

5   Dietmar Larcher, *Fremde in der Nähe*, p. 77.

6   Considering that the populations of most European countries have evolved from many different cultural and ethnic layers caused by migration over hundreds of years, it is difficult to determine after how many generations a cultural group becomes indigenous.

7   Semi-lingualism refers to a reduced competence of a person in his or her mother tongue as well as in the second language, which means that such a person is limited in his or her verbal expression in general. Owing to the interdependence between language and thinking outlined earlier in this book, this implies that semi-lingualism is also a barrier to intellectual development. Research has shown that the development of language proficiency in the mother tongue also contributes to learning a second language and vice versa (see also 'Intercultural learning and language learning' in Chapter 7).

8   This principle is difficult to realize, as can be seen from the ongoing and recent discussion on the universality of human rights. In this discussion, the right of the indi-vidual (or minority) is confronted with the power of the collective (or majority). This reflects the basic dilemma of cultures in general – the relationship between the indi-vidual and the community, between the minority and the majority. Because different value systems determine this relationship differently, it is very difficult to find a common denominator. It seems, though, that in this discussion the demands of cultures are being confused with the demands of nation states.

9   Bh. Parekh, 'The concept of multicultural education'. In Modgil *et al.* (eds), *Multicultural Education*. London: Falmer Press, 1986, p. 28.

10 Dietmar Larcher, *Fremde in der Nähe*, p. 75.

11 EFIL Tenth Anniversary Statement, European Federation for Intercultural Learning, 1981.

12 Alexander Thomas, *Interkulturelles Lernen im Schüleraustausch*. Saarbrücken/Fort Lauderdale: Verlag Breitenbach, 1988, p. 83.

13 Christian Alix has done intensive research on international exchanges. He describes the concept of dialogic learning in detail in his book *Pakt mit der Fremdheit. Interkulturelles Lernen als dialogisches Lernen im Kontext internationaler Schulkooperationen*. Frankfurt/Main: Verlag für interkulturelle Kommunikation, 1990.

14 David Hoopes, 'Intercultural communication concepts ...', pp. 18, 19.

15   Recommendation No. R (84) 18 of the Committee of Ministers on the training of teachers for intercultural understanding, notably in the context of migration, adopted on 25 September 1984. An overview of the work done in this area by the Council of Europe and the Council for Cultural Co-operation between 1977 and 1983 was prepared by Micheline Rey in 1986.

16   UNESCO. Report of the Meeting of Governmental and Non-governmental Officials Responsible for Youth Exchange, Expert Meeting by Intercultura, the Italian Government and UNESCO in Rome, June 1987, UNESCO Youth Division, Paris, 1987.

CHAPTER 6

Educational Objectives of Intercultural Learning

Traditional thinking suggested that in order to know another culture or nationality it was necessary to learn the language. Indeed, for years, schools – and parents – have justified school links and exchanges to France, the United Kingdom and Germany, in particular, as a means of learning French, English or German. Learning the language was the goal, the educational objective. But, as we all know, this isn't all the learning that transpired – or didn't transpire but could have. Stereotypes and prejudices increased or decreased; participants were frustrated at not knowing how to interpret the non-verbal language; 'differences' were undoubtedly identified but never explained or understood; one's own cultural identity was probably confronted but not set in context.

So what are the goals of intercultural learning? Is it possible to be precise about learning objectives so that the benefits or outcomes of intercultural learning can be measured and evaluated? The authors think so, or we wouldn't have written this book. Institutions, exchange organizations and social scientists active in the field of intercultural communication have all demonstrated not only that intercultural learning objectives are possible but that research investigations and evaluation indicate real outcomes, real learning. The difference lies in the nature of the learning, which by and large is experiential, something not altogether comfortable in the traditional classroom setting.

WHAT OTHERS HAVE SAID

There are at least three trends, identified by Margaret Shennan in her book for this same series, *Teaching about Europe*, pushing schools along the path of a European dimension in education.[1] The first is the albeit bumpy but undoubtedly certain road to social and economic integration post-1992; the second powerful trend is the fast pace of technological development, which has created an enormous potential for linking Europeans (without movement); and, finally, the ongoing transitions in

Central and Eastern Europe, which have the effect of expanding the notion of 'what Europe is'. These factual trends make it necessary that more than a language is learned if we are to cooperate and communicate.

The Council of Europe at its Standing Conference of European Ministers of Education in October 1991 adopted a resolution on the 'European dimension of education: teaching and curriculum content' with the following educational objectives: 'to increase awareness of the growing unity between European peoples ... to help make the younger generation conscious of their common European identity ... to foster understanding ... that the European perspective applies and that European decisions are necessary ... to take an active part in shaping Europe's future.'[2] The resolution goes on to suggest that the basic values of political, social and individual life which underlie the educational process should be viewed in the framework of a wider European community, which means

- willingness to reach understanding, to overcome prejudice and to be able to recognize mutual interests while at the same time affirming European diversity;
- receptiveness to different cultures while preserving individual cultural identity;
- the will to coexist in harmony and to accept compromises in the reconciliation of different interests in Europe.[3]

To realize the European dimension in education, schools are encouraged to develop awareness of Europe across the curriculum. The Standing Conference recommended (within a long list) that methods for using school links and exchanges as part of teaching be developed. These learning objectives are affective by nature; they require an approach which is experiential if pupils are to reach understanding, overcome prejudice, become aware of their individual and European identities, be receptive to different cultures, etc. The European Union has also addressed learning objectives in its development of a European dimension in education. In 1988, the Council and Ministers of Education of Member States defined four objectives in pursuit of strengthening the European dimension in education:

- to strengthen in young people a sense of European identity;
- to prepare young people to take part in the economic and social development of the European Union;
- to make young people aware of the advantages, but also the challenges, represented by the enlarged economic and social area;
- to improve their knowledge of the European Union and its Member States in their historical, cultural, economic and social aspects.[4]

It is interesting to note the difference between 1988 and 1991 in the nature of what was resolved. In 1988, ministers were concerned that young people learn to be good European citizens, to acquire the knowledge and skills required for full participation in a wider and united Europe. By 1991 the goals reflected the need to address tensions and conflicts that have openly occurred between cultural and ethnic groups within borders of national states. In 1988 it was a matter of improving pupil knowledge of the Community and its Member States, making young people aware of the possibilities, preparing them for social and economic union.

These aims were cognitive, whereas in 1991 the goals reflected the need for understanding, overcoming prejudice, affirming diversity in Europe, being receptive to cultural differences and accepting compromises. These goals for learning are much more emotional and have to do with the way people feel about their neighbours, both within and across borders. Goals related to both cognitive and affective development are necessary for intercultural learning.

Two interpretations help to explain the differences in aspiration of these resolutions. One is the different nature and goals of the two institutions, the European Community (as it was) and the Council of Europe. The other is the different international perspective. In 1988, Europe was still divided between East and West, and therefore the vision of the European Community for developing a European identity was limited to Western Europe. In 1991, this barrier had been abolished – at least in political terms. The newly evolving visions of Europe had to include numerous countries which had not previously been considered as having a European identity. This cultural and political diversity required a new approach to developing such a vision.

In 1994 the Standing Conference of European Ministers of Education adopted four resolutions, one of which dealt with school links and exchanges. This resolution built on the work previously mentioned. Importantly for the discussion in this book, it encouraged the participation of as many young people as possible in school links and exchanges, and identified the success of such links and exchanges as being dependent on good preparation, supervision and evaluation, as well as on the provision of training and support for teachers. The quality aspects referred to in this resolution are echoed in this book.

These resolutions reflect a group or societal goal orientation. The aims are intended for all people who find themselves living in Europe. They are written not for the individual but for the society. They are political by nature; they have to do with what we want Europe to become.

WHAT RESEARCH HAS TO SAY

Georg Auernheimer, a German researcher who has dealt intensively with intercultural education, identifies four different categories of objectives for intercultural learning, which overlap while describing different priorities:

- intercultural learning as social learning;
- intercultural learning as political education;
- intercultural learning as antiracist education;
- intercultural learning to support migrant children in developing their identity.[5]

With respect to **intercultural learning as social learning**, empathy, solidarity and the ability to deal with conflict are primary objectives. Empathy is seen as the ability to put oneself in someone else's position and thus to be able to see this person's problems from his or her point of view. Solidarity is seen as a principle contrary to rivalry and competition. Solidarity implies common action with others, while there is awareness of the differences between oneself and those one cooperates with. These two competencies are complemented by the ability to deal with conflict in a fair and constructive way. This should result in a better understanding of the situation of migrants, cultural or ethnic minorities and foreigners in general. It should enable one to reflect on one's own behaviour, to become aware of and overcome one's prejudices, and thus to develop new patterns of communicating with and relating to others.

Intercultural learning as political education refers to the socio-economic and political situation of migrants and cultural or ethnic minorities. This implies an education against nationalistic thinking and towards 'intercultural respect'. In this context, intercultural learning is aimed at the ability to analyse institutions and national structures with respect to structural discrimination and structural violence. To achieve this, it is necessary to overcome the monocultural and nationalistic view of existing curricula, school textbooks and educational materials in favour of a truly multicultural perspective, and thus to establish a multi-reference education system. Other cultures and people should not be perceived as objects but as historical subjects. It is crucial which conception the learner develops of society, of history and of international interdependencies and conflicts. This refers especially to history, economics and political education, but also to languages and natural sciences (for example, the Crusades could be described from a Muslim as well as from a Christian perspective).

Intercultural learning as antiracist education aims to raise awareness of one's own racism, which has been adopted during socialization. This racism is very deeply rooted, is usually unconscious and suppressed because it is recognized as not being acceptable, but still affects one's thinking, decisions and behaviour. But racism can also explain social processes and problems, such as unemployment, of people who are not part of the national culture: institutionalized racism resulting in structural discrimination. In this context, intercultural learning is aimed at critically reviewing and overcoming racism in everyday language, media and literature as well as in one's attitudes and behaviour. It is aimed at a constructive cooperation between people of different cultural backgrounds.

The fourth facet of intercultural learning is that it is aimed at **supporting migrant children in developing their identity**. With respect to the development of their identity, migrant children are faced with a very difficult situation since they are permanently confronted with contradicting value systems, with a foreign and sometimes hostile environment, with social isolation and insecure future prospects.[6] The social reality of migrant children is characterized by two cultures – they are travellers between cultures. Migrant children have to learn to deal with contradicting cultural influences. They must be able to participate in two languages and cultures and thus need to develop what is referred to as 'bilingual–bicultural identity'. This requires a bilingual and bicultural education based on a dynamic concept of culture. A major aspect in this process is real bilingualism, which implies that migrant children need to learn and use their mother tongue as well as the majority language. As outlined earlier, the development of the mother tongue is indispensable for the intellectual, emotional and social development education of migrant children – not only to avoid alienation from their original family and environment but also to increase their proficiency in the second language. Another aspect is that the children of the majority culture have to be involved in this learning process. They, too, have to become familiar with the language and the culture of the migrant children – at least at a basic level – to be able to understand and empathize with their colleagues.

With respect to educational structures and methods this requires an approach of immersion rather than submersion. Immersion refers to an approach where the children immerse into a foreign language and culture under guidance that respects their capability and acknowledges both languages as being of equal value. Submersion refers to an approach which, in the past, was traditionally taken with respect to education in multicultural settings, where children are overchallenged with the use of the second language and where their native tongue is neglected.

Although the situation of indigenous cultural minorities is different from that of migrants much of what has been written so far with respect to the development of a bicultural identity can also be applied to them.

Concluding, it can be said that intercultural learning requires new approaches and initiatives in education that are aimed at integration, that acknowledge the right to be different and that consider the language, tradition, religion and culture of migrant children in the curriculum. It has to be pointed out again that education cannot replace politics; it can only contribute to the intercultural competence of individuals. This competence is of great value for the peaceful development of democratic multicultural societies.[7]

In contrast, exchange organizers have paid more attention to the learning taking place during a sojourn abroad. AFS Intercultural Programs, an international exchange organizer that has been operating secondary school exchanges since 1949, deals primarily with individual placements in a family for a duration of one year. In effect, the AFS 'Year Program' is a one-year intercultural communication course for individuals. AFS has identified four areas of learning: personal values and skills, interpersonal relationship-building, intercultural knowledge and sensitivity, and global issues/awareness.[8]

Personal values and skills

1 To think creatively, demonstrated by an ability to view ordinary things, events and values from a fresh perspective, to generate innovative ideas and solutions.
2 To think critically, demonstrated by an unwillingness to accept superficial appearances and by a scepticism of stereotypes.
3 To accept more responsibility for oneself, demonstrated by increased ability to exercise self-control within the context of social norms and expectations.
4 To de-emphasize the importance of material things, demonstrated by an increasing tendency to define one's worth and goals in terms of ideals instead of possessions.

5 To be more fully aware of oneself, demonstrated by increased willingness and ability to view oneself objectively and to see oneself as deeply influenced by one's native culture.

Interpersonal relationship-building

1 To deepen concern for and sensitivity to others, demonstrated by increased ability and willingness to 'put oneself in the other person's place'; that is, to empathize.
2 To increase adaptability to changing social circumstances, demonstrated by greater flexibility in the process of adjusting to new people, social situations and cultural norms.
3 To value human diversity, demonstrated by an eagerness for communication, mutual respect and friendship with others from a variety of backgrounds different from one's own.
4 To communicate with others using their ways of expression, demonstrated by the ability to carry on extended conversations with hosts[9] in their native language, and by the ability to use and to react appropriately to non-verbal signals common in the host culture.
5 To enjoy oneself in the company of others, demonstrated by a diminishing of self-consciousness and an increase in readiness to participate joyfully and whole-heartedly in many varieties of social gatherings.

Intercultural knowledge and sensitivity

1 To increase knowledge of host country and culture, demonstrated by an ability to explain key dimensions of that culture from the perspective of a host national.
2 To increase sensitivity to subtle features of the home culture, demonstrated by an ability to see aspects of that culture not previously recognized and to evaluate its strengths and weaknesses from the perspective of an outsider.
3 To understand the nature of cultural differences, demonstrated by an ability to describe some of the fundamental concerns that must be addressed by all human beings, and by a readiness to accept that a wide variety of solutions to those concerns are possible.
4 To broaden one's skills and concepts, demonstrated by the ability to think and act in ways that are characteristic of the host culture but transferable to other environments.

Global issues/awareness

1 To deepen interest in and concern about world affairs, demonstrated by a sustained commitment to obtaining information from many sources with respect to the problems commonly facing all human beings.

2 To be aware of worldwide linkages, demonstrated by a willingness and ability to make personal choices in certain ways because one cares about the effect of one's choices on people in other communities throughout the world.

3 To gain in commitment to the search for solutions to worldwide problems, demonstrated by the giving of one's personal resources (time, energy, money), whether in a professional or voluntary capacity, to the search for culturally sensitive and technologically feasible solutions.

As a result of research undertaken in the 1970s and 1980s, AFS was able to specify learning objectives in each of the areas that occur for the sojourner and that can be guided to a learning result.

American foreign language teacher H. Ned Seelye, in the most recent edition of his *Teaching Culture* (1993), suggests six goals of cultural instruction for the classroom, particularly classrooms of foreign language learning.[10] The overarching 'super goal' specifies that 'all students will develop the cultural understandings, attitudes and performance skills needed to function appropriately within a society of the target language and to communicate with the culture bearer'. Seelye moves from lofty prose to six more detailed and concrete learning goals for the teacher to use.

1 *Interest.* The student shows curiosity about another culture (or another segment of his or her own culture) and empathy toward its members.

2 *Who.* The student recognizes that role expectations and other social variables, such as age, sex, social class, religion, ethnicity and place of residence, affect the way people speak and behave.

3 *What.* The student realizes that effective communication requires discovery of the culturally conditioned images that are evoked in the minds of people when they think, act and react to the world around them.

4 *Where and when.* The student recognizes that situational variables and convention shape behaviour in important ways.

5 *Why.* The student understands that people generally act in the way they do because they are using options their society allows for satisfying basic physical and psychological needs and that cultural patterns are interrelated and tend mutually to support need satisfaction.

6 *Exploration.* The student can evaluate a generalization about the target[11] culture in terms of the amount of evidence substantiating it, and has the skills needed to locate and organize information about the target culture from the library, the mass media, people and personal observation.

These goals or learning objectives as well as those of AFS are stated in terms of participant or pupil focus and achievement, not in terms of the teaching process. It may be appropriate to develop additional learning objectives that relate to the teaching and teacher process. Learning objectives are stated in terms of the individual but there will also be a learning effect that can be measured in terms of the *group*, the class, including the teacher. George Renwick in his work identifies a number of factors within a class that can be affected in intercultural learning, especially if the group is multicultural in composition:

1 Level of trust between sub-groups and within the class as a whole.
2 Patterns of communication, e.g. who is included, excluded, by whom why; development of vocabulary and non-verbal expression unique to the group.
3 Extent to which group agrees on common objectives.
4 Clarity with which objectives are defined and degree to which pupils are included in the defining process.
5 Emergence of leaders or spokespersons; extent to which support and cooperation divides along cultural lines.
6 Development or dissolution of cliques.
7 Degree of discrimination against one sub-group by another.
8 Degree of any conflict and lines along which conflicts are drawn.
9 Level of tension or suspicion.
10 How the class handles a crisis or challenge.
11 Degree of competition within the class, between the class and other groups.
12 Extent to which the class contributes to other groups, school projects, organizations.
13 Extent to which pupils in the group have a sense of group identity.[12]

Renwick suggests that teachers or facilitators choose those which are most appropriate or interesting – or necessary. The factor list also implies that appropriate objectives should be designed for the areas of interest.

INTERCULTURAL LEARNING GOALS IN THE CLASSROOM AND ACROSS BORDERS

There are four major areas of learning goals which make sense in the context of crossing, in the first instance, European borders, of applying learning schemes in the classroom and of supporting the development of globally minded young adults:

• perception and images
• awareness, knowledge
• attitudes
• skills and patterns of behaviour

The learning objectives for these areas are not substantially different from what has been cited in other sources, but the approach to and sequencing of those objectives follow the needs of the environment in which we find ourselves at the end of the twentieth century in schools in Europe.

Perceptions and images

Stereotypes, images and prejudices abound. Sometimes they are conscious; more often they are not. The media thrive on stereotypes: the mother figure getting stains out of her husband's and children's clothes; the white male banker convincing viewers how to save or spend their money; beautiful women from a tropical paradise selling seats on planes; 'beautiful' people drinking beautiful rum. Magazines promote skin care, health care, hair care, beauty care – all in pursuit of an ideal stereotype. Politicians talk about and sometimes address the voter stereotype.

What is behind a superficial stereotype? Everyone perceives the world differently – has different expectations of the world, thinks differently about it. The perception is unconscious and evolves out of a framework provided primarily by culture, according to David Hoopes.[13] Persons in a culture group share a set of perceptions about the world; another culture group will have evolved a different set of perceptions based on their needs, personality and culture. It is this culture which determines the screening of sensory data, the making sense of noise, odour, sights, texture, tastes. Someone who smokes will not notice smoke in a room nearly as quickly as someone for whom smoke is an unfamiliar odour. A city dweller will not hear the ambulance siren as quickly as a rural resident. A Thai student is likely to find British food bland while a British traveller to Thailand is likely to find 'mildly' seasoned food uncomfortably 'hot'.

The culture framework also enables the world to be categorized. How many cars are seen in a day? Yet some are noticed more than others: looks like a friend's car, it's your favourite colour or an unusual shape, one is speeding, another is weaving from one side to the other. There is a problem with categories in perception. It is possible to move too rapidly from category to stereotype: all people who speed are reckless; cars that weave about the road must have a drunk driver at the wheel. Numerous distinctions must be made about categories – how they look, how they move, how they sound, taste, smell. If we don't encounter weaving or speeding very often, we are less able to distinguish the subtleties that make up the behaviour. The screening and categorizing of sensory data, our unconscious system of perception, gives order and structure to the world. The perceptions are shared by others in the same culture group, while other culture groups have developed different cultural interpretations of the sensory data.

With respect to perception, intercultural learning targets the understanding of how our perception is culturally influenced: what we perceive and what not, how we perceive it, and how we classify and categorize what we perceive. It is necessary to enlarge and develop one's perceptual system to be able to understand and relate to other cultures.

This area seems an appropriate starting-point for learning goals. Pupils, classes, schools – many are taking first steps, having first experiences with 'others' who are different. The focus of this area, then, is to understand that perceptions and images already exist, have been learned and are in a state of continuous development. The learning goals are:

- to have an understanding of self-perception;
- to have an understanding/perception of own culture;
- to have an understanding/perception of other cultures;
- to become conscious of own stereotypes and prejudices;

- to recognize stereotypes and prejudices as superficial images;
- to recognize the influence of one's perceptions of own culture/self on perceptions of other cultures, other people;
- to recognize perceptions of other cultures having an influence on own perception of self/own culture.

Awareness, knowledge

This area follows logically in the approach to intercultural learning as a guided activity – in the classroom, with another class in another country, with a school link project. If perceptions and images exist, what can be known (learned factually) about one's own culture, about the culture being studied or visited, about differences between cultures, lifestyles and values?

Culture can be difficult to 'get at' as so much of it is in the realm of the unconscious. The easy bits – the fine arts, the literature, the foods consumed, dance, dress – are very conscious. But behaviours and values that shape our lives – ideas about the rearing of children, patterns of superior–subordinate relationships, the pace of work, body language, the concept of time – are not so visible, they just are. These parts of culture are more difficult because they are known to the culture group to which we belong and therefore assumed to be universal.

Becoming aware or 'enlightened' is a very Western notion and thereby cultural in itself. The 'Golden Age' of European history saw a move from absolute monarchy to enlightened despotism to real attack on the principle of authority; freedom of thought was encouraged; awareness of a new and modern world, an enlightenment, took place. This trend of thinking, the need for awareness, remains part of our cultural heritage. Pupils in Asian countries may have very different approaches to awareness.

Increased awareness and knowledge show us that we are part of a culture, that this culture affects thinking, feeling and behaviour, that there are other cultures and differences between cultures, and tell us what the reasons for these differences are. Following the idea of enlightenment, it is assumed that awareness and knowledge provide the potential for change.

Becoming aware that culture is not universal, that others solve the problems of everyday existence in ways that are not wrong but different, is the basis of a second set of learning objectives:

- to know one's own culture, including its values, lifestyles and patterns of behaviour;
- to know other cultures (represented in a multicultural classroom, in a bilateral exchange, exchange pupil present in a class, country with which there is a school link);
- to know the influence of (cultural) values on behaviour;
- to know cultural differences as enriching and appropriate.

Attitudes

Attitudes are interdependent with perception and with awareness and knowledge. They are partly conscious and partly unconscious. They reflect the particular perception of the world: curiosity, or indifference, about different cultures, values and lifestyles; confidence, or lack of confidence, in oneself for an intercultural encounter; comfort, or discomfort, with those who are different. Attitudes determine how a person relates to people of another cultural background, how a person deals with differences and conflict. But attitudes also determine what a person wants to know about the self and about another culture. Thus, they have an influence on awareness and knowledge. It is important to realize that attitudes are dynamic and can be changed.

An important aspect of intercultural education related to attitudes is the notion of cultural relativism, which implies that other cultures are not perceived to be less valuable than one's own. This is a prerequisite for relating to people from other cultures on an equal level. Other learning objectives with respect to attitudes are:

- to be aware of own/other attitudes;
- to accept and respect cultural differences;
- to value diversity;
- to be open towards the foreign;
- to be willing to deal with conflict.

Skills and patterns of behaviour

This area is about change and development in the pupils, classes, schools – and teachers – involved in any intercultural learning process. Behaviour belongs to the 'visible' part of culture influenced by perception, awareness, knowledge, attitudes and skills. If we perceive and imagine, if we know and have awareness, if we have developed certain attitudes, which skills do we have to acquire to comply with this new situation; what is it then that we think and do differently?

At the macro-level, we would all like the world to be different, more peaceful, more respectful of human rights, more environmentally conscious. A single intercultural learning project will not bring about world peace. It may enable small steps to changed behaviour in the class, the initial development of skills in pupils which, if we, and they, get it right, will be a continuing education and skills development.

Intercultural learning means the development of certain skills: how to communicate with people from different countries, both verbally and non-verbally; how to relate to and interact with people with different cultural backgrounds; how to behave and function effectively in a foreign environment.

The learning goals are:

- to communicate with others using their ways of expression, both verbally and non-verbally;
- to think critically;

- to analyse own culture, including data gathering, in order to contrast it with other cultures;
- to empathize, to have sensitivity to others;
- to tolerate ambiguity in self and others;
- to adapt to changing social/environmental factors;
- to listen actively to those from a different culture;
- to be able to give – and receive – feedback interculturally;
- to adapt behaviour in another cultural setting;
- to negotiate tension and conflict that is culturally based.

Learning goals and objectives must be clear. They can be adapted, made appropriate to the specific classroom situation or expanded during an activity or project – but you, the teacher or facilitator, will need to know what is to be achieved and learned. If there are too many learning goals, everyone will become confused. Intercultural learning falls within the social science net, which means there are frequently no clear answers, only more questions. It also means that only with clear goals can there be a framework in which to work: orientation for the process as well as evaluation. It is important for pupils to agree with the goals. We all have a stake in our own learning. Intercultural learning is personal and emotional as well as factual and useful. If the authors were young adults, they would certainly point to the fact that there is little evidence in the history of the world that adults have on their own managed to relate and communicate interculturally in an effective manner.

Notes and references

1   Margaret Shennan, *Teaching about Europe*. London: Cassell, 1991, p. 20.
2   Standing Conference of European Ministers of Education, 17th Session, Council of Europe, Resolution No. 1 on 'The European Dimension of Education: Teaching and Curriculum Content', Vienna, 16–17 October 1991 – see Appendix 2.
3   It should be noted that some of these objectives are not completely in line with the concept of intercultural learning as described in the previous chapters. Coexistence of different cultures in harmony seems to be an idealistic concept, while this coexistence implies conflicts. Preserving cultural identities is based on a static concept of culture as opposed to a dynamic interaction between cultures resulting in cultural evolution.
4   Resolution of the Ministers of Education meeting within the Council on the European dimension in education of 24 May 1988 (88/C 177/02).
5   Georg Auernheimer, *Einführung in die Interkulturelle Erziehung*. Darmstadt: Wissenschaftliche Buchgesellschaft, 1990, pp. 175–214.
6   *Ibid.*, p. 202.
7   Dietmar Larcher, *Fremde in der Nähe*. Klagenfurt: Drava, 1991, p. 61.
8   AFS Intercultural Programs, 'Statement of AFS Educational Content and Learning Objectives', pp. 2–4.
9   In the AFS lexicon, 'host' always refers to the country, culture or family to which the

pupil moves during the exchange period.

10 H. Ned Seelye, *Teaching Culture, Strategies for Intercultural Communication*, p. 31.

11 Seelye uses 'target' culture or 'target' language to define the culture or language being studied.

12 George W. Renwick, 'Evaluation: some practical guidelines'. In Margaret Pusch (ed.), *Multicultural Education. A Cross-cultural Training Approach*. Yarmouth, ME: Intercultural Press, 1979, pp. 213–19.

13 David Hoopes, 'Intercultural communication concepts and the psychology of intercultural experience'. In Margaret Pusch (ed.), *Multicultural Education. A Cross-cultural Training Approach*. Yarmouth, ME: Intercultural Press, 1979, pp. 13–16.

CHAPTER 7

Approaches to Intercultural Learning

When one is developing school curricula for intercultural learning, four basic issues must be considered:

- Why should one learn interculturally – the rationale for intercultural learning?
- What does intercultural learning actually mean, what does it imply?
- Who will be involved in this intercultural learning process?
- How is it done?

So far this book has mainly dealt with the first two issues. This chapter will take up approaches that can be used to achieve the learning objectives of an intercultural learning project with a specific group of people. These approaches require a conscious choice of methods that link learners, teachers and subject.

A basic dilemma for this book and its content is that the concept of education is closely linked to axioms and patterns of thinking as well as to values. The methods and tools applied in education are closely linked to habits, patterns of behaviour and norms. At the same time, all this is to a large degree culturally determined. This fact is reflected in the way education systems and thus schools (but also universities and training institutions) function. It is reflected in the general approach to education and learning, in the learning goals, in the curricula, in the structure of education systems and schools, in the didactics and teaching methods, in the relationship between teachers and learners.

This demonstrates the complexity of the task of developing approaches to intercultural learning in schools. Not only is the perception of the subject – culture – as well as the thinking and behaviour of the teachers and learners culturally determined, but so is the educational environment in which the learning should take place.

CULTURE AND EDUCATION

Culture has a great impact on various aspects of education. The purpose of education and the concept of learning are perceived differently in different cultures. In some cultures the purpose of education is learning to cope with the new, with the unknown, with unforeseen situations. It means learning how to learn rather than how to do. Learning thus describes a process in which the individual becomes able to cope with nature, the environment and society at large. The assumption is that learning is for life; it never ends.

In other cultures, learning means acquiring the skills and behaviour needed to be an acceptable group member. Learning is for the young to learn how to do things in order to participate in society. The assumption is that the solutions to all questions and problems of life are inherent to the collective group or society.

A good way to demonstrate the effect of culture on education is through the theory of Geert Hofstede, a Dutch researcher, who is also referred to in the exercise section of this book. Hofstede has compared cultural characteristics in more than fifty different countries (not including the former socialist countries of Central and Eastern Europe) and described five dimensions of culture.[1] According to these dimensions, Hofstede describes differences between school systems in different cultures.

The first dimension, *power distance*, reflects social inequality, the relationship with authority, etc. In a culture with high power distance, school tends to be teacher-centred, the teacher is directing the learning, the students only speak when asked, the teacher is never criticized – the teacher has the correct answer. In a culture with low power distance, the students are treated as equals, the students make interventions, ask questions, express criticism and disagreement. Power distance has a great impact on the relationship between teachers and pupils and thus on the learning methods used by teachers. According to Hofstede's research, power distance is, for example, high in France, medium in Spain and Italy and low in Scandinavia.[2]

The second dimension, *individualism versus collectivism*, describes the relationship between the individual and the group. In collectivist cultures, the performance of the group is more important than the performance of the individual. Consequently, in a collectivist culture students tend not to speak up if not directly addressed, confrontations and conflicts are avoided, it is important not to lose face. In an individualist culture, students expect to be treated as individuals, regardless of their backgrounds, and confrontations and open discussion of conflicts are acceptable or even considered to be good (collectivist cultures often correlate with cultures with large power distance).[3]

The third dimension, *masculinity versus femininity*, describes the social implications of having been born male or female. For Hofstede, 'masculinity' refers to the extent to which the dominant values in a society tend towards assertiveness and the acquisition of things, and away from concern for people and the quality of life. In a culture with a high degree of masculinity, students compete openly with each other and school is very serious – failing is a disaster, school is career-orientated, academic performance is dominant. In a feminine culture, according to Hofstede, mutual solidarity is seen as a goal, school is interest-orientated, social adaptation is important, teachers are friendly, etc. For example, Austria, Italy and Switzerland are considered to be 'masculine' countries while the Scandinavian countries and the Netherlands are considered to be 'feminine' ones.[4]

The fourth dimension, *uncertainty avoidance*, describes different ways of dealing with uncertainty. In cultures with strong uncertainty avoidance, students expect teachers to have all the answers, they do not disagree with teachers, etc. In cultures with weak uncertainty avoidance, a teacher can say 'I do not know' and disagreement is acceptable. Portugal, France, Spain and Belgium have a strong uncertainty avoidance; Austria, Germany and Switzerland have a medium uncertainty avoidance; and Denmark, Sweden, Ireland and the United Kingdom have a low uncertainty avoidance.[5]

The *time dimension* refers to key differences between cultures with a long-term and those with a short-term orientation. Simply speaking, in a short-term-orientated culture, quick results would be expected and students would be directed to learn for their exams. In a long-term-orientated culture there would be an adherence to slow but lasting results and the students would 'learn for life'.[6]

THE EDUCATIONAL ENVIRONMENT

The above illustrates the variety of educational concepts and structures depending on culture. This also applies for Europe: while educational institutions in Europe at first sight look alike, they are in fact very different. Of course, these differences have an influence on the approaches taken to integrate intercultural learning in school curricula and to implement intercultural learning projects and exchanges.

There are different roles for the school within society. In some countries, schools are perceived to be a (disliked) necessity, while in others schools are valued highly – by pupils too. This has an impact on how pupils perceive a special project (possibly involving extra time and energy) and therefore on their motivation to become engaged in it.

The way curricula are designed is very precise, detailed and lengthy in some countries; in others, it is very general, free and brief. There are countries with more rigid curricular requirements, which make it very difficult to implement an intercultural learning project, and there are countries with very flexible curricula, where project work might be endorsed.

The structures of education systems differ greatly within Europe. There are very hierarchical education systems with a strong educational authority, which requires bureaucracy and lengthy procedures to approve a special project, and there are decentralized systems where local and regional school authorities or even schools decide and act independently. The structure has an influence on the motivation of teachers as well as on the recognition they receive from the institution for investing extra time and energy.

In some countries, the grouping of pupils changes depending on the subjects they study; in others, the same group stays together as a class most of the time. This provides for different working situations. The members of a group with which a teacher does a project can have had the experience and history of working together but they also might hardly know each other, and will need time to become acquainted and to develop patterns of cooperation.

The relationship between teachers and pupils has a great impact on the approaches and methods used. This relationship is more distant and authoritarian in some countries and less authoritarian in others. The motivation and participation of pupils will strongly depend on this relationship. It can be said that for an intercultural learning project a more open relationship will be helpful, since the teacher should involve the pupils in the planning and preparation of the project. It is also likely that the teacher will face situations where he or she does not have answers and solutions and thus will be a learner too. This relationship will require mutual trust because both teachers and pupils depend on cooperation.

The approaches taken for implementing an intercultural learning project will depend on the relationship between teachers. In some countries, the teachers of a school perceive themselves to be a team, in others they act mostly as individuals and compete with each other rather than cooperate. Working on a project in a team formation is easier. This situation will be unusual for teachers in some countries and might require extra thought and preparation.

This demonstrates the impact that the culturally determined educational environment has on the way intercultural learning projects are perceived and organized – the objectives pursued, the approaches and methods applied, the materials used and the structure of the project in general. The approach has to be compatible with the 'school culture' or it will be rejected. But traditions have to be questioned in order to introduce concepts like the one presented in this book, which might be relatively new in a number of countries.

The biggest pedagogical challenge in working with bicultural groups – such as during a class exchange – or with multicultural groups in general is to find approaches and methods that are compatible with all the cultures represented. Frequently, this will not be possible and will cause confusion or even conflict with part of the group. There are many examples of this. In a class exchange, the pupils from one country might be used to structured learning situations with precise objectives, detailed assignments and strict timetables. They might prefer situations where there is one correct answer that they can find. The pupils from the other country might find too much structure difficult and prefer open-ended learning situations with vague objectives, broad assignments and no timetables, situations which allow a number of answers or solutions. Obviously, it will be difficult for teachers from two countries to design a project together. And it will be difficult for the pupils from two countries to work together on a given task.

It is necessary for the teacher or facilitator to be conscious of this problem and to address it once it appears. This can be used as an exemplary approach to intercultural learning. Learning about the concept of education in another country and learning about another culture, getting to know another 'school culture', understanding the reasons for the differences, understanding the values as well as views of life and of the world underlying the different education systems, learning to relate to these different concepts and solutions and possibly to make use of them – all this contributes to the intercultural learning process anticipated.

It is not possible to develop a unique approach to intercultural learning in schools but only to develop a generic framework which then can be used to develop approaches that are appropriate for specific countries and cultures.

THE SOCIAL AND CULTURAL ENVIRONMENTS

The choice and design of an approach will also be strongly influenced by the social and cultural environments of a specific school or class integrating intercultural learning into the school curriculum. There are a number of different possible settings.

- *A monocultural class or school in a monocultural society*. Although this is becoming an increasingly rare situation in Europe, there are still many regions – especially in rural areas – where only one cultural group is represented. The community is monocultural, frequently small in population, and the school reflects this. Ideas about 'culture' are likely to be unconscious but strong and untested.
- *A monocultural class or school in a multicultural society*. In this setting, the school, for whatever reason, retains a monocultural profile while situated in a multicultural society. This can occur with migration, where schools have an intake which excludes children of migrant families, or in countries with indigenous cultural minorities where the education system provides separate schools for different cultural groups.
- *A multicultural class in a multicultural environment*. In this setting, the school population reflects the multicultural character of the society and community in which it is situated.
- *Bicultural or bilingual regions and bicultural or bilingual classes*. A special situation exists in countries like Belgium or Switzerland, where there are two or more rather homogeneous language, ethnic or cultural regions.
- *A class with one or a few representatives from a different culture*. Another setting which is becoming increasingly 'normal' is that where a class receives one or more exchangees from one or more other countries. Or a class can receive pupils from another country whose parents have moved there owing to a work transfer, e.g. with a multinational or transnational company or with an international organization.

INTEGRATION OF INTERCULTURAL LEARNING IN SCHOOL CURRICULA

It has been illustrated that culture has a large impact on most areas of life and society in general. The complexity of the nature of culture implies that intercultural learning – as social learning – happens at a different level from the acquisition of knowledge and skills that is normally provided in different subjects at school. It is therefore logical that intercultural learning should not be a new subject but should be integrated into existing subjects and school activities. An interdisciplinary and cross-curricular approach is required, linking different subjects and thus enabling a related and complex understanding of knowledge, perceptions, attitudes and skills.

Since intercultural learning implies practical experience rather than theory, and since many aspects of culture cannot be found within the school environment, an extra-curricular approach may be required. Pupils will have to deal with issues that cannot be integrated into the existing subjects, they will need to explore elements of their own culture that cannot be found within the classroom, and sometimes they will have to leave the traditional school environment to become exposed personally to another culture, which is an integral element of intercultural learning.

Intercultural learning must be viewed as an ongoing and long-term process. Social and intercultural learning do not happen overnight. One cannot expect that prejudices and stereotypes which have been learned from early childhood can be changed as a result of a two-week project or a visit abroad. The integration of intercultural learning in school curricula must happen continuously and for all age groups during the whole school life of a pupil.

The traditional structures in the educational environment, such as rigid schedules and class structures, are frequently incompatible with the approaches described here and thus limit the intercultural learning possibilities. It is therefore useful and some-times necessary to break up these structures at least for a limited time. New and familiar approaches must be subtly balanced to avoid the whole idea being rejected.

There are limits to how far these approaches can be adopted in the different educa-tion systems in Europe. Depending on the specific situation, the following approaches are possible when trying to integrate intercultural learning in school curricula.

- Integrate intercultural learning within a specific subject. This can be done rather easily in language classes, geography, social science, political science, etc., but it is actually possible in all subjects to refer to the intercultural dimension on an ongoing basis. An individual teacher is able to pursue the goals of a project. This approach can be taken in a more rigid educational environment and does not necessarily require close cooperation with other teachers.
- Integrate intercultural learning within a number of different subjects in a specific class group on an ongoing basis. Two or more teachers would be involved, who would plan and implement the project together. They would work and teach as a team and develop a schedule that would meet their needs. The same approach could be taken with two or more class groups. This approach can be adopted most comfortably in a flexible educational environment, allowing for cross-curricular and extra-curricular teaching and learning approaches.
- Combine a long-term project – subject-orientated, cross-curricular or extra-curricular – with intensive phases such as a project week or an exchange. Even in more rigid educational environments, it should be possible to break up the regular schedule or the regular class structure for a few days, possibly involving other class groups or even the whole school.

Such an 'intensive phase' includes personal encounters of pupils with people of another culture. Depending on the social and cultural environment, the intensive phases could be organized in the following ways.

- A multicultural or bicultural/bilingual class can work consciously and intensively on what exists: 'exchanging cultures' by presenting one's own culture, traditions, rituals, symbols, etc., and learning from the others about their culture; 'exchanging languages' by teaching one's own language; addressing the relationship between the different cultural groups.
- It can be the exploration of one's own community through interviews, a field study or the like, to gain awareness of one's own cultural background or to find out more about other cultures living in the community.
- In a monocultural class, a personal encounter with another culture can be achieved either by receiving a class from abroad or by visiting another country (or another part of one's own country with a different cultural or ethnic group). It is preferable that such visits go in both directions so that both sides are experienced: being a 'native' as well as a 'foreigner'. For younger pupils, such visits might be rather short – in elementary school just a day or two – while for older pupils they can last up to four weeks.
- A school link without a physical exchange of pupils can have an intensive phase, e.g. simultaneous work on the same topic for one or two weeks, an exchange of findings via modern technology (electronic mail, fax) and presentation of the results to the whole school (the exercises later give some examples of this), the production of a common (bilingual) publication, etc. It has to be mentioned that personal encounters are more than just sending papers and bits and bytes to each other to be dealt with at leisure. It is important to have a face-to-face contact, which cannot easily be escaped or avoided.

INTERCULTURAL LEARNING CONCEPTS

There is no magic formula to intercultural learning in classroom situations or anywhere else. We know very little about it. Learning as such is a very complex process of acquiring and developing knowledge, awareness, attitudes, ideas and skills. Since the process itself is less known, learning is frequently known by its end results. The evaluation of a social or intercultural learning process is quite difficult owing to the fact that a change in perception, awareness and attitudes is hardly measurable. It is even more difficult to develop an appropriate didactic concept and method design for a challenging set of learning objectives. Therefore, didactics and methods for intercultural learning are in the process of ongoing development.

Basic assumptions

Pupils learn only if they want to. The motivation to learn is essential for achieving a given learning objective. This is nothing new but is mentioned here because a traditional motivation – performance recognized by grades and subsequently career – does not apply to an intercultural learning project. There can be incidental learning, e.g. during a visit abroad, but for a structured learning activity a certain commitment of the pupils is necessary. This can be achieved by involving the pupils in the planning and preparation of the project, by developing the objectives together with the pupils. If the activity meets the interests and needs of the pupils, they will actively participate. If the discrepancy between the objectives of the teacher(s) and the pupils is too big, the teacher(s) might have to do all the work and the pupils will consume the activity without much learning.

One of the assumptions underlying the methods presented in this book is that intercultural learning is not a linear process where one reaches a higher level step by step. The learning process instead takes the shape of a spiral where the learner goes in circles, touching the same themes and issues again and again at different levels. This seems to contradict the concept of timing and sequencing of educational approaches introduced elsewhere in this book, but it does not. Each activity has an impact on various different learning areas at the same time, although there is usually a special emphasis put on one of them. For example, there can be an exercise to become aware of one's own prejudices, which at the same time refers to values and lifestyles. Shifting the emphasis and coming back to the same learning areas at a later stage has been described pictorially as going in circles. For a given situation, the didactic follows a logical process within each learning area. For example, it is useful to become aware of one's own lifestyle before exploring other lifestyles.

Another assumption is that intercultural learning is an ongoing process that is never completely finished. It has a lasting effect. As there are seldom 'right' answers and solutions, as there is no perfect intercultural person, so there is no 'finished learning product'. A visit abroad initializes a process that is not finished upon return home but continues afterwards. Exploring one's own country after an experience abroad is the beginning of a new phase in this learning process, which might eventually lead to exploring yet another culture. Intercultural learning implies learning to cope with the new and unknown; it never ends.

Experiential learning

Intercultural learning implies experiential learning. It is not sufficient to read books about culture, to listen to lectures about other cultures, to deal with the subject on a purely cognitive and intellectual level. It is necessary to experience being confronted with new and unknown situations, to experience insecurity, fear, rejection as well as security, trust and sympathy, and to deal with the subject of culture on an emotional level. It is also necessary to learn *from* and *with* people of other cultures.

These two approaches refer respectively to the left and right hemispheres of our brains. The left hemisphere is concerned with learning that is analytical, rational, intellectual and numerical, whereas the right hemisphere deals with the experiential, the visual, the imaginative, the intuitive, the spatial. Since culture is reflected in both parts of our personality, the learning process also has to address both parts. The experience itself is an initial step, which provides questions as well as solutions in a rather complex and unpredictable way. The reflection which goes beyond the initial reaction to the experience allows analysis; that is, an understanding of the meaning of the experience, and consequently the development of a conceptual understanding of the learning process in which one has been and is continuously involved. This again enables the learner to implement the gained knowledge and skills in future actions and behaviour. The concept of experiential learning means moving in circles from experience to reaction to reflection to conceptual understanding to changed behaviour. This means that a pedagogic concept for an experiential learning activity has to refer to both the cognitive and the affective components of the learning process.

An essential experience to learn from interculturally is the personal encounter with people from other countries or cultures, being confronted and relating with them. In a multicultural class, this experience already exists but it is useful to initiate other experiences than those which the pupils know from everyday school life. This enables pupils to go beyond their traditional patterns of behaviour and relationships. In a monocultural class, this experience has to be induced 'artificially', through an exchange, for example. Exchanges of pupils – no matter if one is receiving a group of pupils from abroad or if one is visiting another country – allow an experiential encounter with the 'foreign' in a relatively protected framework.

A family stay as an integral component of an exchange, be it for one week, three weeks, a school term or an academic year, provides a familiar and comfortable yet different environment for exchange participants. The security of a 'family' enables informal experiential learning to take place. It is ordinary daily life: culture profoundly and unconsciously expressed; lifestyles demonstrated round the clock, seven days a week; values portrayed in family activities big and small. Research shows that the longer the stay, the greater is the benefit (understanding) to both exchangee and family.

The family stay component of any exchange requires planning and guidance, like any other part of an intercultural learning project. Preparation before the stay for families as well as pupils and support during the stay must take place. Families are usually perfectly good at being their own family but not all families are equipped to include an extra son or daughter, even for a short period. If he or she is treated like a guest, the family is exhausted at the end of the stay and the pupil hasn't really had the experiential benefit of being part of another family. If misunderstanding or conflict is not discussed and resolved (understood), the learning becomes negative for both parties.

One has, however, to be aware of the fact that an encounter with people of another culture implies misunderstanding. What seemed to be self-evident suddenly is not so clear. Other people are behaving in a way that one perceives to be strange.

And one's own behaviour, which one perceives to be completely normal, results in surprise or even shock to others. This is commonly referred to as culture shock, different culturally determined actions and behaviours leading to misunderstanding or even conflict.

Intercultural education implies a conflict pedagogy. Having to cope with different value systems, beliefs, views of life and of the world, etc., implies conflicts. These conflicts cannot – and should not – be avoided. They are an important impulse for learning – learning through crisis. It means learning to deal with differences and resulting conflicts and possibly to resolve them. Sometimes there are no solutions. Nevertheless, it is important to learn to recognize, to accept and to carry out the conflict in a democratic way. This process is not always pleasant. It can be painful and therefore requires an adequate pedagogy.

At the same time, the experience of being exposed to a different culture enables the development of a consciousness of one's own values, beliefs, lifestyle, habits, norms and therefore culture. This experience is also a basis for being able to perceive cultures relatively without judging them. To ensure this, however, additional pedagogic steps have to be taken.

Being exposed intensively to another culture bears the danger of being overchallenged and subsequently of withdrawing from the exposure. It is essential that during an intercultural encounter there is a balance between the foreign and the familiar, a balance between risk and security. Pupils have to be challenged with the foreign and unknown but they also need security and familiarity. If there is not sufficient security, if the culture shock is too big and the persons involved are over-challenged, they will withdraw and avoid the exposure to the foreign.

When a class visits another country, the security is provided by the class and the teachers while the confrontation with the foreign often has to be imposed by the teachers. In a multicultural class, the exposure to other cultures is present while security is sought within one's own cultural or ethnic group. This is not possible if a pupil is the only representative of a culture in a class or school (as is the case for individual exchangees) or if there is an extremely disadvantageous proportion compared to the majority culture of the school. Appropriate pedagogic measures are necessary to ensure support for these pupils and to provide the necessary security. It is very difficult to keep this balance because individual pupils will have different needs and abilities. The challenge one pupil needs and can cope with to become actively involved with the other culture might overchallenge another pupil. The need for security will also differ individually.

The above illustrates the need for something like a 'pedagogic security bar' for the pupils, which helps to guide them through this complex and sometimes difficult learning process without damage.

A structured approach to intercultural learning

Intercultural learning does not happen incidentally or by chance. It would be an illusion to assume that the meeting of pupils from different cultures will have all the intended effects. It does not automatically lead to greater competence in communication. Pupils will tend to avoid communication if their language skills are not sufficient or if there is no specific need for communicating with the other cultural group. It is very likely that they will remain in separate groups or withdraw if there is no assignment or task requiring interaction and communication with the other group. Meeting pupils with a different cultural background does not automatically result in a change of prejudices or stereotypes. Unfortunately, the opposite may result. It is likely that selective perception will lead to a reinforcement of existing stereotypes.

Intercultural learning requires a pedagogic concept that provides for the preparation of pupils for each experiential activity, for guidance through the experience and for assessment afterwards. Since part of the learning process within an intercultural learning project of a class or school does not happen individually but in groups, this concept refers not only to the content and the development of the individual pupil but also to the group process. The didactic schemes as well as the exercises in this book follow this reasoning.

An important element of a pedagogic concept for intercultural encounters is a 'triangular didactic' as opposed to a 'dual didactic'. A dual didactic only deals with the 'me' and the 'you' in a relationship, which in the beginning can be very exciting – getting to know each other by communicating about each other's personality – but which might also become superficial after a while. The pupils could lose interest, might tend to see their stereotypes and prejudices confirmed and reject the encounter.

A triangular didactic involves a three-point relationship: you, me and a common theme or project that is pursued jointly. Working together on a specific project makes cultural differences and cultural conflicts visible. Intercultural learning then means learning how to deal with these differences and conflicts when accomplishing a common task. (There is an analogy to any kind of relationship that needs to have a content to be continued.)

In a multicultural class, the curriculum itself could be the common theme. A triangular didactic here means that methods should be applied which advise pupils to do certain assignments in bicultural groups (this is already difficult and working in multicultural groups might overchallenge the pupils). But, again, it can be useful to assign a task which is different from the traditional, school-orientated ones. This might enable the pupils to overcome traditional patterns by doing something else, possibly with enthusiasm, and, therefore, to translate what they have learned into their everyday situation.

In a school link or exchange, the themes depend on the specific situation as well as the interest of the classes or schools involved. It can be something of general concern, like environmental issues, nuclear energy, European integration, etc. It can be related to the politics, economy, society or culture of the countries of the schools involved – such as a comparison of education systems, political decision-making processes, lifestyles, etc. But it can also be related to the specific subjects – for example, the historical relationship between the countries involved and how it is documented in the respective history books, or the present economic interdependence and how it is reported in the media, etc. In any case, the link or exchange should include a project that pupils of two (or more) schools are working on together. In this way, the pupils will be learning together and learning from each other. Working in 'tandems' (bicultural pairs) or in multicultural groups is a pre-requisite.

Although so far the approaches outlined mostly refer to formal learning situations as they are familiar in school, it is important to recognize that intercultural learning to a large degree also happens in informal settings, such as meals, shopping, parties and socializing, by living with a family in the country visited, etc. These situations cannot and should not be structured by the teacher(s) except in that they provide sufficient time in the schedule for them. Informal learning situations leave much of the responsibility for the learning with the pupils, who then have to find their own solutions to the problems they are facing. Dealing with informal learning situations successfully has a strong influence on the success of the formal learning situation. It is for this reason that they also have to be considered in a pedagogic concept for intercultural learning.

Intercultural learning and language learning

Language learning is an essential element of intercultural learning. It would go beyond the limits of this book to deal with the issue of language learning in detail. Only a few aspects of language learning in the context of intercultural learning can be mentioned.

In bicultural or multicultural classroom situations, a major emphasis is put on the minority cultural or language group(s) to learn the teaching language, which is normally the language of the majority culture or language group. Intercultural learning implies that the majority culture group should learn the language of at least one minority culture group. Ideally, teaching would be done bilingually, at least in some of the subjects. Unfortunately, only a few school systems in Europe provide real bilingual or multilingual education for bicultural or multicultural schools.

Frequently, bilingual education is considered to be an unnecessary burden by the majority culture group, while it could be seen as an opportunity. To learn a language from native speakers and be able to use it in everyday life is something that is normal and advantageous. For the minority culture group(s), being able to communicate in the language of the majority culture group and thus to participate – at least to some extent – in its social life is not a choice. Contrary to this, the pupils of the majority culture group find it difficult to take part in the social activities of their schoolmates and do not even understand their social conversation between classes, or their jokes or curses.

An intercultural learning project with a multicultural class could well be used to develop the language skills of the majority culture group. The theme could even be language-focused on proverbs or jokes – something that has a strong cultural dimension and is therefore difficult to comprehend for the minority culture group. A useful approach to language learning in bicultural or multicultural classes is for the pupils to teach each other their languages, establishing 'intercultural language trading'. (Intercultural language trading refers to a pupil–centred language learning methodology where two people from different cultures speaking different languages teach each other their language simply by speaking to the other in their own language until communication is established. The process is interactive; the language learning is reciprocal. The role of the teacher is to structure and monitor the learning process, to suggest themes, to give assignments, to instruct and consult with the pupils on how they can learn the language from each other.)

The situation is quite different for a class or school involved in a school link or exchange. The need to learn the language of the partner class or school is either a consequence of the curriculum – in which case there will be a basic knowledge before the intercultural encounter – or is a temporary need so as to be able to inter-act in a satisfactory way with the pupils of the other class or school. Communication needs for a two–week stay abroad can usually be met by existing language skills (possibly in a third language) and sign language. During an exchange, the method of intercultural language trading could also be used. Frequently, though, there is a fear of speaking in a foreign language. This fear is very often part of a school culture that punishes mistakes – and language learning implies making mistakes. It is essential for teachers to encourage their pupils to speak the other language even with mistakes and to assure them that their language performance during an exchange will not be assessed. (The teacher, for example, who does not speak the language of the country being visited could be a 'model' for making the first mistake. Activating this as an idea may require that the teacher also points out the mistake.)

If the language of the partner class or school is completely new to the pupils, basic language skills would be useful to enable a real intercultural learning process. Language is an essential vehicle for culture transfer. To overcome the lack of foreign language skills, a number of language learning methods and techniques are available, which allow rapid familiarization with very difficult languages in an inter-culturally productive way and the acquisition of at least a functional knowledge of the language.

Research tells us that intercultural encounters result in an increased intercultural communication competence, especially when it involves dealing with problems, conflicts, crises, etc. It goes even further. The improvement of *inter*cultural communication skills results in the improvement of *intra*cultural communication skills. This implies that the concept of learning through crisis as well as the concept of a theme–orientated approach to intercultural learning will also support language learning.

SOME IMPLICATIONS

Intercultural learning projects and exchanges may be perceived as a disturbance of regular school work. Traditionally school has been a national institution which in many countries also served to convey national, religious and cultural values and norms. Depending on the country, more or less of this tradition remains in the 'hidden curriculum' and leaves little room for international or intercultural issues. The disturbance caused by projects or exchanges can be used to develop and introduce new learning methods. There are two dimensions to this.

Traditional learning methods and school structures frequently prevent the didactics necessary for intercultural learning. Intercultural learning cannot always be accomplished in 45-minute units in a classroom. As most of this chapter demonstrates, the integration of intercultural learning in school curricula requires didactic fantasy. It is necessary to think in long-term learning processes; timetables and schedules will require change; longer working units will need to be provided. The physical arrangement of the classroom – the tables, chairs and desks – might require a different layout. The class, the learners and the teacher(s) may need to leave the classroom and school since much of the learning takes place outside school and beyond the official agenda. Usually it is beneficial to involve more than one class or age-group – perhaps even the whole school. And it is advisable and sometimes necessary to break the traditional subject-orientated approach and to apply cross-curricular and extra-curricular approaches.

Intercultural learning projects and exchanges also provide a potential for creative development in terms of content, methods and structures. They can help to overcome the monotony of school life and the resulting lethargy of teachers, pupils and parents. They provide an opportunity to create new interest and enthusiasm in learning.

In fact, curricula and formal school structures in many countries are more flexible than they appear and could allow approaches such as the ones outlined in this chapter. But there are many reasons why this flexibility has not been applied. First, any change requires additional effort. There is a fear of departing from traditional behaviour, of doing something new with which there is no experience, where the outcome cannot be foreseen. On a different level, teachers applying new methods experience something similar to pupils travelling to another country. They are leaving familiar ground, becoming exposed to unknown and new territory.

NEW LEARNING SITUATIONS

Teachers face unusual and new learning situations when integrating intercultural learning in school. The following examples illustrate how these learning situations are different from the traditional setting in classrooms and schools.

A major difference concerns the *role of the teacher*. In an intercultural encounter, teachers are likely to find themselves confronted with questions and problems for which they do not have answers or solutions. They find themselves in the same situation as their pupils. They, too, are learners. (It can be helpful to be open with pupils about this. This can also mean that the teacher has less control over the learning process.)

Sometimes a learning process will be initiated where the outcome cannot be foreseen. Improvisation or revision of class plans is not unheard of and these may be required. Intercultural learning also requires a pupil-centred and participatory approach. This means, for example, that pupils should be involved in defining the learning objectives and in planning and organizing a project or exchange. If the needs and objectives of the pupils are not considered, there is a risk of discrepancy between the objectives of the pupils and those of the teacher(s). This may result in a lack of motivation on the part of pupils to participate and engage themselves in the project and feelings of frustration on the part of the teachers that their message is not understood.

The role of the teacher is to provide a framework for the learning process: stimulating, structuring, monitoring and facilitating the process, referring to resources, asking the right questions at the right time, addressing conflicts and other important issues as they arise, ensuring the well-being of the individual pupils as well as of the group. This can have a significant impact on the relationship between teachers and pupils, who leave their traditional teacher–pupil relationship and become partners in learning. In some countries, this is a very unusual situation that will be more of a new learning situation than in others.

Project work and school links require *teamwork between teachers* within a school. Additional work and effort is not easily or willingly accomplished by a single teacher. In a cross-curricular or extra-curricular project, many things will need to be discussed and negotiated by a group of teachers: the learning objectives, the methods, the schedule, the distribution of responsibilities among the teachers involved, etc. Sometimes it will be advisable or necessary to facilitate a specific learning situation as a team of two or more teachers – for example, in situations requiring small-group facilitating or those requiring conflict resolution.

Working in teams provides opportunities for professional sharing and interchange. It can be motivating, many things can be done more efficiently, problems are often more easily solved in teams, failure and frustration can be shared as can increased recognition and it can be more fun than working alone.

Bicultural or multicultural classes and school links involve cooperation between teachers of different cultures. It is obvious that an intercultural learning process for a bicultural or multicultural group is best facilitated by a bicultural or multicultural team of teachers. This requires intercultural competence on the part of teachers and at the same time implies an intercultural learning process for the teachers themselves.

Bicultural class visits between two schools in two countries imply a minimum of two teachers and two classes. The complexity of adding even a third class with a third teacher from a third country also means, in proportion, that much more stimulus, motivation and possibility for intercultural learning. A statistician or actuarial accountant would have a real task to identify the numerous combinations and possibilities.

In an intercultural learning project or school link, there can be a strong *involvement of parents*. It is likely that parents will be concerned about a learning process that focuses on issues rooted deeply in their own life, like values, attitudes, patterns of behaviour, relating to other cultural/ethnic groups, etc., and that they will take a strong stand on these issues. This will influence the learning process of their children and might support or prevent the learning. It might also be the cause of conflict. For example, parents may insist on prejudices and stereotypes which their child questions. Such a situation is normal during the age of maturation, when children question the solutions and answers to life provided by their parents. But it is unusual for this conflict to be initiated through a learning process at school and this may possibly cause a confrontation between the teacher and the parents.

It is for this reason that parents should be involved actively in the planning, preparation, implementation and evaluation of a larger project. This is especially true for an exchange visit, where parents will also be learners. Through their child visiting another country, parents will be exposed to other values and lifestyles, and even more so when they receive a pupil from another country in their own family. Parents will need preparation and guidance for such an experience, which is new not only to their children but also to them as a family. The exercises in this book do not make special reference to their use with parents but many of them can be adapted and modified for this purpose.

A CHALLENGE FOR TEACHERS

Learning to cope with new learning situations as described is part of an intercultural learning process for the teacher. Teachers become aware of their own 'learning culture', adopt new elements (from other learning cultures) and develop new approaches, methods and tools to respond appropriately to a new situation.

As pupils need to be prepared for an encounter with the unknown, so teachers need to be prepared and trained for the new learning situations they are confronted with. These learning situations frequently involve problems, conflicts and emotions and thus impose additional stress. Adequate training and support for teachers involved with the integration of intercultural learning in schools is required. So far, few training opportunities for teachers are available in this field but new teacher training modules and schemes for intercultural learning situations are being developed by the Council of Europe as well as by educational institutions responsible for teacher training in many European countries. It is also possible for teachers to organize their own training and to draw on expertise from inside or outside the educational field. A group of teachers involved in an intercultural learning project might decide to ask a trainer or consultant for supervision of the group during the course of the project.

Teachers should be aware of the additional demands and challenges they face and ensure that they are prepared for them.

Notes and references

1   G. Hofstede, *Cultures and Organizations. Software of the Mind*. Maidenhead: McGraw-Hill, 1991.

2   *Ibid.*, p. 26.

3   *Ibid.*, p. 61.
4   *Ibid.*, p. 84.
5   *Ibid.*, p. 113.
6   *Ibid.*, p. 166.

CHAPTER 8

Methods and Tools for Intercultural Learning

Chapter 7 focused on a long-term pedagogy with respect to intercultural learning in schools. This chapter will describe specific methods and tools representing short-term measures to realize and implement these approaches. These methods and tools can be applied during the process of intercultural learning projects as they are outlined in Chapter 9.

DESIGNING AND MONITORING AN INTERCULTURAL LEARNING PROJECT

Four basic questions have to be answered when developing school curricula: the questions of why, what, who and how. This has to be done at all levels of the development process – starting at the beginning of the whole project as well as when designing a specific lesson. The following steps need to be completed during the design process:

• define objectives of the project/lesson;
• develop, select or modify methods and tools;
• work out timing and sequence of project/lesson;
• describe resources necessary to run project/lesson (people, materials);
• establish how project/lesson will be evaluated.

It is very likely that the design will have to be revised during the course of the project since the outcome of the various activities cannot be foreseen. There will be planning during the process to adapt the design according to the specific situation and needs that evolve during the course of the project. It is useful and advisable to involve the pupils in this design process since this will increase their motivation for, their interest in and their identification with the project.

The following describes the major steps for designing and monitoring an intercultural learning project.

Getting started

Major objectives during this phase are to approach the theme, to specify it and to decide on the general structure of the anticipated project. The teacher should try to develop curiosity and enthusiasm for the theme and the project but should also take into consideration the specific interests of the pupils. It is important that the pupils have a positive attitude towards the project to ensure their motivation and active participation. This can be done in a creative and playful way, addressing all senses and not only on a cognitive intellectual level. Possible approaches are: the presentation of a film, pictures or music related to the theme or country the class will get in contact with; a brainstorming session; an association exercise such as associative drawings, producing a collage, writing texts; doing role-plays, etc.

It is also necessary to clarify expectations as it is possible that they will have an impact on the design of a project. For motivation and learning, it is important that unrealistic expectations are discussed and declared to prevent disappointment and frustration. Possible fears and lack of confidence concerning the theme or the project should be considered and brought into the open.

Another objective during this phase is to develop a good group atmosphere, which is essential for a successful project. This implies that the pupils have to get acquainted in case they do not know each other yet. Even if they are acquainted, they will need to develop an open and cooperative relationship. During the project, it is possible that they will encounter stressful and conflicting situations that will require a constructive and trusting atmosphere.

Questions to be answered during this initial phase could be:

- What is my interest in the theme?
- What do I expect to learn with respect to the theme? How do I expect to benefit and learn during the course of the project?
- What could I contribute to the theme/project?
- What interest could teachers, parents and other pupils have in this theme?
- What fears do I have with respect to the theme/project? What do I not want to happen?
- What barriers could disturb or prevent the learning?

The questions here refer to the individual pupil 'getting started'. The exercises in this book provide a number of additional recommendations and ideas for starting a project in terms of content as well as process.

Planning

This phase requires creativity as well as a structured approach. It starts with collecting ideas and proposals, fantasizing about what the pupils would like to do without having to be realistic. The pupils can be encouraged to express their ideas and thoughts spontaneously and to associate freely with what is expressed during this process, without yet discussing it. A common tool to be used is brainstorming or an association exercise.

Part of this process can be done in small groups to allow greater creativity and participation. It is important to visualize the ideas and proposals, to document them on flip-charts, which can then be posted on the walls of the classroom.

Questions to be answered during this creative phase could be:

- What areas of the theme are we interested in?
- Which countries would we like to get in contact with (in case this has not been decided previously)?
- What kind of project would we like to get involved in?
- What are the possibilities for an intercultural encounter?
- What would we like to find out about the theme or another country?

In a second step, one has to structure these ideas and proposals, narrow them down, set priorities and decide on specific themes and on a specific project. This is sometimes difficult: pulling it all together. When you have finished planning, all should be clear – the objectives, the theme, the activities, the programme, the timing, the responsibilities, etc. It is useful to describe the theme in a number of different ways and thus to approach it from different angles. This allows each pupil to understand the theme more fully and to find his or her own identification with it.

A difficult task during this phase is the definition of goals and learning objectives. There are two potential problem areas. One is that teachers as well as pupils involved in intercultural learning projects tend to get carried away and to formulate goals and objectives as if the world and society could be changed by pedagogic measures. The result is frequently a discrepancy between programmatic goals and realistic objectives, and subsequently frustration for those involved in the project. The possibilities for intercultural learning in school are limited. School cannot be a workshop to repair the damages and shortcomings of society. The other problem area is the potential discrepancy between the objectives of the teacher(s) and those of the pupils, which could result in either lethargy of the pupils or conflict. It is, therefore, advisable to involve the pupils as much as possible in the development of the objectives of the project and to reach common agreement on them.

Questions to be answered during the planning phase are:

- What are the themes of the project?
- How could the theme be formulated in a number of different ways?
- What are the specific goals and objectives of the project?
- What should the framework of the project be?
- What specific activities do we propose?
- What do we have to do to implement the project?
- What are the next steps to be taken?
- What resources (material, persons) are available?
- What previous experiences can we draw on?
- What are potential problems we might be facing and how will we respond to them?
- Who will be responsible for what?
- How will the project be evaluated?
- How will we know if the goals and objectives have been achieved?

It is important during this process to record the results in either words or pictures. This ensures that nothing is forgotten; discussions are more specific and thus priorities are more easily established. It makes agreements on themes, objectives and responsibilities immediately visible; it enables each pupil to recognize his or her input and thus leads to greater identification with the result.

Monitoring

Good planning is not enough. The process of a learning project must be monitored and guided continuously. This means finding out where the pupils stand and what kind of support or guidance they need, and subsequently adapting and modifying the plans, taking into consideration the progress of the project up to this point. Such monitoring needs to be part of the planning process simply because it is not possible to plan something complex, like an intercultural encounter, from the beginning to the end.

Monitoring the process means sensing open or hidden conflicts and reacting to them. Frequently, teachers tend to avoid addressing conflicts during intercultural encounters and react to them according to their own desire for harmony. Harmony might also be reflected in the learning objectives defined during the planning process, such as 'the pupils of the two classes should become friends'. But intercultural learning implies conflicts and thus a conflict pedagogy. The conflicts have to be addressed and dealt with rather than ignored. Dealing with differences and conflicts in a constructive – and sometimes painful – way is an important part of the intercultural learning process. It is also important to help the pupils to organize their learning themselves: to find out where they stand, what they have experienced and learned, and what they still would like to know. A tool to structure this process is introduced later in this section.

Monitoring the process asks for phases of reflection for the pupils during their encounter with another culture. This refers to the concept of experiential learning, which implies altering phases from experience to reaction to reflection to conceptual understanding to new experience. This is best done by organizing regular sessions where the different classes or cultural groups meet separately and share their experiences. This might also help them to find out that they are facing similar problems and thus to gain security. These discussions should be done partly in small groups to provide for more intimacy and greater openness.

Questions to be answered during this phase could be:

- What have I experienced so far?
- What were the emotions involved? Was there fear, anxiety, joy, satisfaction, frustration, etc.? In which situations?
- To what degree are these experiences similar to those of my classmates? What does that mean?
- Which situations or problems have I dealt with successfully? How did I go about this?

- Which situations or problems have I not dealt with successfully? How could I make use of the experiences of my classmates to deal with them? What other approaches could I take?
- What have I learned so far from my own experience?
- What have I learned from the experiences of my classmates?
- What have we learned as a class or group?
- What do I/we still want to find out? What will I/we do to accomplish this?
- What resources will I/we need for this?
- What do I/we want to ask pupils of the other class or cultural group?

In a second step, one could also form bicultural groups (or have a plenary with both classes or cultural groups) where the cultural groups involved tell each other about their experiences and observations and ask each other directly what they want to know. This could also be done on a regular basis during the encounter phase of a project.

Questions to be answered and experiences to be shared could be:

- What similarities as well as differences with respect to the other country or culture did we discover?
- What was surprising to us? What contradicted the images of the other country or culture we had before the encounter? How did these images subsequently change?
- When did the experience match with the images we had?
- Which situations could we not interpret or understand?
- Which problems could not be solved?
- Which situations did we deal with successfully, in our opinion? Were the approaches we took perceived to be correct by the other class or cultural group?

It is important to consider the methods for monitoring the process while planning a project because it will have an impact on the structure and design of the project itself. More approaches to monitoring the process of a project, such as a journal, are described later in this chapter.

Evaluation

The evaluation of the project has to be planned as part of the design of the whole project because evaluation is integral to the project. The question of evaluation to be planned is how it will be recognized that the goals and objectives of the project have been achieved. If an objective relates to the development of attitudes or skills, one has to investigate the attitudes or skills at the beginning of the project or before the intercultural encounter in order to be able to compare them afterwards. Although teachers are used to evaluating pupil achievement, evaluation is still a frequently neglected aspect of teaching and training.

The approach to evaluation is strongly determined by the concept of education and learning and is thus different in different cultures and countries. There are countries where evaluation is considered to be mostly a tool for teachers that is limited to knowledge and specific skills that are measurable. Such an evaluation often involves assignments, which are solved in either a right or a wrong way. This enables the teacher to compare the learning progress of the individual pupils, to grade and rank them, and subsequently to select the pupils for different educational careers. In other countries, the emphasis of evaluation is on viewing the personal development of the pupils. Since this is very difficult to measure, evaluation then refers more to trends and directions of this development. It also implies that the pupils are directly involved in the evaluation process through self-assessment, while the teacher acts as a facilitator enabling the pupils to use the evaluation for future activities and behaviour. Although both aspects are considered in most European countries, there is a different emphasis on one or the other, which results in different approaches to evaluation.

The evaluation of an intercultural learning process that involves social and ex-periential learning tends towards the second of the two extremes outlined above. Such an evaluation can be complex and requires different tools from those usually applied in a school environment, since learning in this context refers to develop-ment and change of personality.

There are various objectives for an evaluation.
For the pupils:

- to become aware of how they have changed and what they have learned;
- to understand what effect this can have on their actions and behaviour and to decide how they want to implement what they have learned in the future.

For the teachers:

- to find out to what degree the learning objectives have been achieved and to consider this when developing learning objectives for future projects;
- to find out what the pupils have learned that was originally not intended (be it desirable or not);
- to analyse the approaches and methods taken and subsequently to implement the experience into future learning activities (thus evaluation becomes a learning tool for the teachers too);
- to be able to demonstrate the outcome of the activities to colleagues and head-teachers.

Questions concerning the assessment for the pupils are:

- How have I changed? How has the experience affected my attitudes? How has it affected my perception of people of the other countries involved in the project?
- How has my relationship to people of the other countries involved in the project changed?
- What new relationships could I develop? Are they different from the ones I had before? How have my existing relationships changed?
- What have I learned? What knowledge and skills have I acquired?
- What difficulties have I faced and how did I deal with them?
- Which were new answers and solutions to problems I had experienced before the project?

- What new views of life and the world did I gain?
- How will all this affect my future behaviour?

As is true with most processes involving personality and relationships between people, there are very few definite answers to these questions. Often there are no wrong or right answers and the result of the learning experience is hardly measurable. But there are indications and signals that might show trends and suggest (subjective) answers to these questions.

Additional questions concerning the evaluation of the project as a whole are:

- How did the pupils perceive the project in general?
- What did the pupils like or dislike?
- What should be done differently next time?
- Any other comments?

It is important to refer to the effect of the project not only on the individual but also on the group. Questions to be answered with respect to this are:

- What was the effect of the experience on the relationship between the pupils of the class or group?
- What was the effect on the spirit and atmosphere within the group or class?
- What was the effect on the motivation and ability to cooperate within the class or group?

The evaluation must be linked to the learning objectives defined during the planning of the project. The basic learning areas outlined in Chapter 6 – perceptions and images, awareness and knowledge, attitudes, skills and patterns of behaviour – also form the basis for the development of evaluation tools and exercises. Evaluation is an ongoing activity. It is important to plan phases of evaluation and assessment during the course of the project and thus to review the learning process on an ongoing basis. Most of the exercises described later in this book include evaluation of the specific learning achieved through the respective exercise.

There are various methods and tools for evaluation. It would be counterproductive to the content of an intercultural learning project to use tests or give grades. The evaluation, wherever possible, should be self-monitored by the pupils. If written work or questionnaires are used and collected by the teacher, the submissions should be anonymous. Methods and tools suggested for evaluation and assessment are:

- individual reflections (use of journals as described later in this chapter);
- reflections and discussions in pairs or small groups structured by a set of questions prepared by the teacher or developed by the whole group in plenary;
- questionnaires to be filled out individually and to be discussed in small groups;
- summary and conclusions of individual and group work in plenary;
- producing documentation of the project, including texts, photographs, tapes, videos, sketches, etc.

CONSIDERATIONS FOR WORKING WITH GROUPS

Since an intercultural learning project involves working with groups in other than traditional settings in schools, a special section deals with this topic. This refers especially to the use of the exercises described later in this book. There exists a vast amount of material describing group work. Much of what is outlined here applies for training situations with adults but can be used for pupils. Only a small part of what is available in the training field can be described in this book.

What is written here is culturally determined. The recommendations will be familiar in some countries and unusual in others. It is possible that some recommendations cannot be implemented in some countries because they are not compatible with the predominant educational environment.

Guidelines for preparing group work

These are some guidelines for preparing group work. As indicated, some may not be appropriate in certain countries or learning situations:

- plan from the end to the beginning;
- be specific when describing the topic;
- be aware of the target group;
- prepare clear instructions for the group;
- prepare a detailed schedule;
- clarify the role of the teacher or facilitator.

Basic structure of group work

Generally, a working session within a larger project should be structured in the following way (it is assumed that there is a general understanding of the topic and that the expectations of the pupils have been clarified):

- warm-up;
- clarify topic (collect ideas, opinions, etc., structure them, set priorities and narrow down);
- work on topic;
- transfer into action.

Basic guidelines for group work

There are two parts to any group interaction: content and process. Content refers to the subject or task on which the class or group is to work. Process is concerned with what happens between and to members of the group while they work together.

When any group of pupils is engaged in an intercultural learning project, the experiential nature of that learning makes the group process a primary concern for the teacher or facilitator. The 'subject' or content is related directly to each individual in the group. How this is handled and guided will undoubtedly mean the difference between positive and negative learning. There are some basic guidelines, which perhaps will not seem new to the reader, but may serve as a checklist for thinking about and planning a particular intercultural learning component.

Content

1 Clarify the framework or setting within which the group is working. Is it monocultural or multicultural in composition? Is a single class involved, pupils from different classes, the whole school? Does it involve a class or group of pupils from abroad visiting the class or school? Does the work take place inside or outside the classroom or school? How much time is available? What resources are available?

2 Clarify and present the topic – in written form as well. Because this will be, perhaps, a different way of working, the presentation of the topic and the related questions must be clear. Some people visualize more easily than they hear. Check the understanding by writing it down. Ask questions that will elicit a feedback response. A group will work more effectively if it is clear and certain about the task.

3 Clarify possibilities and limitations. What is the objective of the exercise or working session, what will it be able to do, or not do? What incidents, talents, backgrounds, moments of recent history exist to be used, perhaps in a different manner? It is important at this point to refer to the expectations of the pupils. Which expectations are likely to be met, which expectations will not be met realistically?

4 Suggest and agree on procedures and steps to be taken. What are the questions to be pursued? What are the specific assignments and tasks to be performed by the pupils? Suggest alternative procedures and options if necessary. Again, clarity concerning the procedures is essential for successful work.

5 Don't be afraid to change your concept if something unexpected happens. This guideline refers to the concept of planning during the process. A group's work cannot be fully predicted, which means that change is not only possible but probable. If it turns out that the planned approach or procedure is not useful it should be adapted and adjusted to suit changed circumstances.

6 Clarify what happens with what is written and produced by the class or group. Early on in an intercultural learning sequence it may be desirable to ensure confidentiality of the individual's as well as the group's work. Once the trust and confidence level builds within the group, it will be more welcome – less threatening – to share the work. The group itself will be the best judge of when that moment arrives.

Process

1 The class or group should 'warm up' before embarking on challenging topics. People need to feel comfortable with one another before settling down to work. Motivation to overcome possible lethargy and to get involved in the topic is also necessary. This can be difficult because intercultural learning can mean change, which requires effort and is therefore perceived to be uncomfortable. Warming up is covered in greater detail under 'Introduction to the Exercises'.

2 The facilitator or teacher should also warm up before working with a group. This refers to the topic as well as to relating to the class or group. The first is done by reading, talking to colleagues, preparing the presentation, etc. The latter implies participating in the warm up of the group.

3 Meet participants where they are. It is likely that the teacher or facilitator has more knowledge and experience of the topic than the pupils. Consequently, he or she has to find out where the pupils stand with respect to the topic, what their specific interests and expectations are, etc. The pupils will be frustrated if they do not understand what is going on or if they believe that their interests and expectations are not considered.

4 Make use of existing energy rather than forcing the group to work on something where it lacks energy. There is nothing to be gained by presenting the topic of tennis if what people want to talk about is football. Perhaps there is a way of relating the interest in football to tennis. Perhaps the anticipated learning can also be achieved by dealing with the topic of football. Harnessing the available energy to a moribund or hidden reservoir is a real skill.

5 Accept what is there. This – very general – guideline is about being realistic. If pupils are frustrated, lazy, tired, etc., one has to respond to this as being real rather than to ignore or criticize it. Perhaps a break is needed, perhaps the pace of work is too quick, perhaps a different method should be applied, etc.

6 When forming small groups, allow the participants to make their own choices (wherever possible). This guideline refers to the necessity for the pupils to feel comfortable with their group. Sometimes it is necessary to impose certain rules on how groups are to be formed, e.g. groups should be bicultural or multicultural, should have a certain male–female ratio or should be composed of pupils not knowing each other. In this case, the pupils might need more time to gain confidence to form the required groups; they might need to move around until they feel comfortable. Identification with their own group and thus with its work is essential for the process.

7 Procedures are established and/or changed together with the group. This guideline has to do with a sense of ownership or identification with the process. Participants are more likely to achieve a good result if they perceive that it has been within their control. There will be a greater disposition of responsibility.

8 Support the group to recognize what the group members have in common and where they are different. This enables the group to recognize the strengths represented in the group as well as potential areas of conflict. It helps to avoid

misunderstandings and to gain clarity during discussions. It results in constructive cooperation.

9 Disturbances within a group should be addressed immediately. Disturbances divert interest and energy from the topic and the task of the group. Thus, disturbances slow down the group or even prevent it from working. If a disturbance cannot be addressed immediately, it is essential at least to agree on a time when it will be dealt with.

10 Do not offend or attack group members. This would be counterproductive to the cooperation between the facilitator or teacher and the pupils. An offended pupil is likely to withdraw or even to disturb or boycott the group work.

11 Be patient; let things happen. There is a delicate balance in the facilitator role (as opposed to the teacher role), which demands firm guidance and a non-authoritarian stance, which permits a range of opinions and tolerates an open debate. It is a building process that may require a great deal of patience.

12 Clarify your role *vis-à-vis* the group. This guideline refers to the facilitator's presentation of himself or herself to the group. To explain the difference in role if necessary, to be comfortable with the group, to be confident in the group's capacity to develop their thoughts and ideas.

13 Keep eye-contact with the group. Do the pupils understand and follow what you are saying? Are there any questions or concerns? Is there agreement or disagreement with what you are saying? Sometimes the verbal message is different from the non-verbal message. Keeping eye-contact helps.

14 Be able to bear silence. Sometimes the process requires more time than the teacher or facilitator has anticipated. Sometimes the pupils need time to think, reflect, decide, respond, etc. This might result in silence, which is important for the process. Silence can, indeed, be golden.

SOME BASIC METHODS AND TOOLS FOR GROUP WORK

There are a number of basic tools that can be of help in working with groups, of which a few are described here. Some can be applied following the guidelines outlined above.

Warm up/getting to know each other

- *Personal introductions* work well in small groups (seven to ten persons) where interest and attention can be sustained throughout as many introductions. Set guidelines such as name, neighbourhood of residence, a special characteristic of the neighbourhood the group member appreciates, etc.
- *Interviews in pairs.* Divide the group (can be any size) into pairs, whose task is to interview each other according to given structure. Afterwards everyone introduces his or her interview partner to the large group.

- '*Visiting cards*'. This is the same as interviews in pairs, but everyone prepares a visiting card (paper size A3) for his or her interview partner. The visiting cards should have a standard structure, e.g. name, district/region/town of residence/origin, siblings, occupation of parents, hobbies and interests, favourite subjects, favourite animal, specific interest in topic, etc. The results then can be displayed on walls, a notice-board or a string going across the classroom.

More tools for warm up and getting to know each other can be found in the exercises in Chapter 10.

Expectations

- *Completing sentences* like: 'This will be a good session if …', 'I am interested in today's session, because …', 'I expect to learn the following from today's session …', 'I do not want … to happen today'. This can be done in a number of ways: (a) pupils write their reactions on flip-chart paper (one per sentence) placed on different walls in the classroom or on a notice-board; (b) reactions are written on 'pin cards' (one per sentence) and pupils group them according to similarities on the notice-board (see also below); (c) teacher/facilitator simply collects expectations on a flip-chart (this implies a group whose members already know each other rather well); (d) reactions are written individually, some are presented voluntarily. At the end, the teacher or facilitator should summarize the expectations expressed by the pupils and clarify what is possible and what not. Pin the flip-chart lists to the notice-board for easy reference.
- *Draw a diagram*:

Using dots with different colours (or symbols), pupils plot their expectations at the start of the session or day. It is possible to repeat this exercise at the end of the session or day for evaluation and to compare the results.

Presentation of input on the topic

- *Lectures*. Lectures are the most common method for conveying information on the topic to the pupils. It is advisable to keep lectures brief or the concentration of the pupils and their interest might fade quickly. It is useful to introduce people from outside school for lectures – people who are involved professionally in a field related to the topic, experts, representatives of other cultures, politicians, etc. It is also possible to ask pupils to prepare and give a lecture on a given topic.
- *Films*. A useful method for introducing a topic as well as background information is through a film or other medium (tape, slide show, etc.). There are numerous films referring to culture and intercultural situations. In fact, the content and appearance of films is strongly influenced by the culture(s) represented by the director, the producers and the actors.

Collect and structure ideas

- *Brainstorming*, the most common tool for collecting ideas with respect to a given topic or task. Example: what approaches can be taken to explore culture X? The basic rule for brainstorming is that everything mentioned by the pupils is noted on a flip-chart or notice-board without comment or discussion. Continue as long as there are spontaneous ideas and comments. Questions of clarification can be asked right away but can also be dealt with after the brainstorming. In a second step, these ideas are structured according to different categories and priorities.
- *Working with pin cards*. On small cards or pieces of paper, pupils note their ideas about the topic. Limit to one card for each thought, three cards per pupil, three lines maximum per card. Pupils read expectations aloud and then group the cards according to similarities on a notice-board.
- *Creative writing*. A very useful tool for approaching and specifying a theme. Small groups of six to eight pupils write their associations on a general topic on flip-chart paper according to the following rules. The topic is written and circled in the centre (this could be the name of a country, or a word like 'foreigner', 'culture', 'lifestyle', etc.). The pupils write words they associate with this topic next to it, encircle it and draw a line linking them with the topic. In further steps, they associate words with their first associations until there is a network of words on the flip-chart. This can serve as a basis for a first discussion in the small group and then be shared with the other groups in the class.
- *Other association exercises*. A similar approach to creative writing can be taken by associative drawings or producing a collage, etc. Sometimes visualizing associations has more creative results than a verbal approach. There are a number of association exercises described in more detail in the exercises (Associating stereotypes, Associative Drawing, etc.).
- *Ranking/setting priorities*. Once a group has come up with a list of issues or ideas that evolved from a brainstorming session, the question is which ones to work and concentrate on. A useful approach is to give each pupil a number of points to

be distributed according to his or her preference for the different issues or ideas on the list. All points can be given to one issue or they can be distributed to different issues. The number of points each pupil has should not exceed 50 per cent of the issues on the list.

Working on a topic or theme

- *Structured discussions in small groups.* In a group larger than ten to twelve pupils it is difficult to have a discussion actually involving all pupils. It is advisable to divide into smaller groups of six to ten pupils each. Clear instructions have to be given on the objective of the group work, the time limit, the mode of presenting the result of the group work to the whole class and the time limit for the presentation. It should be left to the group as to how they organize their work, if they want to assign a group leader or rapporteur.
- *Discussion of representatives.* For collecting and summarizing the results of small working or discussion groups, it is possible to have a discussion involving just one representative from each small group. The representatives would sit in a smaller circle while the other members of the small groups sit in a wider circle behind their representative without participating in the discussion. An alternative is for the representatives to take turns during the discussion – but there is always just one representative per small group participating in the discussion. Other members of the small groups should have an opportunity at the end to add important things which came out of the small groups but which have not been said by their representatives.
- *Fishbowl.* This is a common method for observing how a group functions and how the members of the group interact. A small group sits in an inner circle and is assigned to discuss a specific issue (it is important that the issue is of relevance and that the pupils really wish to discuss it). The rest of the class is assigned to observe the process of the discussion of the small group without participating in the discussion (there can be different assignments for different members of the outer group). What roles are the different members of the discussion group taking? To what degree are different group members participating in the discussion? How does the group reach consensus or arrive at decisions? How does the group deal with disagreement or conflict? Who is facilitating or leading the discussion? Who is proposing ideas? Who is proposing the procedures? Who is disturbing the process? In a second step, the observers present their observations. It is important that they try to be objective and descriptive, not evaluative or judgemental. In a third step, discussion group members can reflect on and discuss how they perceived the process.

Breaks

Leave sufficient time for breaks. Enable participants to relax, e.g. with music. Do not only work as a group, but also socialize, eat together, etc.

Reflection/interim evaluation

'Flashlight/torch' involves a quick round to allow everyone in the group to express how or what she or he feels, what expectations he or she has, etc. This can also be done graphically on a flip-chart or notice-board, with a scale from 0 to 10 where each pupil plots his or her position.

Feedback

Feedback is a tool which enables a person to find out how others perceive his/her behaviour, what he/she says, and how he/she says it. Feedback can refer to the content of a message as well as to the process of communication. Feedback is an important tool to improve communication skills and to avoid misunderstanding. There are some basic rules for feedback. Feedback should be:

- descriptive as opposed to judgemental;
- specific as opposed to general;
- adequate and fair;
- useful in the sense that the receiver of the feedback should be able to change his or her behaviour in the future;
- requested as opposed to forced upon;
- at the right time (feedback is most useful if given as soon as possible after the event it refers to);
- correct.

Feedback is a tool to be used between teachers and pupils as well as within a group of pupils or within a team of teachers or facilitators. Though it might be unusual in some countries, feedback can also be given to the teacher by his or her pupils.

Be creative and design your own methods and tools, or adapt the tools described above for specific situations as needed.

TOOLS FOR INTERCULTURAL LEARNING

So far we have dealt with general methods and tools for working with groups. The following are some methods and tools that are especially useful for project work and experiential learning situations, particularly those related to individuals.

Individual planning

As has been outlined earlier, it is important that pupils take as much responsibility for their own learning process as possible. The grid in Figure 9 is a useful tool for pupils to plan and monitor their learning. It can be used for a complete project as well as for a single step in it, e.g. for a field study, an interview, etc.

What I want to learn/find out about	Ideas for approaches	Skills and resources I will need for this	Who else do I need to involve?	Fears/risks/ challenges	What will that change for me?	How do I know when I have achieved this?
Sample answer: Use of time in the country visited	Ask ten different people with diverse backgrounds	Interviewing; basic vocabulary for different activities; questionnaire	Pupil of partner class; host family	Speaking in a foreign language; addressing people I do not know	It will help me to understand lifestyles of people here	When I have evaluated basic use of time of ten people

Figure 9 Planning grid for intercultural learning

The pupils should be given a number of copies of such a grid and they should be encouraged during various phases of the project to make use of them. It has to be clear to the pupils that the planning grid will be for the personal use of each pupil only, and that it will not be read by anyone else unless the pupil really wants to show it to someone else.

Letter to myself

This is a tool that can be used for various purposes. One is for the pupils at the end of a project or after an exchange to be able to recall their thoughts and feelings at an earlier stage of the project or before the exchange. For this purpose, they write a 'letter to myself' during the preparation phase, referring to their goals, expectations and anxieties, as well as what they expect to gain from the project. These letters are sealed and collected by the teacher and given back to the pupils during the evaluation phase.

This tool can also be used to support the implementation of what has been learned by bridging the phase of intensive experience with the everyday situation after the project or exchange. There is a big danger that many of the good intentions the pupils develop, e.g. during their stay abroad, are lost on the journey back home and when they are immediately caught up again by everyday life, tests and homework. As part of the evaluation of the project or before returning home from an exchange, the pupils should write how they intend to implement and make use of what they have learned, how they intend to change their behaviour, what activities they intend to undertake within some two to four weeks after the project, etc. These letters should actually be sent by mail so they reach the pupils a few days after the conclusion of the project.

In both cases, the letter to myself becomes useful for evaluation, reflection and implementation.

The journal

The journal is a valuable tool to help pupils think consciously about what they are experiencing, thus creating a greater awareness of the culture they are getting to know as well as of their own personality and their own social and cultural background. The journal is a tool that is used during the whole visit abroad as well as for the evaluation after returning home. There are a number of purposes for the journal.

- Pupils can document and record their experiences in order to be able to recall them when they are back home. It is very likely that the experiences abroad will be more intensive for the pupils than everyday life at home and that they will perceive their life abroad more consciously than at home. It is also likely that they will not remember clearly all their experiences after a while and that they will confuse or modify them in their memory.
- It will serve as a basis for discussions with their classmates and with the pupils of the partner class. During the stay abroad, it is advisable that the pupils of the visiting class reflect on their experiences on a regular basis – in plenary as well as in small groups. This can be done once a day but it is also sufficient to do it every two or three days.
- The recommended format enables pupils to list questions that still need to be asked and serves as a reminder of these questions every time something is written into the journal. This helps to monitor and structure the learning process.
- The journal is a great help for evaluation after the return home. It helps pupils to recall all the phases of the stay abroad, including their emotions. This is especially important because certain feelings and experiences might be suppressed after the visit abroad, which could prevent much of the learning process. The journal becomes an essential tool for realizing what one has learned and how one has changed through the experience.

The teacher must make certain that the purpose of the journal is understood by the pupils. It has to be clear that the journal will be only for the personal use of each pupil and that it will not be read by anyone else unless the pupil really wants to show it to someone else. Especially at the beginning, the teacher has to remind the pupils to keep the journal and possibly plan for 'journal writing time'.

On the next pages, you will find detailed instructions for pupils as well as a sample format for a journal.

Journal (instruction for pupils)

During your visit abroad, you will have many different experiences. Some will be new, unknown and foreign to you; some will be familiar. Some will be familiar and still different from at home, others you will not understand. These experiences can be exciting, challenging, funny, frightening, comfortable, etc. – there is a wide range of possibilities.

Journal – visit in   from   to

Date	What did I do today?	How did I feel?	What have I learned about the country?	What do I still want to ask?

Figure 10 Suggested journal format

Journal – visit in X-land   from 12.9   to 24.9

Date	What did I do today?	How did I feel?	What have I learned about the country?	What do I still want to ask?
12.9	Travel by train to X-land.	Very excited – I have never been in X-land before.	People are very friendly and helpful when changing trains. Our train was delayed and the connecting train waited!	How do people in X-land usually travel? Train, bus, car? Do they travel a lot? Abroad, within the country?
	Dinner with the host family.	Felt a bit tense – did not know how to behave.	Dinner started after 21.00 – we eat usually around 18.00.	Do all families eat that late?
13.9	Breakfast.	Was very tired.	There was almost no breakfast – just a cup of coffee or tea.	How can they make it until lunch? Is it like this every day? Is there a chance for me to eat something in the morning?
	First day at school: we played a game to get to know each other and something about each other's country.	Was very excited and surprised how quickly we got to know each other.	The pupils of our partner school are very outspoken and open. They talked about things we normally would not talk about.	There seems to be so much freedom. Who sets the rules? What are they? What is considered to be private? What is considered to be public?
	Afterwards we attended regular classes.	Have not understood much – everybody spoke very quickly. It is exhausting and frustrating.	The relationship between teachers and pupils is very different from at home – there is less hierarchy. Pupils really seem to be interested and motivated to learn.	What is the image of school in X-land? What is the status of teachers? How are pupils graded?

Figure 11 Sample journal page

It is very likely that these experiences will be more intensive than everyday life at home and that you will perceive your life abroad more consciously than at home. It is also likely that you will not remember clearly all your experiences after a while and that you will confuse or modify them in your memory.

For these reasons, you are asked to keep a journal during your visit abroad. This journal has a number of purposes: it will help you to document and record your experiences; it will serve as a basis for discussions with your classmates and with the pupils of your partner class; it will help you to recall your experiences after you return home when you try to evaluate your visit abroad. The journal will become part of your experience.

Try to write the journal on a regular basis at least once a day – for example, every evening before you go to bed. Only you will read this journal unless you want to show it to someone.

The journal has a number of columns to help you structure your daily experiences (Figure 10). If possible, use an extra page each day. If you need extra sheets, copy them before you start writing on the last page. A sample journal page is attached (Figure 11).

If you are writing a journal or diary on a regular basis anyway, you can of course continue to do so. Nevertheless, we suggest that you keep a journal using the format recommended here.

Vocabulary and communication notebook

Language and communication play an essential role in relating to people of another culture. Learning the language and communication patterns of the other culture is a major objective of any intercultural learning project. The following tool can be used by pupils individually to develop their foreign language and communication skills while visiting another country. It goes beyond an ordinary vocabulary notebook and relates language, communication patterns and lifestyle. The pupils produce their own 'vocabulary and communication notebook' according to the following structure. They should be encouraged to write their learnings and observations on a continuous basis, e.g. immediately when they are confronted with new words, phrases, proverbs, etc. This can also encourage them to ask about the meaning of a specific word or phrase when they are confronted with it. They should revisit their vocabulary and communication notebook once a day – e.g. when they write their journal – to recall what they have learned during the day and to complete it if necessary.

It is useful to structure such a notebook according to different topics, e.g. nature, people, relationships, social life, community, household, economy, politics, institutions, religion, tradition, etc. The structure shown in Figure 12 is recommended for each topic. Additionally, pupils can be given special assignments to observe communication styles and behaviour. The following questions can be asked:

- How close do people stand while having a conversation?
- Do people touch each other while speaking to each other? What are the rules for touching each other in general?
- What are the rules concerning eye-contact? Do you look into someone else's

Topic
New vocabulary and phrases:
Observations about language and communication:
Observations about lifestyle:

Figure 12 Structure of the vocabulary and communication notebook

eyes while speaking to him or her? For how long? Can you have eye-contact with other people without conversation?

- Do people use gestures or special mimicry?
- What other communication habits do you observe?
- Are there differences in communication and interaction behaviour depending on sex, age or status, e.g. with respect to distance, eye-contact, touching each other, etc.?

A special assignment for a class or group of pupils could be to develop a (language) guide for everyday life in the country they are visiting. This could be a main theme for the exchange.

Working in tandem

Positive experiences have been gained using the method of working in tandem. Two pupils – either from the two different countries involved in an exchange or from two different cultural groups within a multicultural class – agree to spend as much time as possible together and to introduce their cultures, their countries, their languages to each other. They work together on the theme of the project, they cooperate on assignments given to them, etc. In between, there are phases where they meet with their respective classes or cultural groups to share and discuss their experiences and what they have learned.

In the case of an exchange involving a family stay, it is apparent that the partners of a tandem will stay with each other's families. Of course, the tandems should be the same for both legs of an exchange.

Interviewing

There are a number of advantages to this method. It enables the use of experience and knowledge available outside the classroom; it implies an interaction with other people, and is thus of an experiential nature; it is to a large degree self-monitored by the pupils; it allows an in-depth involvement with the topic through open-ended questions. It is important to design a plan for the interview as well as to record and document the outcome. Pupils who have had no previous experience with interviewing should do an interview exercise with their classmates as suggested in the 'field exercise' in the exercises of this book. The 'field study' (in the exercises) is also built on interviewing.

Questionnaires

Questionnaires can serve various purposes within an intercultural learning project. They can be used as a structured approach to make pupils aware of their own attitudes, values, lifestyles, etc. But they can also serve as a basis for surveys, which then provide an overview of opinions, attitudes, beliefs, values and lifestyles of a larger group of people, e.g. a class, a school or a random selection of the population of a community. For the latter, it is advisable that the questionnaires are designed by the class under the guidance of the teacher or facilitator.

A number of questionnaires are included in the exercises ('educational path and professional career questionnaire', 'where do I come from?', 'evaluation', etc.).

Role change/mirror

A useful method for becoming aware of one's own lifestyle and behaviour is 'role change'. Pupils from two different cultural groups, e.g. within a class exchange, switch roles and thus act as a 'mirror' for each other. This can be done to illustrate the way the behaviour of the other cultural group is perceived in a specific situation. For example, a group of pupils from one class can play a situation as they perceive it to be normal for the other class or cultural group, like 'family having dinner', 'class during break', 'young people going out in the evening', 'boy meets girl' or 'teacher giving lecture'. The same situation should be played by both classes or groups about the other culture without reaction or discussion. In a second step, they discuss how each cultural group perceives its own behaviour, how it differs from what has been presented by the other cultural group, where they agree or disagree with the presentation, what they found out about themselves, etc.

This method can also be used in the case of a conflict between two (cultural) groups. While discussing the issue they have a conflict about, they take the role of the other group, using their arguments, their gestures, their behaviour. In a second step, they discuss how they experienced taking the role of members of the other cultural group, how they felt in this role, how their view of the issue of conflict changed, etc.

EXERCISES AND GAMES

Exercises are a specific method used to initiate, structure or support a learning process. A basic element of most exercises is a dynamic created by specific rules, assumptions, questions to be discussed and/or objectives to be achieved by the group. This dynamic allows and supports an emotional engagement of individuals in the group and thus enables an effective learning process that would not be possible in an everyday situation.

Most exercises involve experiential learning. Even if they only simulate or portray a specific situation, the actions and feelings of the participants during the exercise will be real and as valid as in real-life conditions. Exercises can accelerate the learning process by inducing an experience that real life might offer only much later. Frequently, exercises are designed in such a way that they encourage participants to take extreme positions, enabling recognition of subtle differences and providing for a vivid process.

It is important that the experiential element of an exercise is complemented by reflection as well as a cognitive learning element to support both an affective and a cognitive learning process. The cognitive learning element allows an understanding of the experience and an implementation of what has been learned in future actions and behaviour. Speaking about the situations that were experienced during the exercise – *how* things were said, *what* was said, *how* one acted – on a meta-communication level strengthens the process of becoming conscious of what has been learned.

Short-term pedagogic measures like exercises can only result in small steps towards a better understanding of others, of the foreign. While one tends to stay within the limits of the known, exercises can provide a stimulus to become curious and more open towards the unknown, the unpredictable, the adverse, the contra-dictory, the inconceivable, the incompatible – which is a major element of intercultural learning. The advantage of most exercises is that the rules allow or even require lethargy, timidity and traditional barriers and limits to be overcome, thus creating situations that would not happen otherwise. This is also why the success of most exercises depends on the group adhering to the rules.

Because exercises deal with emotions, with beliefs and values that people hold dear, that are taken for granted, there can be situations of conflict and crisis when such beliefs and values are challenged. This is all right! Frequently, such conflicts are avoided in favour of the need to preserve a superficial harmony related to ideal-istic objectives attached to intercultural learning – e.g. 'one should be friends with people of other cultures'. Avoiding conflicts, though, would mean giving up a source for learning, which is achieved by dealing with conflicts and trying to find solutions for them. Not addressing an existing conflict can result in an even bigger conflict, which cannot be avoided and might lead to a destructive situation.

On the other hand, one should not stage or create conflicts that do not exist. One should create a setting and atmosphere in which it is possible to deal with existing conflicts. Sometimes such conflicts are not visible and have to be uncov-ered. In this case, one has to be prepared to deal with the emotions and tensions involved or the situation could turn to the opposite of what was intended – lack of understanding and rejection of other cultures.

The exercises given later in this book are not intended to lead to one specific answer or solution for a given situation. They usually allow and provide for a number of different answers and solutions. The question is how people with differ-ent answers and solutions to the same situation and subsequently with different approaches to life can still cooperate and relate to each other in a constructive way. Again, there is no unique answer to this question; it will depend on the specific situation. This is partly what intercultural learning is about.

SELECTING, MODIFYING AND DESIGNING EXERCISES

Intercultural learning implies a long-term process. The ability to learn intercultur-ally will not depend on numerous superficial contacts with many other cultures. Intercultural learning will happen through a few intensive experiences and encoun-ters, through the development of deep relationships. It is the quality rather than the quantity of intercultural situations that will have a positive effect on the learning process.

This is also true for exercises. It is not necessarily useful to do as many exercises as possible, but one or two carefully selected, well designed, prepared, implemented and evaluated exercises are encouraged. The depth of experience with exercises will provoke greater learning. Again, one has to be aware of the importance of breaks, the unscheduled time, the moments that do not seem to be used effectively but during which important learning takes place.

Exercises used within an intercultural learning project have to relate to the learn-ing objectives in general and to those relevant in the specific situation when they are used – the objectives of the specific project, the age group, the setting, etc. A single exercise cannot serve all the objectives for intercultural learning but emphas-izes one or just a few learning objectives. The sequence of exercises follows a certain logic of process depending on the specific setting and situation. There is no unique sequence – one has to develop a didactic scheme for each project and adapt it as the process goes on. Chapter 9 describes a number of such schemes in detail. To design such a scheme, one should have a broad knowledge of exercises.

Existing exercises useful for social or intercultural learning are numerous. It is very likely that there is already a good exercise to serve in a particular setting with a specific learning objective. Nevertheless, as there are no standard recipes for intercultural learning, the exercises described in this book and elsewhere cannot be used as such. They have to be adapted to the specific setting. Perhaps elements of one or more exercises are used to develop something completely new. The point is generally not to *design* a new exercise but to *select* an appropriate one and to *modify* and/or *adapt* it according to specific needs.

Still, it might be necessary to design a new exercise. It is possible; it can be good fun. It is only important to remember that 'unique' and 'famous' exercises are not invented every day. 'Abigale' is probably the most famous exercise in the collection that follows. It is widely used, worldwide, with a variety of age ranges. It is so widely used and quoted (as we have also done) that it is now difficult to trace the original source. Whether you are modifying and adapting or designing a new exercise, the basic elements for any exercise are as follows.

- 'Briefing': introduction into the subject and explanation of goals of exercise; eventually linkage to previous exercise.
- Time for individual thinking and reflection.
- Active involvement of all participants, e.g. breaking into small groups.
- If possible, interaction with representatives of other cultures: this is the actual core of the exercise involving personal emotion and engagement.
- Sharing of results of small groups and/or individuals.
- 'Debriefing': evaluation of exercise. What did the participants learn? Which questions have evolved from the exercise and/or have been left open? How can they be dealt with?
- Continuation: go into more depth; what to do with the results; follow up to open questions, etc. (traditionally known as homework).

There is no unique order for the various elements of an exercise (except that briefing and debriefing are at the beginning and at the end). For example, it is possible to give theoretical input at the beginning as well as more towards the end. Or one can start right away with an experiential element (like an interview assignment) and schedule time for individual thinking and group work afterwards. The sequence within an exercise will depend on the specific situation but also on the learning tradition of the cultural group it is used with.

It is important to realize that the way an exercise is designed – its objectives, its process design, its instructions, its timing, its structure – is also culturally determined. Some cultures are more reserved with respect to physical contact than others. Similarly, in some countries, pupils are more used to learning through exercises and games than in others. For this reason it is advisable that exercises used in bicultural or multicultural settings are selected, modified or designed by bicultural or multicultural teams of teachers or facilitators. This is also true for the design of a complete didactic scheme.

Exercises used with bicultural or multicultural groups will usually require a different approach from that used with a monocultural group. Some cultural groups will need more time for a specific assignment than others. Some discussions will require more time. The process will be more complex and thus will also require more time and monitoring, and it would be counterproductive if the process was interrupted owing to a lack of time. The reflection and evaluation will require more time and attention, especially if an exercise has resulted in strong emotions and reactions.

Although one is tempted to make more use of non-verbal exercises in bicultural or multicultural settings because of the lack of language competence, it is essential to ensure a certain amount of verbal communication and understanding. It would be an illusion to assume that intercultural learning is possible only by non-verbal means. It is important to convey and share verbally on a cognitive level what has been experienced and perceived and how it has been interpreted. To support this, pupils can share their (non-verbal) experiences first in monocultural groups and then in plenary. Nevertheless, it is important to find approaches to overcoming language barriers to enable verbal communication between the different cultural groups involved in the project.

Simulations

Simulation is a very strong experiential learning tool for intercultural learning. It can translate an abstract issue into a situation that is surprisingly close to reality. It can lead to intensive involvement of pupils; it can affect actions, thoughts and feelings, and can serve as resource for discussion and learning. While the instructions for simulations can be very precise, they are rather unpredictable in their outcomes. They can be intensive, exciting and long, and subsequently require much time for discussion and evaluation afterwards. They can turn out not to have the anticipated effect and be brief, superficial and perhaps even boring.

A simulation is especially useful in a monocultural setting where one or more different cultures are simulated and the feelings of the participants resulting from the interaction between the different (partly simulated) cultural groups are real. A simulation, therefore, can be used for preparing for a visit abroad or any encounter with another culture. In this case, a simulation enables pupils to experience the exposure to something unknown, unpredictable or inconceivable. It also enables pupils to observe their own behaviour in such situations and thus to become aware of their own culture.

It is advisable for the teacher or facilitator to have experienced a simulation before attempting to run one. The outcome of a simulation can be quite complex and requires more preparation than just reading the instructions. Changing the rules of a complex simulation should be avoided. Simulations have usually been carefully constructed and even minor adjustments might alter the anticipated dynamic.

There are a number of simulations included in the exercises in this book. A very useful one for an intercultural learning project is 'albatross', which was developed by the Experiment in International Living. Useful simulations not included in this book are 'the owl' and 'bafá bafá', which can also be used for development education or political education in general.[1]

Role-plays

While serving a similar purpose to simulations, role-plays are far less complex. They can be designed rather quickly for a specific purpose and setting. They can involve pupils quite intensely and offer an experience that stimulates thoughts and feelings, which can be translated into understanding and implementation in future actions and behaviour.

There are basically two approaches to role-playing in an intercultural context. One is to perform a role-play about a situation in one's own culture. The fact that it is a 'play' allows for greater distance from reality, and thus exaggeration and subsequently display of the extremes of patterns of behaviour in one's own culture. This can contribute to a clearer perception and greater awareness about one's own culture. By taking roles other than one's own, one can experience the same situation from different perspectives and realize the opportunities and limits of one's own society or culture. It can result in a better understanding of one's own culture for pupils from another cultural background.

Another approach is to perform a role-play about a situation within another culture as it is perceived by oneself and one's colleagues. Such a role-play would demonstrate which behaviour of the other cultural group is perceived to be surprising or peculiar. It would also reveal situations that have been misperceived or misunderstood. It is important to evaluate such a role-play properly to allow clarification of what has been misperceived and to address possible feelings of having been offended.

Some people feel uneasy with role-playing and are hesitant to act in front of others. Frequently, however, the discomfort passes once they are involved in it. In fact, role-playing usually turns out to be great fun – especially as the participants can act in ways not usually possible and can show extreme behaviour. Nevertheless, no one should be forced to perform a role-play. Observing a role-play and participating in the discussion that follows can be as valuable as direct involvement.

As there are no role-plays included in the exercises in this book, some examples and suggestions are given here.

Example role-play: the Smith family on holiday

The Smith family (father, mother, two children and grandfather) decide to spend their holiday in a small village in a Mediterranean country. The prices elsewhere have become outrageous and this small village is 'good value for just half the money'. After lengthy formalities at the airport and a complicated transfer by bus they reach the guesthouse. Communication is difficult because the people at the guesthouse 'do not speak a word of English'. On the second day, Mr Smith discovers that his wallet has disappeared.

Characters
Children: would have preferred to go to the seaside, do not know what to do in this village.
Mr Smith: exhausted businessman, needs to rest very badly.

Mrs Smith: tries to solve all problems and to balance the different needs of the family members.
Grandfather: no specific role assignment.
Other roles: owner of guesthouse, police officer, mayor.

This role-play could be used to make pupils aware of their prejudices and stereotypes and how they influence their thinking, feeling and behaviour. It could well be used for preparing for a trip to another country.

Example role-play: coming home late

The 16-year-old daughter of a family comes home from a rendezvous (with a boy) at 1 o'clock in the morning instead of at 11. The mother has stayed up until her daughter came home. Then she told her that she had been very worried, that she was upset and disappointed, and that she would like to discuss the issue the next day. The discussion next day takes place with the following persons present: mother, father, brother (age 18), sister (age 14), grandmother (mother of mother).

There are no specific assignments to the roles except that everyone should act as they think would happen in their family or in a 'typical' family in their country.

This role-play could well be used to illustrate and compare family life and should be used in a bicultural or multicultural setting. (A monocultural setting gives no result for intercultural learning.) What rules are there? What happens if these rules are broken? What is the role of father and mother with respect to the education of their children? What is the relationship between parents and children, between brothers and sisters, older and younger siblings?

Possible role-plays include the following.

- *Play other situations in family life*: breakfast, lunch or dinner; going out to a restaurant for dinner; mother's birthday; Christmas or other traditional festivity; (preparing for) a weekend trip; children bringing home bad examination results, etc.
- *Play school.* This could be a discussion between a parent of a pupil with bad marks and a teacher; a teacher presenting a project to the class; an oral exam; a pupil telling a teacher why he or she could not do the homework; a teacher conference, etc. Such role-plays could illustrate the relationships among and between teachers, pupils and parents.
- *Play work.* This could be a discussion between an employee and his or her boss about a problem the company is facing (e.g. there is a severe budget overrun and expenses have to be cut or production increased, a machine broke down and production is slowed down, a contract was lost to a competitor, etc. Such role-plays could reveal dominant values at work and within this society in general. They could also illustrate the relationship between superiors and subordinates in this society.
- *Play court.* This could be, for example, the trial of a shoplifter or a person who has injured a pedestrian while breaking a traffic rule (gone through a red light, speeding, etc.). Such a role-play would illustrate the role of law in the society (this

might depend on the offence) and the relationship of citizens towards authority. A variation would be a discussion between a police officer and a driver who has been caught exceeding the speed limit or passing another car illegally.

When these role-plays are used in a bicultural or multicultural setting (e.g. as part of a class exchange) and when they are played by all cultural groups present, they can serve to compare the different cultures involved. As a basis for such a comparison, one could use the different dimensions of cultures as described by Hofstede, outlined in Chapter 7.

There are many more possibilities for role-plays. It is up to the creativity and fantasy of teachers and pupils to set up their own role-plays according to the content and objectives of their project.

Field studies

A field study is an experiential learning tool that lets pupils explore real-life situations. A field study will usually require a lot of time. There needs to be sufficient time for pupils to enter into all aspects of it: preparing, doing, evaluating, documenting and presenting the results.

A field study can be done within one's own culture or country as well as in another country. If a field study is done in one's own country, it can provide insight into a situation or issue one is not quite familiar with. For example, for a group of urban pupils, it could be the exploration of rural life. It could be the living conditions of handicapped people, migrants or other minority groups in one's country. It could be working conditions in general – salaries, social security, benefits, protection of workers and employees, etc. A field study can also provide an overview of what a larger group of people in one's community think with respect to a specific issue, what their attitudes are, their values, their habits, their needs, their professional or educational perspectives, etc.

If a field study is done in another country, its primary purpose is to explore the other country or culture. This can be done to acquire a basic information level or with respect to a specific theme or issue. In this case, it is advisable that the field study is prepared by teachers from both countries. If field studies are undertaken in both home and host countries, parallel instruments would give comparative information for discussion. A detailed example of such a field study is included in the exercises section ('field study').

A field study needs to be well prepared. There need to be clear instructions and assignments. Wherever possible, the pupils should be involved in the design and preparation of the field study. There are a number of exercises in this book that could be used for field studies: 'field exercise', 'educational path and professional career questionnaire', 'time in Europe', 'personal values'.

RESOURCES FOR INTERCULTURAL LEARNING ACTIVITIES

There are numerous resources that can be used to look at one's own or other cultures. The following list describes some of these resources in more detail.

- *Theatre, films, etc.* Plays and films usually illustrate lifestyles and values. Analysing a film that was produced in another country and also plays in your country (or involves people from your country) can result in a better understanding of life and politics in the country. But it can also be misleading – films frequently convey stereotypes, which have to be addressed in the discussions following the film. There are also numerous films that involve the interaction of people from different cultures, which can serve as a source for discussion on the topic.
- *Newspapers.* Exploring the newspapers of another country can contribute a lot to a better understanding of its people. How many different newspapers and what types of newspapers are there? What are the topics they write about? How long are the articles? How do they relate to issues and the persons involved? What and how do they write about one's own country? And what does that all mean? Of course, newspapers are also a valuable resource for what is happening in another country and what seems to be important for the people there.
- *Advertising.* Few things are as culturally determined as advertising. Commercials relate to values, traditions, prestige, lifestyle, etc., and consequently give a good insight into another culture. But it is not only the message that is culturally determined, it is also the way they are made – the casting, the screenplay, the cuts, the music, etc. Commercials that are successful in one country are not necessarily so in another.
- *Comics, cartoons, jokes, humour.* What do people laugh about? Who are the heroes, heroines, underdogs? What do they represent? This is very different depending on culture. Comics, cartoons, and jokes frequently touch on taboos, relate to contradictions inherent to the respective society, approach the limits of what is perceived to be acceptable. A joke in one culture might not be perceived to be funny in another because there is no contradiction or taboo to be touched, or, even worse, because it has gone beyond the limits of good taste.
- *Tales.* Tales relate to the traditions and wisdom inherent to a society or culture. They tend to emphasize symbols and to touch on beliefs and values that people hold dear, sometimes in an idealistic, romantic and nostalgic way.

There are numerous other resources that one can draw on to explore one's own or another culture. The following list is provided without further explanation and can be expanded with creativity:

- rituals
- symbols
- books
- children's games, rhymes, toys
- clothing, hair fashion

- recipes, cooking
- handicrafts
- sports
- drawings, photographs
- festivals

Note

1   'The owl' is in Donald Batchelder and Elizabeth Warner, *Beyond Experience*. Brattleboro, VT: The Experiment in International Living, 1977. 'Bafá bafá' is published by Smile II, Del Mar, California.

CHAPTER 9

Model Schemes for Intercultural Learning Projects

Every intercultural learning project is unique. Each one has its own characteristics, making it different from others: specific topics, a specific structural setting,
specific organizational aspects, a specific structure of relationships, a specific ambi-
ence – all owing to the variety of countries and regions where the projects can take
place, to the characteristics of each school and teachers, pupils and parents. And
because such projects are unusual – at least in many countries – those involved
consider their project to be unique.

The six didactic schemes that follow this discussion of models demonstrate the
model framework and elements. The schemes described might not exist in that
specific form in reality. They combine the experiences of various successful projects
and can be used as a frame of reference for designing and developing a new project.
The elements of different schemes can be combined, adapted or modified according
to specific needs and the particular environment, and thus a vast number of projects
can be designed.

The model discussion and the scheme descriptions are not complete and are not
eternally valid. The structure and content of intercultural learning projects depend
on educational, organizational, economic, political and social environments that are
in the process of permanent change. Some models may become obsolete while
others will undoubtedly be added. The model schemes follow the descriptions of
settings contained in Chapter 7.

The concept of learning, the concept of culture and, consequently, the concept
of intercultural learning are culturally determined. Intercultural learning projects
will be designed and organized differently in different countries and cultures. It is
very difficult if not impossible to describe model schemes for projects that are
universally valid. The model schemes outlined in this chapter implicitly reflect the
cultural background of the authors.

DIFFERENT ENVIRONMENTS FOR INTERCULTURAL LEARNING PROJECTS

The social and cultural environments in which a school is situated have an essential impact on any intercultural learning project. In Chapter 7 we described a number of settings for the integration of intercultural learning in school curricula. The following settings refer to the same environments but provide specific suggestions on how intercultural projects can be implemented in those settings.

A monocultural school in a monocultural society

To achieve intercultural learning in such a setting, it will be necessary to establish direct contact with people of a different cultural background in a different part of one's own country or with people in another country. The usual means of accomplishing this is a link or an exchange with a class or school abroad. Although modern technology allows quite intensive and instantaneous communication (fax, electronic mail) and thus actually allows work on the same project simultaneously in two different countries, this does not replace a personal face-to-face contact. A school link which incorporates a personal encounter with people from another culture provides the possibility of developing deeper relationships from which one can learn. In many countries, but especially in Switzerland and Belgium, this can also be achieved by exchanges within the country.

A monocultural school in a multicultural society

In this setting, it is necessary to leave the classroom to explore cultural diversity. How do people of a different cultural background live in one's own community or region? What is the relationship and interdependence between the different cultural or ethnic groups? Sometimes the relationship between different cultural groups within one society is so tense (and results in separate schools for different cultural or ethnic groups) that traditional patterns of relating to the other group can hardly be overcome. Simply going out 'to meet the others' might not work and possibly increases the aversion to the other group. In this setting, the appreciation of cultural diversity and intercultural interaction and communication skills might be acquired by exposure to a culture further away, where the pupils do not have a preconceived and/or negative attitude, e.g. by a class exchange.

A multicultural class or school in a multicultural society

In this case, the situation in the class or school usually reflects the situation in the society – or at least various elements of it. The necessity as well as the potential for intercultural learning is inherent to the class composition. For such a class, intercultural learning means learning for life in a wider society. This setting provides a potential for intensive intercultural learning, but again it is possible or even likely that existing patterns cannot be overcome for many reasons, not the least of which is that a class or school cannot detach itself from society. Therefore it can also be very useful to travel abroad with a multicultural class.

When a class includes migrant children, travel could be to the country of (cultural) origin of some of the pupils, which would reverse the usual situation. The 'foreigners' in the class would become 'natives' (which they actually are not any more if their parents have migrated long ago) and those who are normally 'natives' would become 'foreigners'. Such a class could also travel to a country where there are no cultural links represented in the class and experience a situation where all pupils are 'foreigners'. It is likely that the migrant children will be better able to deal with this situation simply because they are accustomed to being considered foreign, and those who are normally 'natives' could learn from them. The cultural composition and the size of the different cultural groups will play an important role in choosing and designing methods for such a setting.

Bicultural or bilingual countries

There are many regions in Europe where there are indigenous cultural or ethnic groups that are referred to as 'ethnic minorities', although they might be a majority group within a certain region. Such a group is usually defined through a language that is different from the language of that country, usually the language of the majority of people in that country. Frequently one cannot refer to these regions as being bicultural because assimilation or integration has resulted in a common cultural 'layer' with roots in deeper 'layers' of both original cultures, though with a different accent.

Educational institutions and schools have been organized very differently in these regions – they can be anything from truly bilingual to separate systems for the different language groups. For a class or school in such a setting, the approaches suggested under 'multicultural class in a multicultural society' or 'monocultural class in a multicultural society' can be adapted.

A class with one or a few representatives from a different culture

The assumption for this setting is that the 'minority cultures' represented in the class are not represented otherwise in the society of which this class is part. This setting can occur when there is an individual exchangee from another country or pupils whose parents have moved for professional reasons. This setting differs from a multicultural classroom in a multicultural society significantly. The exchangee usually cannot refer to his or her cultural group within this country; the relationship between the pupils in the class is not as strongly imposed on him or her by the society the majority of the class is part of, except for the usual prejudices and stereotypes; the pupils in the class have little or no experience or history of coexistence with each other.

This enables such a class to make use of the potential for intercultural learning more freely and openly. There are fewer barriers to finding out more about the other(s), there is more willingness to help the 'foreigner(s)', there is less fear about losing one's cultural identity. It is commonly assumed that the 'visitor from abroad' will learn interculturally in such a setting – this is one of the main objectives of most exchange organizations. It is less common, however, to make use of such a setting for an intercultural learning process for the 'native' majority of the class. The exchangee is perceived to disturb the regular work of a class. This can be turned around by making use of the exchangee as a resource for learning and for relating to another country and culture.

A DIDACTIC APPROACH TO INTERCULTURAL LEARNING

A didactic approach to intercultural learning implies two factors: timing and sequencing. Timing refers to the schedule of specific learning activities within an intercultural learning project and the amount of time allocated to each of these activities. It does not make sense to hold an intensive preparatory session relating to stereotypes about another country on the day before anticipated travel, or to assess and evaluate a trip on the day after returning home.

Timing or duration also refers to the length of time available for intercultural learning. Is it the time required for a two-week visit to another school abroad, the preparation, the visit, the follow-up? Is it ongoing, perhaps including the hosting of a class from another country, but where the overall focus is a joint project? Does ongoing mean a school term, an academic year?

Sequencing refers to the order in which the different learning objectives are addressed in order to obtain a desired learning result. It makes sense from a didactic point of view to pursue learning objectives in a specific sequence. For example, it makes sense to reflect on stereotypes and prejudices about the people of another country before going there. Being aware of their own stereotypes and prejudices enables pupils to question them actively, while not being aware of them could result in their reinforcement of negative stereotypes through selective perception.

It is likely that even with planned sequencing, with the greatest input of common sense, the group will revisit subjects and issues time and again, totally out of sequence. The subjects and learning objectives are interrelated. This spiral process of learning was referred to in Chapter 7. It is hoped that as subjects are touched again and again, each time there will be a new perspective, thanks to increased awareness or consciousness on the part of participants.

There is no unique timing and sequencing of the different learning steps and activities for intercultural learning. But there is a 'logic' to the didactic of each intercultural learning project, depending on the composition of the pupils, the social and cultural environment, the framework of the project and the context within which it is organized.

There are several assumptions underlying this approach to intercultural learning.

- There needs to be security within one's own culture. Everyone has a (cultural) self-perception, be it unconscious or conscious. During an intercultural learning experience, the learner should be or become conscious and confident of such a self-image. Without this, the individual might withdraw from the process.
- Intercultural learning implies confrontation with other cultures. The nature of culture can only be realized if one is confronted with lifestyles, behaviours, values and beliefs other than those so far taken for granted.
- There has to be an 'initializing event'. People need to be motivated in order to learn interculturally. Sometimes this motivation is created by the arrival of a new pupil in the class from another country, or it could be an intercultural conflict inside or outside the school environment. If this is not the case, it may be necessary to start an intercultural learning project 'artificially' with an 'initializing event' that will effect an emotional response and motivate the pupils to participate actively in the project.

ELEMENTS OF A MODEL SCHEME

The following describes the chronological flow of an intercultural learning project. In spite of the large variety of intercultural projects, there are a number of elements which comprise the model scheme framework and which can be applied generally. These elements have proved to be necessary or useful for the effective organization of projects and for enhancing their pedagogical value.

Searching for a partner school

Many factors play a role in the search for a partner school: the goals being pursued in the project, the partner country, the geographic distance, the presence or absence of a common language for communication (at least between the teachers), the type of school, the age of the pupils, etc. It is likely that the exact partner school being searched for will not be found. This is normal and implicitly caused by differences in motivation, ideas, objectives and structures in different countries and schools. This is a step in an intercultural learning process. It can be very intercultural to become involved in something that is different from what is expected or familiar.

Schools in countries with main vehicular languages (English, French, German) may have less difficulty finding a partner school than schools in countries with less frequently taught languages. This is because a major objective when organizing a school link or an exchange is still the learning of another language – in a majority of cases this is one of the above-mentioned languages.

Planning

It is difficult to organize a project involving one class. It is more difficult to organize a project involving more than one class. And it is even more difficult to organize a project together with people in another country, who have a different culture and speak a different language. Bad telephone connections are the least problem in such a situation. Good planning is a prerequisite for the success of any intercultural learning project. Chapter 8 addressed planning with respect to the content and theme of the project. Here we add some thoughts to be considered when planning a project in general:

- If the project involves a partner school abroad it is essential that the planning is done together with teachers (and pupils) of the partner school. This is especially important with respect to the objectives of the project, which can be different. It is not necessary that the two schools involved pursue identical objectives but they do need to be compatible and should complement each other.
- The planning should involve all people concerned with the project – pupils, parents, teachers, headteachers – to ensure maximum participation. Those excluded from this process can become an obstacle to the success of the project.
- It is impossible to plan from beginning to end something that might go on for a whole year, involving learning and intensive experiences of pupils from different cultural backgrounds. Planning will have to be dynamic; the plans will undoubtedly be modified and further developed during the project.
- Planning allows for overview during the project. Finding out where the project stands, what has been already accomplished, what still has to be done – all is possible with reference to a plan. Such planning provides clarity and, therefore, security during the project.
- Sufficient time should be scheduled for which no activities are planned, to allow for spontaneity and unplanned activities.

The planning of an intercultural project needs to take into account the following aspects:

- Content and structure of the project: themes, learning objectives, approaches, methods, etc. In the case of an exchange one also has to consider the accommodation of the pupils (families, youth hostel, etc.).
- Programme and process of the whole project: preparation, evaluation and documentation.
- Cooperation and communication: with partner school, colleagues, pupils, parents.
- Organizational/technical aspects: travel, insurance, accommodation, finances, legal aspects, etc.

Setting goals and objectives

For any educational activity, it is essential to reach a certain clarity concerning goals and objectives (this also applies to intercultural learning projects), the development of knowledge, awareness, attitudes and skills of pupils.

Learning objectives are not static. They can be changed and further developed during the course of the planning process and of the project itself if circumstances make this useful or necessary. Where there is to be an exchange or link with a class in another country, the objectives must be mutually agreed or compatible with the partner class or school. It is important to involve the pupils as much as possible in defining the objectives.

Objectives must also be achievable. An intercultural learning project will not eliminate prejudice. A project will give participants different ways of examining prejudice and confronting their own attitudes. An intercultural encounter may help them to change their way of thinking. But achievable objectives will not change the world, they will be small steps.

Preparation

It would be an illusion to assume that an encounter of pupils from different cultural backgrounds will have all the positive effects that are anticipated. Intercultural or international encounters of pupils are no magic tool. Achievable objectives, a decrease of prejudices and overcoming rejection can be realized if the encounter is well prepared. Not to prepare the project or encounter well might mean that existing prejudices are enforced rather than questioned.

An important element of any preparation for an intercultural project is a reflection about own lifestyle, values and cultural identity. This reflection should also lead to an awareness of what is taken as being obvious. Another aspect of preparation is becoming conscious of the images one has about the other cultures or countries involved in the project. These images strongly influence behaviour and actions when one is discussing, meeting or relating to people of these cultures or countries. Only if these images are conscious can they be questioned and possibly corrected as a result of the project or encounter.

During the preparation for the project, it is important to learn certain techniques and tools to explore the foreign and unknown – learning by discovery and through project work. The pupils themselves should define what they want to find out, what questions are meaningful to them, what issues they want to work on. They should develop their own approaches and methods to explore another country or culture through work, play, festivities and everyday life.

For an encounter, it is useful to deal with the history, geography, society, politics and economy of the partner country. Nevertheless, the total experience cannot be anticipated in the preparation, nor should it be – the possibility of discovery and experiential learning through the encounter with people of the other country is paramount to the project. The information collected should be compared with the presentation of the other country by the pupils of the partner school. The purpose of preparation is not so much to find answers but to devise questions.

Other elements of preparation, especially for an exchange or intercultural encounter, are:

- clarification of expectations, addressing unrealistic expectations;
- addressing possible fears of the pupils;
- exercises, role plays, simulations referring to communication and encounters with the foreign;
- establishing contact with the pupils of the partner school through letters, tapes, videos, exchange of pictures or other material objects, etc.

Preparing for an intercultural learning project also involves working on the theme of the project. How this is done will largely depend on the theme itself.

It is important to involve parents in the preparation for an intercultural encounter, especially if the family will be receiving a pupil from another country during an exchange. In this hosting situation, parents, like their children, must confront differences, become conscious of their own ethnocentric behaviour, and at the same time realize that the pupil they are receiving is also behaving in his or her own ethnocentric way and that this way of thinking and behaving is not 'wrong' but simply different. They, too, are learners. Receiving a pupil from another country in a family requires understanding. Parents need to be sensitive to the pupil's effort to speak continuously in another language. The hosting of a pupil from abroad requires understanding that the pupil has to learn rules and behaviour that their own children learned in early childhood.

It is an illusion to assume that the shorter the duration of an encounter with pupils from abroad, the less preparation will be needed – the opposite is true. The shorter the encounter, the greater is the danger that existing prejudices and stereotypes will be reinforced. More preparation is needed for a short intercultural encounter than for a longer encounter.

Guidance

Intercultural encounters do not automatically result in an increased communicative competence. If the insecurity in a foreign environment becomes too great, there is a danger that the pupil might escape or withdraw. To avoid this, a 'pedagogic security rail' or pedagogic guidance of the project needs to be provided.

Such guidance implies an awareness of where the pupils stand and what kind of support they need. It also means empathizing with the pupils, understanding their situation. It means sensing problems individual pupils might have, sensing open or hidden conflicts, and reacting to these situations appropriately. But it also means providing an environment and structure for the project where a constructive intercultural and social learning process can take place for the pupils. For this, regular sessions of the class(es) or cultural groups could be organized to allow room for reflection and sharing what has been experienced. This was outlined in more detail in Chapter 8.

While the pupils are being guided through a project it is important to keep the right balance of closeness and distance: on the one hand, to provide opportunities to be confronted with the foreign and to be able to explore the unknown; on the other hand, to allow pupils to withdraw, to share the experiences with friends, to reflect about the experiences, to cheer up and prepare for new events. This pendulum, this oscillation between the foreign and the familiar, is necessary for discovery and exploration.

When an exchange involves pupils living with families in another country (usually families of pupils in the partner class), guidance for parents receiving a pupil from abroad in their home must be catered for. Regular meetings during the exchange could be organized for parents. Another possibility is to organize individual contact, by, for example, telephone conversations or meetings, with each family during the visit to find out how the pupil is adjusting, how they as a family are adjusting and learning. This enables possible misunderstandings and problems to be addressed.

Experiencing a reality different from the one a pupil has grown up with can cause confusion. In the case of a stay abroad this can result in a need for readjustment after the return home, especially if the visit abroad has been long and intensive. Parts of the lifestyle abroad may become more attractive than that at home (particularly if the hospitality is over indulgent); the terms 'normal' and 'self-evident' become less powerful, even confused. This is all right and does not result in a general judgement that one lifestyle is better than another. The question for teachers to explore with pupils is how the experience abroad can be applied, made use of in the home cultural environment. Nevertheless, it must be understood that this environment cannot be changed by an individual. The transfer of behaviour found adequate and useful abroad to the home culture can cause problems and conflict at re-entry.

This means that a pupil returning home from a stay abroad can face similar situations to those encountered in the other country. The pupil will view his or her own cultural environment with a new and different perspective. Things that seemed 'normal' before will be perceived as 'strange'. Sometimes the pupil might feel like a 'foreigner' in his or her own country. Pupils in the re-entry phase of an exchange might require pedagogic guidance, referred to as 'reorientation', to deal effectively with this situation.

The teacher plays an essential pedagogic role in guiding the pupils (and their families) through the process of an intercultural encounter. It is important to realize, though, that this role is not to solve problems and conflicts for those involved or to act as a judge in any confrontation. The role is that of a facilitator, a stimulator, a questioner, a listener. It is also important to realize that there might not be a solution. Nevertheless, it is important to recognize and accept misunderstandings or conflicts, and to deal with them in a fair and even-handed manner.

Final event

Intercultural learning has an affective and social component. This means that it not only includes working and learning together in a traditional way but also includes celebrating feasts together, socializing, making music, dancing, cooking, eating – enjoying life together. This implies not only that pupils from different cultures involved in an intercultural project will have working relationships but also that during the course of the project they will develop personal relationships and friendships. The degree to which this happens could be an indication of the success of the project. (To express it in a slightly exaggerated way: if as a result of a two-week exchange pupils aged 15 or older from one school have not fallen in love with pupils of the partner school something has gone wrong!)

An important element of any project is some form of closing event. It gives importance to the project, it provides recognition of everyone involved, it leads to satisfaction about what has been accomplished, it allows the application of knowledge and skills acquired during the project, it allows for relaxation after intensive work and it provides a lasting learning experience about how a festivity is celebrated in a different culture. Such an event provides the opportunity to involve people from outside the class or school and especially to involve even more people from different cultural backgrounds, helping to create a truly multicultural situation.

A part of this component cannot be planned and structured intentionally. A cramped and tight schedule not leaving time for individual use will prevent enjoyment and personal relationships, important parts of the experience. Festivities and social rituals do need a framework and preparation. But, more than in any other part of an intercultural learning project, the pupils need to be the organizers and actors. The role of the teacher is to arrange time in the schedule, give advice, and monitor and support the respective activities. To make this component a constructive part of the project, creativity and common sense from teachers and pupils are needed.

An important part of planning and preparing for the event is to reach agreement on its objectives, content and structure, and who will be responsible for what. There is no limit to creativity during planning and preparation. Some suggestions are:

- music performances
- learning and singing a song as a multicultural group
- dancing
- cooking and eating
- photograph exhibitions
- theatre performances
- games

Documentation

Documentation can serve a number of different purposes. It can contribute to further reflection on and assessment of the experience; it conveys what has been experienced to parents and friends as well as to pupils and teachers who have not participated; it can help pupils to remember their experiences later on; and it can contribute to publicity for the project and for the school. The last will be especially important if the project has received funding or other support from public or private sources.

It is essential to envision the documentation as part of the project planning because otherwise possibilities for documenting the project will be limited. The planning of the documentation has to include a clarification of who will be responsible. The responsibility can be taken by a small working group but could be shared by the whole class, with different pupils being responsible for different parts of the documentation.

There are numerous possibilities for the documentation of a project:

- a video or film (to avoid boring and lengthy films this needs good preparation and editing);
- tapes with interviews, statements, music, live recordings, special sounds, etc.;
- slides, pictures;
- an exhibition of 'pieces of culture';
- artistic presentation of the experience through drawings, posters, collages, prose, poems, sketches, pantomime, dance, etc.;
- a newspaper or other publication containing stories, factual information (facts and figures about the other country or the cultures involved in the project), interviews, excerpts from journals/diaries, cartoons, photographs, etc.;
- a group journal which is written on a daily basis, the pupils taking turns;
- a combination of the possibilities outlined above.

The presentation of the documentation can be integrated into a final event and can serve as a 'thank you' for all who have supported the project.

Evaluation

Evaluation is a standard element for an exchange or any intercultural learning project. This has been dealt with in detail in Chapter 8 and does not need any further elaboration here.

DIDACTIC MODEL SCHEMES FOR INTERCULTURAL LEARNING PROJECTS

Common to each of these model schemes is that they generally have three phases:

- a preparation phase during which pupils prepare for some form of intensive experience;
- an intensive phase which usually contains an intercultural encounter (this could be a visit abroad, a visit of a class from abroad, a field study within the community or country, a work project related to intercultural learning);
- a phase of reorientation and evaluation.

During each of these phases, all areas of intercultural learning have to be dealt with, though each in a different context. For example, during the preparation phase, pupils become conscious of prejudices and stereotypes; during the intensive phase, they relate them to the reality they are experiencing; during the evaluation and reorientation phase, they assess how they have changed.

The order in which the models are discussed is not hierarchical but represents a number of class situations that the reader, more often than not a teacher, initially has to consider. The models are set forth on a basis of what exists in terms of class composition and resources available.

The composition of the class, monocultural or multicultural, raises a political question about the intercultural learning to be achieved. Will it be internally directed and focused because the class is made up of two or more cultural groups? Will it take its lead or motivation from the fact that the monocultural class composition does not reflect the national multicultural environment, and so requires an external focus? Does the pupils' age prevent travel? Are the financial realities such that travel is not feasible? The final two models assume travel as a possibility and a reality.

Intercultural learning project for a monocultural class without a school link

The first didactic model describes the pedagogic process in an intercultural learning project for a monocultural class that is not part of a link with a school or class abroad (see Table 1). At local level, many school classes remain culturally homogeneous through residential patterns and school boundary policies. But instead of introducing another culture to the classroom through an exchange, this model suggests the use of the intercultural learning potential provided by the presence of other cultures within the country. This implies that during the project the pupils have to leave the classroom for a field study or that people from outside school are brought into the classroom. This would be the heart of such a project.

The framework of this model can be described as follows:

- *Content.* The basic content of a project within this scheme is intercultural learning: gaining greater awareness of one's own culture as well as becoming aware of

Table 1 Didactic scheme for an intercultural learning project for a monocultural class without school link
Timing: ongoing
Theme: intercultural learning

Area of learning	Learning objectives	Questions	Exercises/tools
Initializing event	To motivate pupils for intercultural learning.	Why should we learn interculturally? Which present issues in my country/Europe have an intercultural dimension?	Research into media for events which could have an intercultural dimension (e.g. legislation on immigration, rightist actions, migrant worker rights, bilingual education). 'Let's look at the world', 'Europe, yesterday, today, tomorrow'. Issue with an intercultural dimension presently dealt with in a specific subject (e.g. history, political education).
Stereotypes, prejudices	To become aware of stereotypes and prejudices and where they come from. To become aware of results owing to prejudices and stereotypes. To become aware of stereotypes about own culture.	What prejudices and stereotypes towards other cultural groups do we have? Where do they come from? What stereotypes do people in other countries have about us? Where do they come from? How do we present ourselves to others through the media, etc?	'Apartment exercise', 'Completing sentences', 'Associative drawing'. Searching for prejudices conveyed by newspapers, school books, TV, publicity, literature, etc.

Topic	Objectives	Questions	Activities
Lifestyles and behaviour	To become aware of own lifestyle.	How do I (want to) live?	'Ways to live', 'Time in Europe', 'Where do I come from?' Compare with other lifestyles, e.g. observed in films or during a trip abroad.
Cultural differences	To become aware of differences between societies and cultures. To recognize differences as possible source of tensions and conflict.	Is it like here all over the world? What differences do we know about? Why are there tensions, discrimination, conflicts?	Work through newspapers, TV, etc.: look at images of other places. Brainstorming. 'Albatross'.
Own culture, cultural identity	To become aware of own culture. To understand concept of culture.	Who am I? Where do I come from? What are we like? Why are we the way we are? Is there a 'typical' representative of our culture? What is 'typical' about our culture? How do we present ourselves to others through media?	'Personal maps'. Drawing: 'something cultural about me'. Role-play and/or brainstorming and/or 'associative drawing' on 'what is typical about our own culture?' (national, provincial, local). 'Playing regions', 'Cultural quotations', 'Sunshine and rain', 'Maps and atlases'. Analyse national literatures, films, advertisements, e.g. tourist promotion. 'Concept of culture', 'Cultural differences'.

Table 1 – *continued*

Area of learning	Learning objectives	Questions	Exercises/tools
Communication	To become aware of importance/ role of non-verbal communication. To recognize limitations of interpreting symbols and words. To gain motivation for language learning.	How do I communicate? Are there other means of communication?	'Humming exercise', 'Yes/no game', 'Babel', 'Building a tower'. Refer to 'Albatross'. Feedback exercises.
Other cultures	To experience another culture. To increase adaptability to changing social circumstances. To value cultural diversity.	How can I experience the possibilities of another culture? How can I become exposed to another culture? Where do I want to go? How do I want to do it? What do I want to gain? Would I like to relate to local inhabitants? If yes, how?	'Field exercise' involving other than own culture. Discuss possible class exchange/ field trip (domestic/to neighbouring countries). Discuss individual exchange possibilities. 'My next summer holiday', 'My last summer holiday'.
Values	To become aware of values. To learn how/that values influence behaviour and lifestyles.	What values do I have? What values do others have? How do values influence my behaviour?	'Who am I?', 'Personal values', 'Abigale', 'Cave Rescue'.
Global perspectives	To gain commitment to search for solutions.	How can I contribute?	'Community project', 'Where is it from, where is it going?
Evaluation	To review learning.	What have we experienced and learned as a result of the project? How do we think/do differently as a result of the experiences? How do we want to continue intercultural learning?	'Evaluation' (1 and 2).

cultural diversity and cultural differences, relativizing one's own culture and ethnocentrism, overcoming fear of the foreign, developing competence in dealing with intercultural situations. There can be additional themes for the project depending on its objectives and on the cultural group the class relates to as part of the project.

- *Duration*. Such a project can be done very intensively over a few days, e.g. as a project week, but it could also be pursued over a longer period – a month, a term, a school year.

- *Age of pupils*. Such a project can generally be organized with pupils of any age. With younger pupils, an affective and emotional learning approach must be taken. With older pupils, the cognitive component of the learning process must also be addressed.

- *Structure*. Such a project can be organized in one specific subject (or in two or more subjects at the same time), which implies that it is pursued over a longer period. But a cross-curricular approach could also be taken, with an intensive project being organized over a few days to include a number of classes or even a whole school. The project should provide for an experience with people of a different cultural background outside school.

A class with a multicultural composition

The premise for an intercultural learning project in a class with a multicultural composition is different. There is an existing necessity for intercultural learning within the class resulting from the fact that it is multicultural. Additionally, the multiculturalism is permanent, not temporary. While the presence of different cultures in the class provides an essential prerequisite for intercultural learning, the history behind it and the fact that this setting usually reflects the situation of the social environment of the school can make an intercultural learning process more difficult.

A lot of research and work has been done in the past with respect to education in multicultural societies. It would be impossible to refer to it sufficiently in this book. The didactic model for this setting is one of many that can be used to pursue intercultural learning in a multicultural class. Table 2 details this didactic scheme.

This model is based on the following framework:

- *Content*. While earlier educational concepts for multicultural classes aimed at assimilating the pupils of cultural backgrounds other than the national culture of the school, this model aims to establish a mutual learning process where the pupils learn from and with each other. A basic element of this learning process is to become aware of and secure within one's own cultural background, and then actively to introduce it to the others. Gaining an understanding of the other cultures represented in the class then follows. An important aspect of this process is the development of new forms of communication and relationships with pupils of different cultural backgrounds and the overcoming of traditional patterns that

Table 2 Didactic scheme for an intercultural learning project for a class with a multicultural composition
Timing: ongoing
Theme: cultural identity, cultural differences, intercultural learning

Area of learning	Learning objectives	Questions	Exercises/tools
Initializing event	To recognize necessity for intercultural learning.	Why should we learn interculturally?	Refer to existing tensions/issues within class/school. Refer to misunderstanding or non-understanding which has actually occurred.
Theme	To become aware of differences between cultural groups in the class. To recognize differences as possible source of misunderstanding and tensions.	What are the misunderstandings/tensions about? Where do they come from? What do you like about me/my cultural group? What do you not like? What are the differences between the cultural groups in the class?	Brainstorming; discuss results in bicultural pairs. 'Personal maps', 'Piece of culture', 'Associative drawing', 'Role-play'.
Stereotypes, prejudices	To become aware of stereotypes and prejudices, and where they come from. To become aware of the results owing to prejudices and stereotypes.	What image do the different cultural groups in the class have about each other? Are there stereotypes/prejudices about each other? What? How do they affect attitudes and behaviour? What prejudices and stereotypes towards cultural groups not represented in our class do we have?	'Images in the mind', 'Completing sentences', 'Role change/mirror', 'Apartment exercise'. Searching for prejudices conveyed by newspapers, school books, TV, publicity, literature, etc.

Cultural identity, own culture, cultural differences	To become aware of own culture. To learn about other cultures. To understand concept of culture. To appreciate cultural diversity.	Who are you? Where do you come from? Who am I? Where do I come from? Why are we the way we are? What is 'typical' about the cultures represented in the class? How do cultural differences affect the relationship between the cultural groups in the class?	Refer to 'Personal maps' and 'Piece of culture'. Use language and behaviour of 'minority group' for specific situation. 'Cultural quotations', 'Maps and atlases', 'Sunshine and rain', 'Field exercise' or 'Field study', 'Concept of culture', 'Cultural differences'. Bicultural pairs prepare lists why class/school/community is a better place because of us.
Lifestyles, behaviour	To learn about own/others' lifestyles and behaviour. To become aware of limits in understanding symbols/behaviour.	How do I (want to) live? How do you (want to) live? Why do you do what you do?	Refer to 'Personal maps', 'Where do I come from?', 'Ways to live', 'Eating rituals'. Bicultural interviews.
Values	To become aware of own/others' values. To learn how values influence behaviour.	What values do I have? What values do other cultural groups in the class have? How do these values influence our behaviour, working together in the class, our relationship? What do we like about 'us' and the 'others'? What can we contribute to and gain from each other?	'Personal values', 'Cultural values checklist', 'Abigale', 'Cave rescue'. Multicultural happening (food, dance, music, dresses, poetry, etc.).

Table 2 – *continued*

Area of learning	Learning objectives	Questions	Exercises/tools
Communication	To recognize need for intercultural communication. To gain motivation for learning others' language.	How can we improve our communication and interaction?	Bilingual teaching. Regular feedback. 'Building a tower', 'Charades', 'ABA–ZAK'. 'Community project'.
Global perspectives	To gain commitment to and search for solutions. To design/implement a project.	What are the issues in our community? Do these issues have a cultural dimension? What are possible approaches, actions, solutions?	
Assessment/evaluation	To recognize change. To review learning. To agree ongoing steps.	How have we changed? What do we do/think differently? What more do we want to know and how can we find it out?	Revisit associative exercises ('Images in the mind', 'Associative drawings', 'Completing sentences', etc.). Reflect on experience. 'Evaluation' (1 and 2).

might have prevented constructive relationships. Since intercultural learning also implies language learning, this issue has to be addressed during the project. While it is impossible for pupils to learn all the other languages represented in the class, a functional or at least passive knowledge of one other language can be achieved with adequate methods over a longer period, such as a school year.

- *Duration*. Intercultural learning in a multicultural class has to be an ongoing process. More intensive projects (perhaps once during a term) would enable some distance from everyday school life to be gained and thus the questioning of traditional attitudes and behaviour.
- *Age of pupils*. Activities related to intercultural learning in a multicultural classroom have to be pursued beginning in primary school. Especially for younger pupils, the way the teacher relates to other cultures will be taken as an example for their attitudes and behaviour.
- *Structure*. Most activities related to intercultural learning in a multicultural class will take place within the framework of the class (but perhaps also outside the classroom). It is advisable that similar activities take place in all classes of a school as part of a larger concept. This would allow the occasional organization of bigger events involving the whole school and, possibly, parents.

School link without exchange

There are many links between schools where an actual exchange of classes or groups of pupils is very difficult or even impossible. School links without an exchange or direct personal encounter tend to focus more on international and/or political education (see Table 3). They are particularly valuable when it is possible for the teachers of the linking partner schools to meet and plan the project.

There seem to be two categories of links without exchange. There are links where the combination of age and geography factors of the partner schools does not allow a visit in the other country. This applies for primary and lower secondary schools linked with schools further away, e.g. a primary school in Austria linked with a school in the United Kingdom. The objectives for such a link can be to practise initial foreign language skills through correspondence, to deal more intensively with the history and geography of another country or simply to confront pupils with the concept of different countries – to open up to the foreign, to gain an international perspective.

There are also links where an exchange is difficult because of financial limitations. This applies to links involving long distances that incur high travel costs but also for exchanges between schools where there are insufficient resources or where priorities dictate different expenditures. If an exchange visit is planned for a whole class to travel and it is necessary to charge a fee to supplement available resources, how does the teacher ensure that the economically disadvantaged pupils in the class are not excluded because their families are unable to pay the fee? Teachers must also contend with parental fears about their children's travel to another country.

School links based solely on humanitarian action or material support cannot be

Table 3 Didactic scheme for a class with a school link, without exchange
Timing: Ongoing (duration of project depending on theme, age of pupils, etc.)

Emphasis	Learning objectives	Questions	Exercises/tools
Initializing event (direct intervention after teachers of two schools agree on project)	To motivate pupils for intercultural learning and to work on a theme.	Why should I/we learn interculturally? Which present issues in my country/in Europe have an intercultural dimension? What is our/my interest in other country? What theme(s) would we like to work on?	Brainstorming. Research into media for events which could have an intercultural dimension. 'Europe, yesterday, today, tomorrow', 'Let's look at the world'. Issue with an intercultural dimension presently dealt with in a specific subject (e.g. history, political education).
Theme	To define theme(s) to be worked on. To become aware of theme, to understand dimensions of theme here and for school link. To define learning objectives with respect to theme.	What theme(s) do we want to work on? What do we want to find out about theme? What do we want to accomplish? How can the link with the partner school contribute?	'What we know, what we don't know'. Brainstorming, 'Creative writing', 'Pin cards'. Planning session. Periodical research. Correspondence with partner school by mail, fax, e-mail.
Expectations	To become aware of expectations in link with partner school.	What do I/we expect from school link partner?	'Apartment exercise', 'Completing sentences'.

Topic	Aims	Questions	Activities
Stereotypes, prejudices	To become aware of stereotypes and prejudices and where they come from. To become aware of results owing to stereotypes and prejudices.	Do we have a stereotype of country where our school link partner is located? Where does it come from? Do we have stereotypes of other culture groups/countries? Are we prejudiced? Where do our attitudes come from? How do stereotypes and prejudices affect our attitudes?	Search for prejudices, descriptions of stereotypes in press, school books, TV, publicity, literature, etc. Share findings by way of drawings, slides, letters, etc., with school link partner.
Lifestyles and behaviour	To become aware of own lifestyle. To find out about lifestyle in country of school link partner.	How do I/we (want to) live? How do partner pupils (want to) live?	'Ways to live', 'Where do I come from?', 'Time in Europe'. Compare with lifestyle in partner country through exchange of results of exercises, videos, etc.
Cultural differences	To become aware of differences between cultural groups.	How is culture in school link country different from ours?	'Personal maps'. Refer to results of exercises on 'Lifestyles and behaviour'.

Table 3 – *continued*

Emphasis	Learning objectives	Questions	Exercises/tools
Own culture, cultural identity	To recognize differences as possible source of tensions and conflict. To understand concept of culture. To become aware of own culture. To value cultural diversity.	Who am I? Who are we? Where do I/we come from? Why are we the way we are? Is there a typical representative of our culture? What is 'typical' about our culture? What is 'typical' about culture of school link partner? What do I not understand concerning life in country of school link partner? How do/did differences in culture affect work on theme? Could/did these differences result in tensions or conflicts?	Role-play and/or brainstorming and/or associative drawing on 'what is typical about our own culture'. Drawings/videos on everyday life, like 'family life', 'my classroom', etc. 'Playing regions', 'Cultural quotations' (or proverbs), 'Sunshine and rain', 'Educational paths and occupational options' questionnaire. Exchange results of these exercises with school link partner. Search newspapers, periodicals, TV, cinema for images of school link country. Exchange 'Pieces of culture'. Analyse national literature, films, advertisements, tourist promotion, etc. – do same for school link country and exchange findings. 'Concept of culture', 'Cultural differences'.
Other cultures	To experience another culture without going to another country. To increase adaptability to changing social circumstances.	Can I/we experience another culture without leaving own country? How? How can I become exposed to another culture? How can I/we understand the culture of the school link?	'Field exercise'. Brainstorm other (individual) exchange possibilities than the ones already practised. 'My next summer holiday', 'Our class exchange next year'.

Communication	To become aware of importance and role of non-verbal communication. To recognize limitations of interpreting symbols and words, whether spoken or written. To gain motivation for language learning.	How do I communicate? Are there other means of communication? How do the pupils in the link school communicate? How is it different from how I communicate? How do/did these differences affect work on theme?	'Yes/no game', 'Albatross', 'Babel', 'Building a tower'. Exchange videos with school link group which demonstrate a particular communication.
Values	To become aware of values. To find out values in culture of school link partner. To learn how values influence behaviour and lifestyle.	What values do I/we have? What values do others have? How do values influence my/our behaviour? How do/did differences in values affect work on theme?	'Who am I?', 'Personal values', 'Abigale'. Refer to 'Educational paths and occupational options' questionnaire. Refer to 'Field exercise'.
Global perspectives	To gain commitment to search for solutions of global issues.	How can I/we/school link class contribute?	'Where is it from? Where is it going?' 'Community project' – do in both schools and share. Exchange project outcomes/results. Were they different? Why?
Evaluation	To review learning.	What have we experienced and learned as a result of the project? How do we think/do differently as a result of the experiences?	'Evaluation' (1 and 2).

It is assumed that the themes identified at the beginning are pursued throughout.

considered real intercultural encounters, as they imply an unequal partnership. Partners must be able to give as well as receive, to exchange something, even when what is exchanged is different and cannot be directly compared.

The framework of this model can be described as follows:

- *Content.* Since for most pupils involved in the link there is no personal encounter with pupils from the partner school, the content of the school link usually refers more to international and political education than to intercultural learning. None the less, such links should, if possible, incorporate an exchange of the teachers involved. Perhaps smaller groups of pupils, eventually from different classes, possibly including parents, might be exchanged. It would also be possible for pupils on an individual basis to visit pupils of the partner class during holidays.
- *Duration.* There are no rules for the duration of a school link without exchanges. Usually, a link between schools will last for a number of years, while the different classes might be involved in the link only for a period of some weeks or up to a year. Communication and interaction will require more time if the pupils do not meet each other and communicate only by mail.
- *Age of pupils.* A school link of this kind can be organized for pupils of any age group. The content, the themes, the means of communication, the role of the teacher, etc., will differ depending on the age of the pupils involved.
- *Structure.* As indicated, the link can involve the whole school, while different classes or groups of pupils might pursue different themes and activities. The link will be stronger, be more dynamic, if the teachers of the two schools meet, e.g. on an annual basis, to plan, coordinate and evaluate the activities.
- *Means of communication.* Especially for younger pupils, visualized communication will play an important role – drawings, pictures, collages, the exchange of material objects, possibly of videos, tapes with music, different sounds, etc. (even if they do not understand each other's language, it is interesting to hear the sound and the phonetics). Once the pupils can communicate in a common working language, they can also correspond through letters, fax or even electronic mail if the necessary equipment is available.

This didactic model scheme describes the intercultural learning process for a class or group of pupils linking with a class or group of pupils abroad. A link of this type can deal with a variety of different themes that are not reflected in this scheme but could be integrated according to the specific situation.

The classic exchange model

This model is referred to as classic because it has the longest tradition and is most frequently used within Europe. The original objective of this model was the development of foreign language skills through practical experience abroad. Therefore, it was implemented originally and mostly between France, Germany and the United Kingdom. In the late 1970s and early 1980s, teachers and educators realized that exchanges provided an opportunity not only for language learning but also for social and intercultural learning. Subsequently exchanges took place between other than the traditional 'popular language countries' and the content of exchanges was expanded to a variety of issues and themes other than language. This, in turn, resulted in additional activities between the schools involved in the exchanges and in a greater continuity of their relationships. Exchanges became a part of a more complex relationship, referred to as 'school links' or 'school partnerships'.

The framework of this model can be described as follows:

• *Content*. The content of an exchange can be two-fold. Frequently, the intent is to continue curricular work in language learning, geography or history, but it can also relate to social and intercultural learning.
• *Duration*. The different education systems in Europe have different regulations concerning the duration or length of an exchange, which actually prohibit some exchanges if the maximum length in one country is less than the minimum in another. Usually, the exchanges within this model last between one and four weeks, the majority taking place for two weeks. The preparation phase usually starts at least three months before the exchange and the assessment phase can go on for another two months, so that the duration of the whole project is at least half a year.
• *Age of pupils*. Considering the duration of the exchange, the age of the pupils usually will be 15 years or older, but there is an increasing number of one-week exchanges involving pupils aged 13 and 14.
• *Structure*. Exchanges usually involve a class or part of a class but a group of pupils from different classes could make up the exchange (which makes it more difficult to organize the preparation and assessment). For specific parts of the project, the whole school can be involved, especially during the visit of a group from abroad. It is advisable to organize reciprocal exchanges linking two classes (or groups of pupils), leaving a gap of some months between the two visits. Sometimes this may not be possible and a visit is made in only one direction.

The didactic schemes detailed in Tables 4 and 5 refer to this model, describing the pedagogic process for a class going abroad and for a class receiving a group from abroad. Though the processes are actually similar, it is necessary to describe them separately because they take place in different environments. The class going abroad is moving into a foreign environment and thus needs a different and probably greater preparation to cope with the unfamiliar, while the class receiving a class from abroad is remaining in its familiar environment and thus needs to be prepared to open up towards the visiting pupils.

The planning and preparation for the exchange need to be coordinated by the receiving school and the sending school to avoid discrepancy with respect to the objectives, content, process and structure of the activities during the actual visits. It is recommended that the teachers of both schools responsible for the exchange meet during the planning phase.

Table 4 Didactic scheme for a class visiting a class in another country

Timing: 2 weeks for exchange, 10 to 20 weeks for preparation, 4 to 8 weeks for evaluation and follow-up

Week	Emphasis	Learning objectives	Questions	Exercises/tools
−20 to −10	Theme	To become aware of theme, to understand dimension of theme here and for school link. To define learning objectives with respect to theme.	What do I/we know about theme? What do I/we want to accomplish? How can the visit abroad contribute?	Planning session. Brainstorming. Periodical research. Correspondence with partner school.
−10 to 0	Expectations, assumptions Stereotypes, prejudices	To become aware of expectations. To become aware of own prejudices and stereotypes and how they influence expectations. To become aware of own stereotypes about one's own country.	What expectations do we have concerning the visit in the other country? Are they realistic? What image(s) do I/we have of partner country? What is my/our self-image? What forms a stereotype?	'What we know, what we don't know'. Drawing or role-play: 'Life/school in the country we will visit'. Completing sentences like 'The partner school will be . . .', 'We will learn . . .', 'Our presence will mean . . .', 'The partner pupils will expect us to be . . .', 'Our visit will be . . .'. 'Images in the mind'. Letter to myself.
	Cultural identity, own culture, cultural differences	To become aware of own cultural background. To prepare for encounter with different culture.	How do I/we live? What is important to me/us? What traditions do we have? How will I relate to and communicate with people in the other country?	'Where do I come from?', 'Field exercise', 'Cultural quotations', 'Albatross', 'Playing regions'.

	Theme	Objectives	Questions	Activities
0	Initializing event (arrival in other country)	To get to know each other. To establish relationships. To become familiar with life in the country visited.	Who are the partner pupils? Who am I/are we? How do we present ourselves?	'Assumptions', 'Personal maps'. Drawing: 'this is me in the partner classroom'. 'Slogans'.
1	Communication skills	To establish communication with partner pupils. To gain motivation for language learning. To develop language learning skills.	How do I/we communicate with partner pupils? How can we improve communication? How can we learn the language of the others? Do we use the same language to talk about the theme?	'Humming exercise', 'Charades', 'Yes/no game'. 'Tandems' – pairs of pupils, one from each class. Vocabulary and communication notebook.
	Lifestyles and behaviour	To learn about and appreciate own and others' lifestyles and behaviour.	How do I/we (want to) live? How do partner pupils (want to) live? What is school like in the other country? How is education organized? What are the benefits?	Refer to 'Where do I come from?' and other exercises done during preparation. 'Ways to live', 'Lifestyles', 'Time in Europe', 'Eating rituals'. Role-playing, e.g. play 'family' or play 'school' in own and visited country. Reflect on everyday activities in country visited (e.g. cooking and eating, dancing, singing, sports, showing slides). Refer to journal. Compare questionnaires.

Table 4 – *continued*

Week	Emphasis	Learning objectives	Questions	Exercises/tools
1 to 2	Theme	To work together on a common theme.	Depending on theme.	Field study, interviews, questionnaires.
	Cultural differences and cultural identity	To become aware of cultural differences. To become aware of own culture. To understand others' culture. To value cultural diversity. To describe cultures involved.	How are the partner pupils different from me/us? What is the partner culture? What is my culture? What are we like? What am I like? Why are 'we' as we are? Why are 'they' as they are? How do cultural differences affect how we work on theme?	Follow-up to 'Images in the mind'. Refer to 'Personal maps'. Demonstrate an activity according to own culture (e.g. cooking, eating, dancing, singing, sports, photographs). Observe 'school' in partner country. 'Concept of culture'. 'Cultural differences', 'Field study', 'Educational paths and occupational options' questionnaire. Role change plus most exercises under category 'culture'.

Values	To become aware of own and others' values. To understand that and how values influence behaviour, norms, etc.	What values do I/we have? What values do the others have? How do they affect the respective behaviour? How do differences in the value systems influence the relationship between pupils of the two countries?	'Who am I?', 'Personal values', 'Cultural values checklist', 'Abigale'.
Assessment	To recognize change and effect of experience. To plan and agree further steps and activities.	What did I/we learn? How have I/we changed? How have the others changed? How has the work on the theme proceeded? How will it continue? What do I/we want to take away from the experience? How will we continue our relationship?	'The most important part of the experience for me was . . .'. Why? Refer to exercises concerning stereotypes. What has changed? Refer to 'Journal'. 'Evaluation' (1 and 2). Start work on documentation.
Final event	To close visit. To learn how festivities are celebrated in different cultures.	How do we say farewell to each other? How can we celebrate a festivity together? How do we celebrate a festivity in different countries?	'Final event'. Intercultural festivity/party.

Table 4 – *continued*

Week	Emphasis	Learning objectives	Questions	Exercises/tools
4 to 8	Evaluation, assessment	To review learning. To implement what we have learned.	How will I/we apply what I/we have learned? What do I/we do differently as a result of the experience? What do we still want to know and how are we going to find it out? How do I/we describe the experience to others? How will we continue personal relationships?	Refer to expectations and questionnaires. Refer to 'Letter to myself'. Refer to exercises on stereotypes, cultural identity/own culture, values. Reflect on the experience. What can it mean for me/us? (Refer to 'Journal'.) Produce 'active' presentation for school. Produce and present documentation. Correspond with partner school.

Table 5 Didactic scheme for a class receiving a class from another country

Timing: 2 weeks for exchange, 10 to 20 weeks for preparation, 4 to 8 weeks for evaluation and follow-up

Week	Emphasis	Learning objectives	Questions	Exercises/tools
–20 to –10	Theme	To become aware of theme, to understand dimensions of theme here and for school link. To define learning objectives with respect to theme.	What do I/we want to find out about theme? What do I/we want to accomplish? How can the visit of the partner school contribute?	Planning session. Brainstorming. Periodical research. Correspondence with partner school.
–10 to 0	Expectations, assumptions, stereotypes, prejudices	To become aware of expectations. To become aware of stereotypes and prejudices, and that they influence expectations. To become aware of stereotypes about own country.	What do I expect? What image do I have of the partner country? Why do I have this image? What other stereotypes and prejudices do I have? What image do I have of my own country? What will the exchangees expect our country/us to be like?	'What we know, what we don't know'. Drawing or role-play: 'the exchangees in our class'. Associative exercises. Completing sentences like: 'The exchanges will be …', 'We will learn …', 'The presence of the exchanges will mean for us …', 'The exchangees will expect us to be …', 'For the exchanges the stay here will mean …'. 'Completing sentences', 'Apartment exercise', 'Images in the mind'.

Table 5 – *continued*

Week	Emphasis	Learning objectives	Questions	Exercises/tools
−10 to 0 (continued)	Cultural identity, own culture, cultural differences	To become aware of own cultural background. To prepare for encounter with different culture.	How do I/we live? What is important to me/us? What traditions do we have? How will I relate and communicate with the exchanges?	'Where do I come from?', 'Field exercise', 'Cultural quotations', 'ABA–ZAK', 'Playing regions'.
0	This part of the scheme is, of course, very similar to the previous scheme for a class receiving a class from abroad.			
	Initializing event (arrival of exchangees)	To get acquainted. To establish relationships.	Who is/are the other(s)? Who am I/are we? How do we present ourselves?	'Assumptions', 'Personal maps'. Drawing: 'this is me in this classroom'. 'Slogans'.
1	Communication skills	To establish communication with pupils from abroad. To gain motivation for language learning.	How can I/we communicate with the others? How can we improve communication? How can we learn the language of the others? Do we use the same language to talk about the theme?	'Humming exercise', 'Charades', 'Yes/no game'. 'Tandems' – pairs of pupils, one from each class.

	Theme	Objectives	Questions	Activities
	Lifestyles and behaviour	To learn about and appreciate own and others' lifestyles and behaviour.	How do I/we (want to) live? How do partner pupils (want to) live? What is school like in the other country? How is education organized? What are the benefits?	Refer to 'Where do I come from?' and other exercises done during preparation. 'Ways to live', 'Lifestyles', 'Time in Europe', 'Eating rituals'. Role-playing, e.g. play 'family' or play 'school' in own and exchangees' country. Have exchangees demonstrate an activity according to their culture (e.g. cooking and eating, dancing, singing, sports, showing slides). Compare questionnaires.
	Theme	To work together on a common theme.	Depending on theme.	Interviews. Questionnaires. Field study.
1 to 2	Cultural differences and cultural identity	To become aware of cultural differences. To become aware of own culture. To understand others' culture. To value cultural diversity. To describe cultures involved.	How are the others different from me/us? What is my culture? What is the others' culture? What are we like? What am I like? Why are 'we' as we are? Why are 'they' as they are? How do cultural differences affect how we work on theme?	Follow-up to 'Images in the mind'. Refer to 'Personal maps'. 'Concept of culture', 'Cultural differences', 'Educational paths and occupational options' questionnaire. Role change plus most exercises under category 'culture'.

Table 5 – *continued*

Week	Emphasis	Learning objectives	Questions	Exercises/tools
1 to 2 (continued)	Values	To become aware of own and others' values. To understand that and how values influence behaviour, norms, etc.	What values do I/we have? What values do the others have? How do they affect the respective behaviour? How do differences in the value systems influence the relationship between pupils of the two countries?	'Who am I?', 'Personal values', 'Abigale'.
	Assessment	To recognize change and effect of experience. To agree and plan further steps and activities.	What did I/we learn? How have I/we changed? How have the others changed? How has the work on the theme proceeded? How will it continue? How will we continue our relationship?	'The most important experience during the exchange programme was ...'. Why? Refer to exercises concerning stereotypes. What has changed? 'Evaluation' (1 and 2). Start work on documentation.
	Final event	To close visit/encounter. To learn about festivities in different cultures.	How do we say farewell to each other? How can we celebrate together? How do we celebrate in different countries?	'Final event'. Intercultural festivity/party.
4 to 8	Evaluation, assessment	To review learning. To implement what we have learned.	How do we apply what we have learned? What will I/we do differently as a result of the experience? What do we still want to know and how are we going to find it out?	Refer to expectations and questionnaires. Refer to exercises on stereotypes and cultural identity/own culture. Reflect on experience. Produce and present documentation. Correspond with partner school.

Class with an individual exchangee

One of the roots of individual pupil exchanges lies with the engagement of idealistic organizations and people after World War II who wanted to build bridges between the former enemies and thus to contribute to a better understanding between people of the respective countries. In the beginning, most of these exchanges took place between the USA and countries in Europe. The duration of the exchange was one year and it involved staying with a family and attending school. In the 1970s, a number of developments took place: the exchanges were organized multilaterally, i.e. between countries within Europe as well; exchanges were also offered for shorter periods, of a term, three months or even just a few weeks; the number of organizations offering such exchanges and thus the number of pupils involved expanded dramatically. As a result, the presence of an exchangee from another country became something common in secondary schools in many European countries.

Since the objective of these exchange programmes was primarily the personal growth of the individual exchangee, the effect of their presence on the class they attended was mostly neglected. The presence of the exchangee was and frequently still is perceived as a disturbance to the regular work of the class, which in some countries resulted in a limitation of the number of exchangees accepted in a class or school.

The last didactic scheme (detailed in Table 6) suggests a way to turn this situation around, to make use of such a setting for an intercultural learning process for the 'native' majority of the class as well as for the exchangee.

The framework for this model can be described as follows.

- *Content.* The exchangee can serve as a resource for learning about the country of his or her origin, which can be useful for a number of subject matters, not the least of which is language learning. The presence of the exchangee can be used for political, international and social education by comparing the different political and social systems. The exchangee must be 'used' as a resource but he or she is a learner too with respect to the country and culture of the school he or she is attending, and thus needs adequate support and guidance during this process. The situation of the exchangee is especially difficult because he or she is alone in a foreign environment, lacking the security of the other pupils in the class. Additionally, the exchangee might need support with respect to the family he or she is living with.
- *Duration.* Individual pupil exchanges normally last from three months to a year. The preparation of the class should start a few weeks before the arrival of the exchangee. If the exchangee arrives at the beginning of the school year, the preparation must be done at the end of the previous school year. An evaluation of the experience in the class should take place a few weeks after the departure of the exchangee. Again, if the exchangee stays until the end of the school year, one has to postpone this to the beginning of the next school year. The scheme can also be applied to shorter visits of individual exchanges.

149

Table 6 Didactic scheme for a class with an individual exchangee

Timing: ongoing, depending also on length of stay of exchange

Emphasis	Learning objectives	Questions	Exercises/tools
Prior to arrival of exchangee			
Expectations, assumptions	To become aware of (unconscious and hidden) expectations.	What do I/we expect? What will the exchangee expect us to be?	Drawing/role-play: 'the exchangee in our class'. Completing sentences like: 'The exchangee will …', 'People from the exchangee's country are …', 'We will gain/learn from the presence of the exchangee …', 'The presence of the exchange will mean for us …', 'The exchangee will expect us …'. 'What we know, what we don't know', 'Apartment exercise', 'Images in the mind'.
Stereotypes, prejudices	To become aware of stereotypes and prejudices and how they influence expectations. To become aware of stereotypes about own country.	What image do I have of the exchangee's country? What stereotypes and prejudices do I/we have with respect to exchangee's country of origin? What image do I/we have of own country?	
During the stay of the exchangee			
Initializing event	To get to know each other. To establish relationship.	Who is he/she? Where does he/she come from? How can he/she become part of the class?	'Personal maps', 'Piece of culture'. Drawings and role-plays: 'our class'.
Communication skills	To establish communication patterns between class and exchangee. To support exchangee in learning the language of the class.	How can I/we communicate with the exchangee? What language do we use in everyday life – to talk about school, family, etc.?	'Humming exercise', 'Charades', 'Albatross'. Introducing exchangee to local dialect ('Intercultural language trading').

Lifestyles and behaviour	To learn about exchangee's lifestyle and behaviour. To become aware of own lifestyle and behaviour.	How do I/we (want to) live? How does exchangee (want to) live?	'Where do I come from?', 'Ways to live', 'Lifestyles', 'Time in Europe', 'Eating rituals'. Role-playing, e.g. play 'family' or play 'school' in own and exchangee's country. Ask exchangee to demonstrate an everyday activity in his or her country (e.g. cooking and eating, dancing, singing, sports, showing slides). Have class respond with demonstration of same/similar activity according to their culture.
Cultural differences and cultural identity/ own culture	To become aware of cultural differences. To become aware of own culture. To understand exchangee's culture. To value cultural diversity. To be able to describe cultures involved.	How is the exchangee different from me/us? What is the culture of the exchangee? What is my culture? What are we like? What am I like? Why are 'we' as we are? Why is the exchangee as he or she is? How does culture affect the way people relate to each other?	Follow-up to 'Images in the mind' and other exercises. Referring to stereotypes and prejudices. Refer to 'Personal maps', 'Cultural quotations', 'Concept of culture', 'Cultural differences', plus other exercises under category 'culture' ('Sunshine and rain', etc.).
Values	To become aware of own and others' values. To learn how values influence behaviour, norms, etc.	What values do I have? What values do my classmates have? What values does the exchangee have? How do these values influence our/his/her behaviour?	'Personal values', 'Cultural values checklist', 'Abigale'.

Table 6 – *continued*

Emphasis	Learning objectives	Questions	Exercises/tools
Assessment (1 to 3 weeks prior to exchangee's departure)	To recognize change and the effect of exchangee's presence in the class.	What have I/we learned? How has the presence of the exchangee changed the situation and behaviour of the class? How has the exchangee changed? How has the exchangee contributed to the class?	'The most important experience during the presence of the exchangee was ...'. Why? Refer to exercises concerning stereotypes. What was different? What has changed? 'Evaluation' (1 and 2).
After departure of exchangee			
Evaluation	To review learning.	What do we miss since the exchangee's departure? What do we do or think differently?	Refer to expectations. Reflect on experience. Establish school link with exchangee's school. Correspond with him/her/school in other country.

- *Age of pupils*. Individual exchanges tend to be limited to pupils aged 14 and older. As developmental maturity moves down the chronological age range, there are increasing opportunities for individual exchanges for younger pupils. These occur as organized offerings from outside the school environment but also as a result of a school link where school and family have established trust and familiarity.
- *Structure*. The presence of an exchangee offers a number of options. The exchangee and the country and culture of his or her origin can be related to the subject work of the class whenever it seems appropriate and feasible. An intensive project dealing with the country of origin of the exchangee as well as with intercultural learning in general could be organized. Other classes or even the whole school could be involved in some of these activities. These activities become even more intensive and relevant if there is more than one exchangee present in the class or school.

Of course, a similar scheme can also be used for a class with one or more pupils whose parents have moved to this country for professional reasons for a limited period of time, e.g. for a working assignment with a branch or subsidiary of the company they work for.

OTHER SCENARIOS

The six model schemes demonstrate an intercultural learning process for specific, albeit ordinary, scenarios. The schemes have been used to illustrate a variety of situations in which intercultural learning is appropriate and to suggest that the process varies according to the needs and opportunities of the situation.

There are many more situations, more than this book can begin to detail, but it is worth mentioning several other scenarios. The reader will undoubtedly have still others in mind. In contemplating 'different' scenarios, it is important to ask several questions. What are the realities of the scenario, i.e. who is involved: one class, two classes in the same school or different schools, multicultural, monocultural, single subject or cross curriculum, travelling, not travelling, etc.? What needs to be achieved, i.e. what will the benefits be? What time is available? Depending on the answers to such questions, the entry point for intercultural learning may be very focused, or it could require a look at a larger learning process. Whether you look through a telescope or a microscope, the design of any scheme will depend on the time and resources obtainable. We now briefly discuss some scenarios.

Class where an individual pupil goes to another country for a limited period of time

Objective: to bring the experience of a single pupil into the classroom for shared learning.

This could happen by corresponding with the pupil while he or she is abroad and making use of him or her as an 'out-posted' resource for the class in subjects such as history or geography, or as part of an intercultural learning project according to the model scheme for a monocultural class without a school link. The presence of this pupil in the school abroad could also serve as a stimulus to the establishment of a link between the two schools, which could continue even when the pupil has returned home.

Once the pupil has returned from abroad, his or her experience can be drawn upon in the appropriate lessons, e.g. with respect to the history, geography, language and socio-economic fabric of the culture the pupil has visited. If the native language is one taught in the school, the pupil is a resource for pronunciation and inflection.

Bicultural or multicultural class visiting migrant country of origin

Objective: to enable pupils of a migrant culture in the sending class to gain self-esteem and confidence in their identity through a process that puts these pupils in the majority culture situation; to explore the roots of the migrant culture and thus to gain a greater understanding of migrant pupils.

This scenario was practised with success between classes in Luxembourg (bicultural) and Portugal (country of origin) as well as between classes in the Netherlands and Turkey, and was organized by EFIL during the 1980s for pupils aged 12 to 14. The class visits enabled both 'minority' and 'majority' groups to gain a different view of each other. Exploration of cultural differences and ideas about stereotypes before and after the visit gives quite different results. One has to be aware, however, that the culture of the migrants is not identical with that of their country of origin. The culture of the migrants has evolved differently from the culture of their country of origin, so they, too, will be 'foreigners' there. Visiting their country of origin – possibly for the first time – enables them to gain a greater understanding of their own cultural background and to realize that they are not 'natives' of this country any more. This can be painful and requires adequate preparation, support and assessment.

Teacher exchanges and other international activities for teachers

Objective: first-hand training to enable increased confidence and intercultural competence by the conscious building-in of an intercultural learning component to any teacher exchange.

Teacher exchanges have a long tradition. Originally intended to increase the language proficiency of foreign language teachers through practical experience, they have been increasingly used for gaining an insight into pedagogy and teaching systems in other countries as well as for specific training with respect to different subjects, such as geography, history, economics and political science. There are a number of different schemes: actual exchanges between two schools for a year or a semester, study visits abroad for individual teachers as well as for groups of teachers, internships abroad for language teachers as 'teaching assistants', seminars for teachers (from) abroad, seminars with international participation, etc. Some of these schemes are organized by the Council of Europe (e.g. within its In-Service Training Programme for Teachers) or the European Union (e.g. within the actions of the SOCRATES programme).

A special facet of such activities is visits by teachers of classes with migrant pupils to the country of origin of these pupils (or of their parents or grandparents), which enable the teachers to understand the cultural background of their pupils. Among others, EFIL has organized such visits for teachers from Germany, Austria and the Netherlands to Turkey. These visits were not easy to organize because of the cultural differences between the countries. None the less, they were successful for the teachers who participated. Frequently these exchanges concentrate on the learning experience of the teachers going abroad and do not actively involve the staff of the school of origin or the school visited. The provision of adequate pre-paration, support and assessment − not only for the teachers travelling but also for their colleagues at home and abroad − could expand the effect of such visits to teachers and pupils of both schools involved in the activity. Teacher exchanges and visits abroad can serve as a very effective tool for developing school links, class visits and exchanges, integrated projects and correspondence exchanges, as outlined in the model schemes.

Domestic exchanges

Objective: to experience cultural differences without crossing borders; to understand that linguistic differences can also imply cultural differences.

In Switzerland classes move from canton to canton, from Swiss language (German) to Swiss language (Romansch), to Swiss language (French) to Swiss language (Italian), within an exchange scheme run by Jugendaustausch in der Schweiz. Also, the Portuguese Ministry of Education funds domestic exchanges on a large scale to enable understanding of local, urban–rural and north–south cultural differences within the country. Such exchanges could be organized in many other countries with different language groups and/or minorities. They may also become increasingly popular as national cultures become blurred, where borders change and where there is increased attention to decentralized, local, regional, border cultures.

In Belgium or Switzerland where there are two or more different linguistic and/or cultural regions, domestic exchanges provide the structure for intercultural learning projects. In many ways, these exchanges are similar to international or cross-border exchanges. The same barriers exist in the education systems, which in these cases are subject to regional authority. But one does not need a passport and it is possible to use the same currency.

These exchanges could follow the 'classic exchange model'.

Short–distance school links in border regions

Objective: to overcome borders in a practical sense; to provide international/intercultural experiences for primary school pupils.

Since schools are national institutions they tend to be orientated towards the centre rather than towards the periphery. Schools in peripheral regions have an easy opportunity to find out what the world looks like on the other side of the (national) border and therefore to overcome national views and attitudes. We know what school is like hundreds of kilometres away as long as it is within the same country; but what is it like 50 kilometres away in the neighbouring country?

Since such a short distance can be travelled easily both ways within a day, a link can also be established for primary schools, although it should not be limited to them – a school link of this type is valuable for any age group. In fact, short distance links have existed for a long time, for example between France and Germany. Many such links have been developed in the past years along the border between Western European countries and the former socialist countries in Central and Eastern Europe.

Multilateral school links and exchanges

Objective: to develop a truly international perspective.

Although they are complicated to organize, multilateral links and exchanges are worthwhile. With three or more cultural groups involved in a common activity or in an exchange, the polarity between the 'we' and 'they' can be replaced by an identification as an *international group*. Following a conference on school links and exchanges in Barcelona in 1991, the European Community established a pilot project for multilateral school links involving some forty schools from all over Europe.

Language classes

Objective: to understand that language is influenced by factors of culture as well as verb conjugation or sentence construction, that it is one important part of culture.

Intercultural communication exercises, in particular, can help to bring 'language' alive and to demonstrate that any language is only a part of communication. When pupils from Leicester go to Lyons, the language learned in the classroom may require communication skills additional to those of verbal language.

Correspondence links

Objective: to experience intercultural communication through the written word – until pupils decide to exchange videos!

An individual correspondence activity can be quite rewarding but it does have the limitation of being an individual activity rather than a class or group engagement. Among others, the Fédération Internationale des Organisations de Correspondance et d'Echanges Scolaires (FIOCES) has long offered the challenge of correspondence exchange to pupils. Having a correspondence link, being a pen-pal, gives free rein to the artistic and literary in the class.

International schools

Originally intended to provide a 'standard' or 'elite' (depending on the point of view) education to middle- and upper-middle-class children of parents working abroad on temporary work placements, 'international schools' increasingly use the multicultural composition of their classes for intercultural and international educa-tion. In fact, these schools can serve as a 'laboratory' for intercultural learning. International and intercultural education has always been an objective of these schools and underlies their existence. A similar idea forms the basis of bilingual schools in monolingual or monocultural regions where a foreign language, e.g. English or French, is being used also to teach subjects other than this language. The approach implies the use of a foreign language in areas where it is not normally used and it thus becomes a tool for everyday life. In this setting, a link with a school in the country of that second language seems to be a logical consequence.

CHAPTER 10

Exercises

This chapter contains a collection of useful exercises for intercultural learning. They can be used in all kinds of settings: in monocultural classes doing an intercultural learning project, in multicultural classes or groups, in classes or schools involved in an international school link, in classes or groups involved in an exchange with a class or group abroad. Some of the exercises can be integrated into regular subjects and curricula, some can be used for cross-curricular work, some are of an extra-curricular nature. Most exercises can also be adapted for situations out of school; for example, for youth groups, youth centres and youth exchanges generally.

Intercultural learning cannot be learned out of a book; nor is it easily examined in the traditional manner. To become interculturally literate, one needs experiential learning. These exercises, and many others that exist or can be designed, form an experiential vehicle for use in the classroom. They are a different form of textbook, where there are seldom 'right' answers, where the solutions arise out of the doing of the exercise.

Some of the exercises are 'games' in that they simulate or portray a specific situation, i.e. they are not real. However, the reactions, feelings and learning experienced by participants during the game will be as valid or real as in real-life conditions. Because the exercises deal with emotions, with beliefs and values that people hold dear, that are taken for granted, there can be moments of crisis when such beliefs and values are challenged. This is *all right*! In fact, the literature shows that young people on international exchanges learn and develop in a positive sense most dramatically as a result of experiential crises.

The descriptions of the exercises vary: some are described in great detail and can be done without much preparation, others are drafted more roughly and need further development in order to be appropriate to a specific situation for which the exercise is to be used. In other cases, the procedure is obvious and can easily be outlined by any teacher. We trust that, in any case, the reader will be able to plan and prepare the exercises in detail using the recommendations outlined in Chapter 8. Most exercises were designed without reference to a specific subject. Since the exercises might be used by teachers in a range of different subjects, they still need to be adapted to the specific curricular situation.

It has to be pointed out that a number of the exercises here are based on exercises published in *Projektunterricht 'Interkulturelles Lernen in der Schule'* (Intercultural Learning Project in Schools). This publication was developed in 1984 by the Austrian Ministry of Education in cooperation with AFS Österreich, Austauschprogramme für interkulturelles Lernen (the Austrian member organization of EFIL), and was aimed at teachers trying to integrate intercultural learning into the curriculum.

STANDARD FORMAT FOR AN EXERCISE

The following format is used to describe the exercises.

- *Learning area/category*. Although there is a main emphasis for each exercise, it will normally also relate to other learning areas. For example, the 'Assumption exercise' has been allocated to the 'getting acquainted' category while at the same time it deals with 'stereotypes and prejudices'. Sometimes the learning area is different depending on the setting in which the exercise is being done. For example, the exercises under 'lifestyles' have been placed there on the assumption that they are done with monocultural groups, but when they are done in bi-cultural or multicultural settings they could be listed within 'cultural differences'.
- *Learning objectives*. Learning objectives are an indicator of what is possible in the use of the exercise. They also form a basis for evaluation of what has happened. Again, an exercise can be used to achieve very different learning objectives depending on the setting in which it is being used, or by adapting or modifying it to a specific situation and need.
- *Duration*. The times indicated in the descriptions of the exercises represent a minimum. With respect to using the exercises within a school environment, we have tried as much as possible to provide a design that allows the integration of the exercises into a regular schedule, although intercultural learning cannot normally be accomplished in 45-minute units. Sometimes it is useful or even necessary to work for longer periods than usual to allow for the anticipated learning processes. Some of the exercises need sessions of two or more hours at one time and could involve a full day, or more, of work. Some of the exercises require sessions or individual work on more than one day. Some even include longer working cycles over some weeks.
- *Group*. The description under this title refers to recommended group size and group composition. Some exercises are especially useful for monocultural groups or classes, others for multicultural groups and others again for use within an exchange. Nevertheless, in most instances it is possible to adapt an exercise for a situation other than the one given. Experience with group size shows that a plenary session with more than 30 to 35 pupils is hardly useful. For plenary sessions with groups larger than 35 pupils one should divide the session into

smaller groups with one teacher or facilitator for each sub-group. For real discussion, groups of six to ten pupils will give a good result.

- *Supplies*. For many exercises, worksheets or questionnaires are included. Most of these need to be adapted to the specific situation in which they are being used. When they are to be used in a non-English-speaking country or school they will have to be translated. For use in a bilingual setting – for example, within a class exchange – it is advisable to use bilingual worksheets or questionnaires to provide equal understanding for all participants. Bilingual material, in general, is a good tool to support language learning. For some exercises, working material still has to be developed and therefore more time is needed for preparation.
- *Description of exercise*. This part provides a telescopic view of what the exercise looks like.
- *Instructions*. Sequenced (step-by-step) guidelines for doing the exercise. The time indicated for the various steps is usually a minimum and can be extended depending on the situation. For most exercises, the instructions are based on specific assumptions concerning the application and setting and have to be adapted and modified if used in a different setting. For some exercises, the instructions have been kept general and have to be further detailed for specific use.
- *Variations*. Other possibilities for using the exercise – either for a setting different from that assumed in the instructions or for different learning objectives. It can also refer to possible expansion of the exercise.
- *Evaluation*. This part refers to the learning objectives and how far they have been achieved. Frequently, a number of questions to be discussed by the pupils or answered individually are outlined and should enable an evaluation. For a number of exercises the guidelines for evaluation are included in the instructions.
- *Comments*. Unusual perspectives not otherwise covered under other headings. Very often they refer to possible tensions and conflicts which may arise during the exercise. Generally these conflicts should not and cannot be avoided – usually they have been present already and are only brought to the surface through the exercise. As already outlined earlier in this book, conflict or crisis is an important source for learning processes.
- *Reference*. Some of the exercises described in this book were originally developed and designed by the present authors – many others are based on and developed from ideas or exercises we (the authors) have found during the many years we have been active in the field of intercultural learning. We have tried as far as possible to make reference to their origin. Sometimes this has been difficult or even impossible. Some exercises are so widely used and quoted (as we have also done) and others have been changed and modified by the many users in such a way that it is now difficult to trace the original source. If an exercise is used widely in such a way, it usually means that it is a useful and good exercise. And if an author of an exercise is presented with his or her own exercise after it has been handed on by word of mouth and used by many people, it is probably the best recognition he or she can get.

As indicated earlier, the ideas for a number of the exercises come from the publication *Projektunterricht 'Interkulturelles Lernen in der Schule'*, which was developed by the Austrian Ministry of Education in cooperation with AFS Österreich, Austauschprogramme für interkulturelles Lernen, in 1984.

EXERCISE CATEGORIES: AREAS OF LEARNING

The exercises in this book have been grouped according to the 'areas of learning' referred to in the didactic schemes described elsewhere in this book. Most exercises, though, also relate to other areas of learning – the grouping in this section has been made according to the main emphasis. The following is a short description of these areas of learning, with reference to further exercises.

Getting started (GS)

As outlined earlier, the start of an intercultural learning project is crucial with respect to its success in terms of content as well as process. Different aspects have to be considered.

Getting to know each other

It is essential that members of a group working on a project get to know each other rather quickly – this will help to improve the process and to avoid unnecessary misunderstandings later on. It is especially important if some members of the group know each other quite well while others do not – this might result in the larger group splitting into 'insiders' and 'outsiders' or into different parties (for example, if pupils from two or more different classes go on a trip abroad).

There is a vast number of exercises for getting acquainted in general that can be used with any monocultural group. One has to consider, though, that many of these exercises do not work in bicultural or multicultural settings or might even be counterproductive. Usually, adaptation to the setting is necessary. It is also recommended that an exercise for getting acquainted for an intercultural learning project has an intercultural component and that the exercise refers to the content of the project.

In this sense, getting to know each other is possible in a number of ways: through an exercise referring to the assumptions one makes about someone else one does not know ('Assumption exercise'), an exercise where one compares individual lifestyles or preferences for lifestyles ('Lifestyles', various questionnaires), an exercise referring to one's values (most exercises under 'values'), or an exercise dealing with communication.

Warm up (GS/WU)

Social learning sometimes involves reflection and discussion of rather personal issues, sometimes it implies overcoming traditional barriers, approaching people one has no or only a superficial relationship with, etc. This is not done easily – it needs time, a process of slow immersion. A class or group has to warm up just as a football team has to warm up before a match. Warming up refers not only to the process but also to the content. It means becoming familiar with the theme(s) of the project, starting at a level that is understandable by everyone and that also allows immersion in the content of the project. This is part of the didactics in any intensive learning process.

There is a large number of warm-up exercises. Again, one has to consider the intercultural context of the setting in which they are applied (see Getting to know each other) and adapt them accordingly. Of course, when members of the group starting an intercultural learning project do not know each other a getting acquainted exercise can serve as a warm-up exercise.

Initializing events (GS/IE)

Initializing events provide a stimulus to get an intercultural learning project started. Such a project is usually not started simply when the teacher presents the idea – it requires a motivating element for the pupils, it needs to catch interest and enthusiasm, even for a project involving a visit abroad, especially in a country with a not so frequently spoken language. There has to be something generating a dynamic that almost logically results in the project starting. In the following, this will be referred to as an 'initializing event'.

An initializing event can take many forms:

- a new pupil in the class from another country;
- a parliamentary/public discussion or vote on an issue such as ethnic minorities, bilingual education, migration, European integration;
- a book or film on any of these issues which created intensive public discussion;
- a 'critical incident' in the class, possibly resulting in a conflict;
- neo-fascist, racist or anti-foreigner movements;
- a war or violent conflict.

Stereotypes and prejudices (SP)

A frequent attribute of prejudices and stereotypes is that many of them are unconscious. For many prejudices, it is even more complicated: we have been taught not to hold them. So, on a cognitive level, we will deny having them even if we do and if subsequently our behaviour is still guided by them. The primary objective of most exercises in this category – to become aware of one's stereotypes and prejudices – is difficult to achieve. Since we have learned to hide our prejudices so well, most exercises ask for spontaneous and intuitive responses, associations and reflections that should enable the pupils – and teachers – to gain access to the (unconscious) images in their minds about other groups, societies and cultures. often we can also do this by analysing our feelings and behaviour in certain ions that have been created by the exercise.

ly once we really become aware of our prejudices will we be able to question and possibly correct them and the behaviour guided by them. One has to be modest about achieving this objective. These prejudices have been learnt in early childhood and they have been reinforced over many years. It would be an illusion to think that an exercise lasting several hours would eliminate prejudice.

Since the image one has about one's own cultural or ethnic group is also based on stereotypes, many of the exercises refer to those. It is useful in the case of bicultural settings to confront the image group A has about itself with the image group B has about group A and vice versa (group A representing one culture and group B representing the other culture). In such a setting, exercises in this category can also be used for learning about cultural differences, one's own culture and cultural identity.

Again, there are many more exercises available on prejudices and stereotypes, most of which can be adapted for intercultural learning projects.

Culture (CU/CD or CU/CI)

The exercises in this category suggest a number of approaches to learning more about one's own culture as well as about one or more other cultures. A frequently used approach is to enquire into specific aspects of another culture and to compare the findings with those from one's own culture. Realizing that there are different views of life and the world, different values, different lifestyles and behaviours, different social structures, etc. – realizing that there are cultural differences – enables us to understand the nature and concept of culture. And subsequently learning about one's own culture and becoming aware of one's own cultural identity is interdependent with learning about another culture.

By their nature these exercises have an experiential component: it is not enough to collect information and data about another culture; there must be an interaction with persons from the other culture. Intercultural learning requires talking to people from another culture, relating to them, working together with them on a specific task, eating together, experiencing school, free time, everyday life together.

Interaction between people of different cultures implies misunderstanding, that one will not understand or even resist the attitudes or behaviour of others, that one will offend others without intent or without even realizing. Frequently, existing stereotypes and prejudices are confronted with a divergent self-perception or reality.

Exercises dealing with this learning area represent the 'heart' of an intercultural learning project and therefore require special attention with respect to preparation, guidance and evaluation.

Lifestyles and behaviour (LB)

Lifestyles have an individual component, which has been developed according to family traditions, personal preferences, etc. Simply speaking, some individuals usually have tea for breakfast, some have coffee, others have something else or even no breakfast at all. But there is also a component of lifestyles that is common to a larger group – be it regional, socio-economic or cultural. There are habits and routines that are considered to be 'normal' within a certain culture and that are subsequently common to many people in this culture. For example, there are cultures where people usually have their main meal at noon and there are other cultures where people have it in the evening – while individual habits might still differ.

What is common to these habits and routines is that they are followed automatically and unconsciously. Most exercises in this category have the objective of enabling consciousness and awareness of one's lifestyle and behaviour. A common approach is the use of questionnaires or surveys that record an individual's activities as well as those activities common to a larger group or society – everyday activities as well as exceptional activities. These can then be consciously reflected on.

Most of these exercises can be done in monocultural groups – for example, as a preparation for a visit abroad. But most of them can also be applied in bicultural or multicultural settings to compare different lifestyles. In this case, the exercise has to be associated with the category 'culture'. Trying to describe the cultural component of a lifestyle bears the danger of stereotyping: this fact must be pointed out by the teacher or facilitator to avoid stereotypes being developed or existing stereotypes being reinforced through these exercises.

Global perspectives (GP)

This category enables an understanding of the interrelatedness between a larger world – beyond the local community (or even school), beyond the county or region, beyond national borders – and what we know, feel and do locally. What is the degree of 'globality' already present in our lives and communities? What is the effect of local action on others at a distance? What is the effect of international action on the school and local community? What is the impact of events, actions, movements in 'other locales' on me, my school, my community? What happens with the spread of technology all over the globe? Music?

It also concerns solidarity. Feminist organizations, environmental movements, human rights bodies, world development groups tend to be globally aware about their particular concern or issue. Such organizations are also very good at making the global interest understood at local level.

The aim of the exercises is to broaden the nature of 'global' so that it is not the purview of a single, albeit important, interest. One of the exercises in this category, 'Where does it come from?', can be modified and used as a model for numerous variations. It could also be turned around to 'Where does it go to?' depending on the modification desired. This exercise could be used as an initializing event as well.

A rather famous exercise that can be used for developing an awareness of global interdependence is 'Bafá bafá' by Gary Shirts (published by Smile II, Del Mar, California). Although this exercise is geared towards a better understanding of the concept of culture and intercultural communication, it also leads to a better understanding of the mechanisms of interaction and communication and therefore the interdependence between different groups and societies.

Values (V)

Values have a great influence on the way we think, feel and act. They direct our decisions, they influence our emotions, they affect our actions, lifestyle and behaviour. As a matter of principle, values refer to a group. Nevertheless, there can be different – possibly even contradictory and conflicting – values within a society (or culture). Obviously, values play an important role in the relationship and interaction between people in general and between people of different cultural backgrounds specifically. In fact, most exercises relating to culture, cultural differences, lifestyles, etc., also have to do with values.

For most of the exercises in this category, the objective is to become aware of one's value system and how it influences thinking, feeling and doing. One approach taken is simply to rank a number of things – abstract or material – according to one's values. A more subtle approach is to rank a number of persons in a given story according to their behaviour and actions – which are based on values. Value exercises can usually be done in monocultural as well as bicultural or multicultural settings. In a bicultural or multicultural setting, they could also be referred to as culture exercises.

Since values are rooted very deeply in a personality and since values also influence our feelings these exercises tend to become emotional. Especially when doing such an exercise in a bicultural or multicultural setting, one has to be prepared to deal with tension and conflict.

Communication (CO)

Obviously, communication plays an essential role in an intercultural learning process – verbal as well as non-verbal communication. While for most exercises in this book verbal communication – language – is a major tool for conveying information, ideas, attitudes, beliefs, feelings, etc. (and thus for relating to other people), non-verbal communication plays an equally important role. Much of what we communicate is conveyed by gestures, mimicry, behaviour, etc. These non-verbal communication tools have a specific meaning depending on the culture: nodding the head will mean consent in one culture and rejection in another, the gesture for waving farewell in one culture might be interpreted as 'come here' in another.

Frequently, non-verbal messages are not perceived consciously, especially if they support and complement verbal messages. We become aware of non-verbal messages if we do not understand them or if we are confused by them because they are unexpected or because they contradict the verbal messages. This is exactly what frequently happens in intercultural communication. Because of insufficient language skills, gestures and non-verbal communication tools are used under the assumption that they are globally used and understood – which they are not. Even if language skills are sufficient, the lack of competence in non-verbal communication in the respective country can result in misunderstanding, confusion and even offence.

This issue is addressed specifically in the exercises in this category. They mainly refer to non-verbal communication or to a very restricted verbal communication with only a few verbal expressions or acoustic signals. A major objective of these exercises is to understand that gestures, mimicry and behaviour have different meanings in different cultures and that this unspoken communication must be learned just like the language. Another objective is to experience the irritation and frustration resulting from the lack of understanding and misunderstanding as well as from the inability to make oneself understood. Learning to cope with such situations is an important element of intercultural learning.

There are a number of other exercises in the field that can contribute to the development of intercultural communication skills. One of them, 'ABA–ZAK', is listed in the 'global perspectives' category. Other exercises that can be used to practise observation and communication skills are 'The Zeezoos and the Yahoos' (Cross-Cultural Orientation, The Experiment in International Living, Brattleboro, Vermont, 1984) and 'The owl' by Theodor Gochenour (*Beyond Experience*, The Experiment Press, Brattleboro, Vermont, 1977).

Evaluation (E)

Some basic ideas and approaches concerning the evaluation of an intercultural learning project were described in Chapter 8. As outlined there, evaluation is an ongoing activity. The individual exercises provide for their own evaluation; it is possible to 'take stock' at appropriate moments during the course of a project; a concluding evaluation gives the opportunity for summing up the project or activity; it is possible to 'revisit' the learning some months later or as a warm up exercise for a new project. The timing and frequency of evaluation are a matter of choice and professional judgement.

There are numerous evaluation tools available in the educational field. Two sample questionnaires for evaluation are enclosed in this chapter and contain various standard elements: open questions, check lists, ranking, scales, sentence completion. Questionnaires like these can be easily developed for specific situations during the project and for closing it.

CATEGORIES AND LIST OF EXERCISES

Here we provide a list of all the exercises described in this book according to the categories outlined above. Since many of the exercises fit into more than one category, they appear twice or more on this list. This enables the user to find all the exercises belonging in one category with reference to other learning areas they can be used for. (Pages vi and vii give the page numbers on which exercises appear.)

The didactic schemes in the tables in Chapter 9 have a column of suggested exercises, which also refer to this listing. The categories make it easy to identify other exercises that can be used or substituted to achieve the same learning objectives.

Category/Exercise	Reference
Getting started (GS)	
Getting to know each other	
Assumptions	SP 5
Who am I?	V 4
(See also Chapter 8.)	
Warm up (GS/WU)	
What we know, what we don't know	GS/WU 1
What's in your wallet	GS/WU 2
Assumptions	SP 5
Initializing events (GS/IE)	
Initializing events	GS/IE 1
Europe, yesterday, today, tomorrow	GS/IE 2
Let's look at the world	GS/IE 3
Personal maps	GS/IE 4
Stereotypes and prejudices (SP)	
Slogans	SP 1
Apartment exercise	SP 2
Images in the mind	SP 3
Completing sentences	SP 4
Assumptions	SP 5
Playing regions	CU/CI 4
Associative drawing	CU/CI 5
Culture (CU)	
Cultural differences (CU/CD)	
Concept of culture	CU/CD 1
Cultural differences	CU/CD 2
Field exercise	CU/CD 3
Field study	CU/CD 4
Images in the mind	SP 3
Piece of culture	CU/CI 1
Associative drawing	CU/CI 5
Sunshine and rain	CU/CI 6
Maps and atlases	CU/CI 7
Eating rituals	LB 2
Time in Europe	LB 3
Albatross	CO 1

Category/Exercise	Reference
Cultural identity/own culture (CU/CI)	
Piece of culture	CU/CI 1
Cultural quotations	CU/CI 2
Educational paths and occupational options questionnaire	CU/CI 3
Playing regions	CU/CI 4
Associative drawing	CU/CI 5
Sunshine and rain	CU/CI 6
Maps and atlases	CU/CI 7
Personal maps	GS/IE 4
Lifestyles	LB 1
Where do I come from?	LB 4
What's in your wallet	GS/WU2
Lifestyles/behaviour (LB)	
Lifestyles	LB 1
Eating rituals	LB 2
Time in Europe	LB 3
Where do I come from?	LB 4
Field study	CU/CD 4
Educational paths and occupational options questionnaire	CU/CI 3
Global perspectives (GP)	
Community project	GP 1
Where is it from? Where is it going?	GP 2
ABA–ZAK	GP 3
Slogans	SP 1
Values (V)	
Personal values	V 1
Cultural values checklist	V 2
Cave rescue	V 3
Who am I?	V 4
Abigale	V 5
Piece of culture	CU/CI 1
Cultural quotations	CU/CI 2
Educational paths and occupational options questionnaire	CU/CI 3
Time in Europe	LB 3
Lifestyles	LB 1
Where do I come from?	LB 4
What's in your wallet	GS/WU 2
Communication (CO)	
Albatross	CO 1
Humming exercise	CO 2
Babel	CO 3

Category/Exercise	Reference
Charades	CO 4
Building a tower	CO 5
The yes/no game	CO 6
Slogans	SP 1
ABA–ZAK	GP 3
Evaluation (E)	
Evaluation questionnaire	E 1
Evaluation: completing sentences	E 2

What We Know, What We Don't Know   GS/WU 1

Categories
• Getting started: warm up
• Initializing event

Learning objectives
• To become aware of what we know already about a culture, project, country, each other.
• To become aware of what we want to know.

Duration
Can be an informal assignment outside class time but should take a class period of 40 minutes to do the group brainstorming.

Group
From 20 to 30 pupils.

Description of exercise
Brainstorming session to develop focus on a specific activity, be it a school visit, either going away or receiving another class, a subject-specific project, an exchangee in or away from the class.

Instructions
It is possible before the class brainstorming session to ask pupils to think about what they know or don't know about whatever the subject is, e.g. for an exchange or school link, this could be the country of the partner school. Introduce the brainstorming as a means of finding out what we know (can already share with each other) and what we want to know about the topic. Ask for two volunteers to be board recorders to write the lists on the chalkboard. First, take the list of what we know. Anything contributed by a pupil is listed – no judgements or corrections are allowed at this point. When the list is exhausted, i.e. there are no more contributions, ask for a second list about what we want to know. Again, the board recorders list everything without judgement. Only after the lists are completed can the class and/or teacher make factual corrections.

It is possible to continue with this exercise for the purpose of taking responsibility for the various questions. Organize the ideas by similarity. This can be a class process with volunteers to each set of questions. Questions could include: How do we know what we know? Why do we want to know what we do not know?

Variations
Could be used as an introductory session with a visiting school group – what do we want to know about each other? It is also helpful to use this exercise with parents of pupils going on an exchange.

Reference
S.B. Simon, L.W. Howe and H. Kirschenbaum. *Values Clarification* (New York: Hart Publishing Company, 1978).

What's in Your Wallet   GS/WU 2

Categories
• Getting started: getting acquainted
• Values

Learning objectives
• To become aware of own/others' values through ordinary belongings.
• To get acquainted.

Duration
One class period.

Group
From 20 to 30, monocultural or multicultural by composition, any age range.

Description of exercise
It is possible to learn something about who we are and what we value from simple or ordinary aspects of our lives. In this case, pupils are asked to look at their wallets (or purse or school case – whatever is the most common container).

Instructions
Ask the pupils to take three things out of their wallets (or whatever it might be) that illustrate something they value. The items can be anything at all; the mere fact that you carry them with you indicates a degree of importance. Put the items on the desk and think about why they are important to you so that you can describe this to the rest of the class. Take notes for yourself.

Ask for volunteers to describe why and how an item means something to them, how it relates to their values. Be prepared for some pupils to deny having anything. Say that's OK and pass on to another participant. Pupils can also add objects during the exercise. Try to have everyone take a turn.

Variations

This exercise can be conducted as a way of forming small groups. Ask a pupil to choose another pupil on the basis of one of his or her items (similar or different). The other pupil is then asked to choose a pupil to join the other two, thus making a trio. Continue forming trios in this manner until all pupils are involved. The trios could carry on with a discussion about their items and why the items are important to them.

Comments

This can be used as an introductory or warm-up exercise for a new group.

Reference

S.B. Simon, L.W. Howe and H. Kirschenbaum. *Values Clarification* (New York: Hart Publishing Company, 1978).

Initializing Events GS/IE 1

Category
• Getting started: initializing event

Learning objective
• To create interest.

Duration
One class period.

Group
From 20 to 30 pupils, monocultural or multicultural.

Description of exercise
A group discussion, visit or activity that engages the pupils' interest in intercultural learning. Whatever the initializing event, the aim will be to enable the class to see how the topic relates to their specific experience and therefore is important to pursue.

Instructions
To start the project in a class or school, an 'initializing event' may be necessary to create interest for the topic. Such an event must have an emotional dimension. The list of ideas below is by no means complete. Before starting such a project, the teachers involved should go through a brainstorming session on possible initializing events in their specific environment before looking at this list. The 'event' ideas listed below can then be added:

• political conflict based on culture/minorities/migrants, environmental conflicts;
• conflicts related to regional/national identities;
• story related to topic covered by media, film or book;
• a conflict between two different cultures represented at the school, other religious/social/ethnic conflicts in class/school;

- presence of foreigners in class/school;
- foreign teacher (e.g. language assistant);
- promotion of an exchange programme;
- accents, dialects, languages in general;
- school trip abroad or visit by class from another country;
- students in class who participated in an exchange programme;
- vacation abroad.

Europe, Yesterday, Today, Tomorrow   GS/IE 2

Category
- Getting started: initializing event

Learning objective
- To create interest in intercultural learning.

Duration
One class period.

Group
Between 20 and 30. Can be either monocultural or multicultural.

Description of exercise
Probably a discussion activity based on investigation or an assignment prepared by the pupils. As with the first approach or 'initializing event', the purpose is to engage and focus the class in such a way that they want to learn more. The issues listed below have a common denominator in that they induce fear and often a negative reaction. The introduction to this book might satisfy the intellect of the reader, but it would hardly shake anyone up and create a need for intercultural learning: a different approach has to be taken to address emotions. Possible issues to be reflected on could look like this:

Inside Europe

- Economic situation, recession, unemployment. Will other Europeans come to my country, city, town and take our jobs? Will we have an equal opportunity to work in the rest of Europe? Do I want to work away from my community?
- AIDS. What prejudices have become visible? How is discrimination created and increased? First homosexuals, then Africans, then Americans, then British, then athletes, then rock stars, then actors, then. ... How will our community change? What role do media play? Or the politicians?
- Eastern Europe. Many wish that the wall was still there. They take away our jobs; they destroy our economy with cheap labour and cheap imports. We cannot support the whole world.
- Conflict in Northern Ireland, the Basque country, Bosnia, Serbia, Croatia, the former Soviet republics. What are these conflicts about? Do we become

involved? What is our role as fellow Europeans?

- Should we supply arms to areas of potential conflict if it means more jobs in our country? Should the UN/NATO or our army interfere to stop wars?
- Environmental waste. Do we allow ships loaded with nuclear waste to dock in our harbours? Can we send our nuclear waste to other countries?

Outside Europe

- Should we be involved in the internal conflict of a country outside Europe? Isn't this like Northern Ireland, the Basque country, Bosnia, etc.?
- India. What do we know about domestic conflict in India?
- China. Do we remember seeing the events in Tiananmen Square?
- South Africa. What is the impact for us of the new, democratically elected government?
- Middle East. Do we think that the peace process will succeed?
- Hong Kong. Will Hong Kong Chinese flood our country when Hong Kong ceases to be a British colony in 1997?
- And much more, in Peru, Iran, Afghanistan, Chad, Nicaragua, Guatemala. Do we remember headlines from a year or more ago?

The inflation of news makes us forget quickly what has happened. The immediacy of news by way of satellite television brings conflicts, riots, terrorism and hunger into our daily life. What do we do? How are we affected? What stereotypes result? What is the cultural dimension? Why are refugees returned to their countries? Why are migration policies strengthened against people seeking work?

Comments

There is, unfortunately, no limit to the issues that can be used. In order to avoid overkill or non-response, it may be more useful to find one or two issues that are of particular interest, to investigate and discuss them at more length and then to extend the list with the pupils so that they connect the issues to a common thread.

Some of the issues cited may be (we hope) out of date by the time this book is published. Unfortunately, there will be other issues that can be used.

Most of these issues are written from a British point of view, which means that if you are in another country the reflections may need to be restated.

Let's Look at the World   GS/IE 3

Or at least Europe for the moment, or perhaps just the part of Europe that is England (or Scotland or Wales or ...)

Category
- Getting started: initializing event

Learning objectives
- To create interest.
- To make young people aware of stereotypes.

Duration
One class period.

Group
From 20 to 30 pupils. Can be monocultural or multicultural.

Description of exercise
This exercise can be carried out in one of two ways. Using the list of comments below, facilitate a discussion about the stereotypes as portrayed in the list. The list contains comments which are very exaggerated in order to make the point of how people commonly talk about other cultures.

The second way would be to ask the class to do 'street interviews' in order to create their own list, which would then be followed by discussion. A list of comments acquired first-hand will be more credible than one that is prescribed and may produce more discussion, but it will take more time.

Prescribed list
What is England and being English about?

We look at American television and films and make fun of their way of life – cars, Hollywood, riches, their lack of 'culture', their politicians – but we envy Americans for their economic strength and dream of going to work there (although we would never admit it, and rather criticize their spend, spend, spend way of life and unjust society).

We thrive on tourism but resent the Americans, Germans and Japanese for crowding places like Bath, York and Stratford-on-Avon, never mind London. The Americans will buy anything as long as it is old and 'quaint'; the Germans have no sense of humour; and the Japanese, well, who can tell except they're always in a group and have a lot of cameras? Still, we wish our standard of living was as high.

We like to go to countries where there is a lot of sun and beach. The reason for going on holiday is to find the sun and to be able to buy cheap beer and wine. That's why Spain and Greece are so popular.

But since 1 January 1993 we can take the ferry across the Channel for a day of shopping. The French sell wine really cheap. Mum likes that smelly cheese, too.

Italy, too. It really is the grand art tour but terribly dear. Who would think a plate of spaghetti could cost £6! And to learn the currency, which has the same 'sign' as the pound but you need so many of them to do anything.

And speaking of currency. You would think that Europe would understand about the pound. After all, it is our heritage – we can't just give it up in the hope that there might be a stable European currency.

Foreign policy: well, our future is in Europe. I guess it's fine to be able to move about, take a job in another country and all that. But, I wouldn't want to live far away anyway.

Foreigners have such a strange notion about us. They're more interested in the royals than the British. Why can't they realize we're ordinary folk who want a good job, that we don't all live in country houses?

Comments

This list can be described as quite negative. Is it possible that self-denigration is part of our culture? As the list is written to highlight British stereotypes, it can and should be adapted to other national stereotypes when being used in another country.

Personal Maps   GS/IE 4

Categories
• Getting started: getting acquainted
• Own culture

Learning objectives
• To become acquainted.
• To become aware of own culture.
• To create interest.

Duration
One class period.

Group
Almost any size, but needs to be broken into small groups of minimum 8 to maximum 15 persons. Works best in a multicultural setting but is possible with monocultural class.

Supplies/resources
Flip-chart, paper, felt-tip pens (paper and pen for each participant).

Description of exercise
'Self-portraits' are used as a means of understanding participants' own culture and as a way of introducing a group at a more fundamental level.

Instructions
Prepare your own 'self-portrait' by way of introducing yourself in such a way that you will answer the question: 'What is something about me that is cultural?' The self-portrait may be a representation of yourself or be drawings that demonstrate aspects of your daily life. You may use other artifacts that you may have in your bag or pockets. Try to pinpoint those factors which distinguish you in relation to other major world cultures, not in relation to other subcultures within your local society.

Explain that culture affects everything we do and are – assumptions about life and the world, values and attitudes, habits of thought, patterns of behaviour, relationships with others. It is possible to select anything about oneself and relate it to one's culture. Listed here are a small number of examples of what culture affects:

• types of foods you typically eat;
• clothing and self-decoration you wear;

- the rites of passage you have gone through in life (coming of age, marriage, religious ceremonies, etc.);
- relationships you have with your nuclear/extended family members;
- nature of your religious beliefs/practices;
- approach you prefer in socializing children (authoritarian or more liberal);
- beliefs you hold about the division of labour by age and sex;
- behaviours you typically exhibit in the presence of a socially superior person;
- concept you have of the meaning of cleanliness;
- frequency and location of body contact that you make with people in various social categories;
- patterns of decision-making and problem-solving you prefer;
- the way you use your eyes when in conversation;
- the way you segment and handle time;
- patterns of behaviour you exhibit with strangers, acquaintances, friends.

Provide each participant with a piece of flip-chart and felt-tip pens. Ask them to prepare self-portraits to introduce themselves, answering the question: 'What is something that is cultural about me?' (20 minutes)

Ask each participant to introduce himself or herself by using the self-portraits. Be certain that each one addresses the question: 'What is something cultural about me?' (15 to 60 minutes)

Ask everyone to think about the question: 'What do these introductions suggest about what "culture" means?' Have the pupils reflect individually and ask everyone to jot down a brief definition of 'culture'. (5 minutes)

Ask for volunteers to give their definition of or ideas about 'culture'. Write these on the chalkboard or provide poster pads to pupils and ask them to post their definitions on the board. After a number (at your discretion) have been presented, discuss.

Evaluation
Do not feel compelled to arrive at a common or agreed definition. It is valuable to use the range of ideas to emphasize the point that culture is interwoven through everything we are and do.

Comment
This exercise can be used as the first part of a series of three exercises. Part 2 can be found as the exercise 'Concept of Culture' (CU/CD 1). Part 3 is 'Cultural Differences' (CU/CD 2).

Reference
Based on material from *AFS Orientation Handbook, Vol. IV* (New York: AFS Intercultural Programs, 1984). Copyright © AFS International Programs, Inc. Used with permission.

Slogans   SP 1

Categories
- Stereotypes and prejudices
- Global perspectives

Learning objectives
- To become aware of one's own prejudices and stereotypes about Europe.
- To realize the importance and quality of communication.

Duration
One class period, 40 to 50 minutes.

Group
From 20 to 30 pupils, in a monocultural or multicultural class.

Supplies/resources
Chalkboard and chalk or flip-chart and marker pens.

Description of exercise
A group exercise which asks pupils to identify/defend their beliefs about a particular topic. Can be related to value clarification exercises.

Instructions
Present a set of slogans one at a time and ask the class or group to indicate their agreement or disagreement by physically moving to different parts of the room. For each slogan the two groups of pro and con should then debate the slogan, trying to change the perceptions of the other side. If any pupils change their views, they should move to the other group. The debates can continue until it appears that the reasoning and arguments have been exhausted. Sample slogans are:

1 The further development of the EU depends on the creation of a European army.
2 Being European means being white, Christian and broad-minded.
3 Loyalty to Europe is nothing but a new form of nationalism.
4 A unified Europe ensures its supremacy over developing countries.
5 The EU means one president, one parliament, one government.
6 Europe exists for business interests only.
7 A unified Europe means a stronger voice in world affairs.
8 A European identity means a single flag, currency, passport.

Add slogans used in your country.

Evaluation
What do our positions on the debate say about our values? Is there a relation? What is our image of Europe as a region? What is our image of the European Union as a

supranational body? What does Europe mean to us – as a cultural/historical region, as a political/economic region? Is there a European culture?

Comments
Useful in a group comprised of more than one European nationality but not necessary.

Variation
Slogans could be developed about a topic, such as a country to be visited or a project to be investigated, but then the focus of the exercise is limited to learning about stereotypes and prejudices. This could be useful for a monocultural class as preparation for a visit to another country.

Reference
Modification of an exercise used in an EFIL seminar at the European Youth Centre, Council of Europe, Strasbourg, 1991. Used with permission.

Apartment Exercise: 'With Whom Would I Like to Live in the Same House?' SP 2

Category
• Stereotypes and prejudices

Learning objectives
• To become aware of one's own prejudices.
• To become aware that prejudices influence one's decisions.

Duration
One class period, or 50 minutes.

Group
From 10 to 30 participants; can be either a monocultural or a multicultural group.

Supplies/resources
Copies of pupil worksheet, one for each participant.

Description of exercise
Individual and group activity with the aim of heightening awareness of prejudices and how prejudices influence our decisions.

Worksheet

With whom would you like to live in the same building?

You are living in a nice old building on two floors. Since your family cannot afford to maintain it, you have decided to rent out some rooms. After you have renovated the building, there are three apartments (flats) to be let. The newspaper ad results in applications from a number of people (listed below), all of whom are unknown to you. Choose at least three of them to whom you would let the apartment. Also select three you definitely would not rent the apartment to.

   Mark those you wish to live with by indicating a '+' next to them. Mark those you definitely would not rent the apartment to with a '−'.

1 A single mother with a 3-year-old child, whose father is Tunisian. He visits his son occasionally and sometimes brings along a few friends.

2 A Serbian family with six children aged 1 to 12. Father would take on the job of caretaker.

3 A family with a 17-year-old daughter in the lower sixth at school. Father is an accountant in a bank, mother is a teacher.

4 A single 70-year-old lady, living on a small pension.

5 A group of seven Polish young men, all working in the kitchen of a large restaurant.

6 A group of five people living an alternative lifestyle, who reject the materialistic ideology of consumption.

7 Three Palestinian students, who are politically engaged.

8 An Asian family of five persons. Father works occasionally and otherwise is unemployed. They are part of a larger family which has strong relationships. The extended family frequently comes to visit. They all like to have parties.

9 An American couple without children. Husband is working for the UN, wife takes care of the household and three poodles.

10 Two artists, about 40 years old, who live a rather bohemian and unconventional lifestyle. They have many friends who also are artists.

11 A girl studying the piano and singing at the music academy, who has to practise regularly in the afternoon.

12 A black male American with a white girlfriend, who is trying to get a work permit as an engineer.

13 A religious Muslim family, which lives strictly according to the Koran. The mother always wears a veil when going out.

14 A Bosnian refugee family, mother with two children and her sister. Her husband has been missing for three months.

Instructions

1 Introduction of exercise. Straightforward. (5 minutes)
2 Hand out list of potential tenants. Each participant should take 5 minutes to read the list and decide, individually and spontaneously, three people to whom he or she would rent the apartment, and three persons (families) to whom he or she would not let the apartment. This can be done by marking a '+' by those you would choose to live with and a '−' by those you would not wish to live with.
3 Split up into small groups of 6 to 8 participants. Groups should share their lists and produce a chart reflecting their choices with '+' and '−'. Discuss the results in small groups. Why did participants choose the way they did? (20 minutes)
4 Discuss in large group. (20 minutes)

- How close do you let others get to yourself?
- Why do you resent certain groups? Why do you sympathize with certain groups?
- What are the reasons for discrimination against others?
- Which preferences, likes and dislikes, underlie the choices?

Evaluation

What have the participants learned from the exercise personally? What prejudices have the participants become aware of? Will this awareness change their behaviour in the future?

Comments

The first selection process has to be done very quickly – while reading the list the participants should immediately mark the persons/families with '+' or '−'. There is no 'right' score.

Participants in this exercise are frequently confused about the basis of making choices. Some people prefer noise, others quiet. Some people are predisposed to being helpful and therefore might feel responsible towards certain choices. Such preferences do not necessarily mean prejudice, although there may be assumptions and stereotypes about who is likely to be noisy or quiet or just doing 'good'.

Reference

H. Fennes *et al.*, *Projektunterricht 'Interkulturelles Lernen in der Schule'* (Vienna: Bundesministerium für Unterricht und Kunst, 1984). Reproduced with permission.

Images in the Mind   SP 3

Categories
- Stereotypes and prejudices
- Cultural differences

Learning objectives
- To become aware of one's own prejudices/stereotypes about one or more other countries and cultures.
- To understand that prejudices are 'learned' and not a factor of current invention.
- To find out about prejudices and stereotypes which people from other countries have about one's own country/culture.
- To know that it is possible to change one's prejudices and stereotypes.

Duration
Ideally 90 minutes, but could be divided into two class periods.

Group
Ten or more participants from at least two different countries.

Worksheet
Divide a flip-chart into four quarters and describe a cultural/ethnic group that is assigned to you by the teacher/facilitator according to the following instructions:

In this quadrant write three to five characteristics you associate spontaneously with this cultural/ethnic group	In this quadrant, draw a picture of typical representatives of this cultural/ethnic group
Which animals would you spontaneously associate with this cultural/ethnic group? Which car?	What do you think is so important to this cultural/ethnic group (e.g. a tradition, an institution) that it would cause a riot if it was taken away or prohibited?

On top of the flip-chart indicate cultural/ethnic groups or countries represented in the group producing it.

Supplies/resources
Flip-chart(s), copies of worksheet (each group of 10 to 12 will require a facilitator).

Description of exercise
Group-focused, the exercise enables participants to become aware of their own prejudices as well as those of others towards them. It can be confrontational; discussion needs to be handled adroitly so that participants understand that the offence is not personal towards individuals but generalized as a group stereotype. The crisis in learning in this exercise can be very positive.

Instructions
1 Introduction of exercise. Should be straightforward. (5 minutes)
2 Split the total group into an even number of small groups (five to seven participants) each. Groups should be culturally/regionally homogeneous, e.g. Scots, Welsh, English or, in the case of a class visit from another country, the host class and the visiting class. Give groups names or numbers.
3 The first group selects a cultural/regional/ethnic group represented in the second group, while the second group does the same for the first group. And so on, depending on how many small groups you have. Each group prepares a flip-chart about the selected cultural/regional/ethnic group according to the attached worksheet.
4 The paired groups get together and share their flip-charts. First group presents its flip-chart to second and describes possible reasons or origins for the image of the other group. Group 2 should not yet react. Group 2 presents its flip-chart to the first group in the same manner. Group 1 does not yet react. Reactions: both groups compare the image they have about themselves with the image presented by the other group.
   • Where do the two images match/agree?
   • Where do the two images differ/disagree?
   • By which parts of the images presented by the other group do members of the groups feel offended?
   • Which parts of the images presented by the other group made members of the group feel proud?
   Discuss together where the underlying stereotypes/prejudices could come from and how they were possibly developed. Ensure that participants understand that these images have not been developed by the persons in the exercise but that many of the prejudices and stereotypes have been 'learned' long before. Keep the discussion focused so that the images are always generalized, never personal. Ask the groups about their view of their own cultural/regional/ethnic group. Isn't that also a stereotype?
5 If the size of the total group has meant additional pairs doing the exercise, it is possible to meet in plenary (flip-charts on walls). Get brief reports from the groups on what has been learned. Short input on prejudices and stereotypes: how are they learned, what are their functions, what effect do they have on

people? Were any stereotypes common to all groups? Does that have any relevance?

Variations
This exercise can also be done with a monocultural class/group as preparation for a visit abroad. In this case, half the small groups should produce a flip-chart about the country to be visited and the other half one about their own country. These flip-charts should be discussed again after returning from the visit abroad. Has there been any change? What caused the change?

If this exercise is being used during a class exchange, it can be done twice: once at the beginning and once towards the end of the visit (possibly also during the counter-visit). Compare the flip-charts and discuss what has changed and why.

Comments
Be careful in discussions that nationalistic attitudes are not being enforced. Concentrate on cultural/regional/ethnic groups. This can be an excellent exercise for both a visiting class from another country and a multicultural classroom.

Reference
Intercultural Centre, Vienna. Used with permission.

Completing Sentences   SP 4

Category
• Prejudices and stereotypes

Learning objectives
• To become aware of own stereotypes and prejudices.
• To become aware of others' stereotypes and prejudices about own country/ culture.
• To learn that it is possible to change one's stereotypes.

Duration
Forty-five minutes but can be expanded to up to 90 minutes.

Group size
This exercise can be used in a monocultural class in a multicultural society as well as in a multicultural class. For use in a bicultural setting within a class exchange, the exercise has to be adapted and modified appropriately. If the group is larger than 25 pupils, it is better to divide into two groups with one teacher/ facilitator for each.

Description of exercise
The pupils spontaneously complete sentences referring to another cultural/ethnic group. They discuss the results and how they came to them. If possible, pupils of

the respective cultural/ethnic group react to the completed sentences and present their views and feelings on the situations the sentences referred to.

Supplies/resources

Worksheet with incomplete sentences – one copy per pupil. When there are two or more cultures represented in the group one needs a different set of worksheets for each cultural/ethnic group.

The worksheet can include sentences like:

- In our country X-ians are...
- People do not want to rent apartments to X-ians, because...
- People want to rent apartments to X-ians, because...
- The apartments of X-ians are...
- X-ian pupils in school are...
- X-ians make their income/work mainly on/in...
- In their free time X-ians prefer to...
- X-ians educate their children...
- When I meet an X-ian...
- X-ians came to our/this country, because...
- The relationship of X-ians to their native country is...
- I like X-ians who...
- I dislike X-ians who...

(X-ians stands for members of a cultural/ethnic group that the sentences refer to. In a monocultural class, one will refer to another cultural/ethnic group of the same society. In a multicultural class, one will refer to another cultural/ethnic group within the class.)

Further incomplete sentences could refer to the values, norms and lifestyle of the X-ian cultural/ethnic group as well as to the relationship of people of one's own cultural/ethnic group to X-ians. Of course, all these questions have to be phrased in detail depending on the specific situation.

Instructions

1 Ask pupils to complete the sentences individually and spontaneously. Ask the pupils not to make judgements but rather to be descriptive. Tell them that the worksheets are only for personal use and will therefore not be collected. (5 to 10 minutes)

2 Discuss the results sentence by sentence in plenary. Ask the pupils how they came to their conclusions and discuss the underlying prejudices and stereotypes. In a multicultural setting, let groups react to each others' sentences. Discuss how this affects the relationship between the different cultural/ethnic groups and what can be done to improve this relationship. Ensure that the participants understand that the underlying stereotypes and prejudices have not been developed by themselves, that most of them have been 'learned' long before. Explain that stereotypes and prejudices are always based on generalizations and normally do not reflect a personal attitude.

Variation

The exercise can be adapted to a bicultural setting in a class exchange. Since the relationship between the two cultural groups involved is of a different nature from that within a multicultural society the questions will mostly refer to values and lifestyles of each other's cultures.

Evaluation

One can draw various conclusions by comparing the completed sentences of pupils: for example, if a sentence is completed in a similar way by most pupils it is very likely that – unconsciously – they have completed it based on an existing prejudice. Another approach to evaluation is to examine the sentences for judgements and to discuss how these affect the relationship to the respective cultural/ethnic group.

Comments

In a multicultural class, the discussion can become quite emotional. Normally, the underlying conflict has not been caused by the exercise but will have been suppressed so far or expressed in other ways. An open discussion allows the class to deal with these conflicts in a constructive way. If an open conflict is foreseen, it can be advisable to do the exercise with two teachers.

Reference

Idea developed from H. Fennes *et al.*, *Projektunterricht 'Interkulturelles Lernen in der Schule'* (Vienna: Bundesministerium für Unterricht und Kunst, 1984). Used with permission.

Assumptions   SP 5

Categories
• Prejudices and stereotypes
• Warm up, getting acquainted

Learning objectives
• To realize that one automatically makes assumptions and suppositions about other people when seeing them.
• To become aware of one's own stereotypes and prejudices.
• To understand that these assumptions are helpful in relating to people one does not know.

Duration
Between 40 and 60 minutes.

Group
Can be used for a group of any size. Can be used in monocultural as well as bicultural and multicultural settings. This exercise is best used in groups whose members meet for the first time or when there has not been much personal contact with each other so far.

Description of exercise
Pupils who do not know each other make assumptions and suppositions about each other. Afterwards they share with each other how they came to these suppositions as well as how they felt about the suppositions made about themselves.

Instructions
1 Without prior explanation ask participants to form small groups of 3 to 4 (maximum!) pupils each, in such a way that they do not know any of the other pupils in their small groups.
2 Taking turns, they are asked to make suppositions about pupils in the group one at a time. The pupil about whom suppositions are made is not allowed to react to these suppositions – verbally nor non-verbally. The suppositions could be about where the pupil is from, what his or her interests and hobbies are, his or her family, if he or she is the only/youngest/oldest/middle child etc. Advise pupils to start each sentence with 'I suppose that …' to underline the fact that it is a supposition which could very well be wrong, too.
3 In a second round they again take their turn and react to the suppositions made about themselves. What was right/wrong? How did they feel about the suppositions made about themselves? They should also try to express why they made specific suppositions about the others and thus which stereotypes and prejudices were underlying their suppositions.
4 Share results of small-group discussions in plenary. Explain the nature of stereotypes and prejudices, how they develop, how they are learned and what functions they have. Talk about selective observation/perception and intuition and the role this plays when relating to an unknown person. Ask pupils for a final reflection on the exercise and try to clarify any remaining dissatisfaction.

Comments
This exercise can also be used with adults and thus could serve as an exercise for a first-time teachers' meeting when working together on a project or exchange.

Reference
Developed by Intercultural Centre, Vienna. Used with permission.

Concept of Culture   CU/CD 1

Categories
• Culture
• Cultural differences, own culture

Learning objectives
• To appreciate the complexity of the concept of culture.
• To understand several ways of looking at definitions of culture.

Duration
One class period, 40 to 50 minutes. This exercise is Part 2 of a series of three exercises. Part 1 ('Personal maps', GS/IE 4, page 175) takes about one class period; Part 3 ('Cultural differences', CU/CD 2, page 190) requires 2 to 3 hours.

Group size
Can be done with normal size class, 20 to 30 pupils.

Supplies/resources
Photocopies of handouts.

Description of exercise
This is a workshop that focuses on cultural differences. Part 3 is based on research findings by Geert Hofstede (Institute for Research on Intercultural Cooperation, Maastricht, The Netherlands) that first appeared in 1980. A more recent book, *Cultures and Organizations, Software of the Mind*, 1991, updates these findings and relates his research to the school environment. The first part of the workshop is contained in GS/IE 4, 'Personal maps'. Part 2, which presents a number of concepts of culture, can also be used on its own. Part 3 makes use of the research data from 50 nations. This part of the workshop will be difficult to use with reference to countries other than these 50. Check the list on page 196 to make sure your participants will be able to find data for their own country.

Instructions
Introduce four ways of looking at the concept of culture, presenting each briefly as outlined, and providing photocopies of concept handouts where appropriate.

The participant group might be asked to describe their collective and to identify other groups, first in the same geographical area (old age pensioners, young mothers, etc.), then in a different geographical area.

Continue with Part 3 ('Cultural differences', CU/CD 2).

Variations
May be used as part of the total workshop; independently but still an integral part of the workshop, which may be run as a series over a specified time period; or Parts 1 and 2 may also be used on a stand-alone basis, but it is not recommended that Part 3 be used without having first used Parts 1 and 2.

Reference
Based on material in *AFS Orientation Handbook, Vol. IV* (New York: AFS Intercultural Programs, 1984). Copyright © AFS Intercultural Programs, Inc. Used with permission.

Concepts of Culture

'Fish-in-water' analogy for understanding culture:

Trying to understand culture is a bit like a fish trying to understand water, for we are trying to be objective about something of which we are already a part. It is something that completely surrounds us at all times. Even the way we approach the task of understanding – the terms of the language we use, the process of thinking – is affected by culture. As we are unable to get away from culture, as a fish cannot get away from water, we find it very difficult to understand our own culture objectively.

The 'Iceberg' concept of the nature of culture:

Culture is like an iceberg in that only 10 per cent of culture is visible. About 90 per cent of what makes up culture is beyond or below our conscious awareness. This does not mean that culture has less influence on our daily lives but rather more. It is possible to monitor and attempt to control that of which we are aware but we are unlikely to monitor, control, change that of which we are unaware. Aspects of the culture about which we are aware include sculpture, painting, literature, theatre, music, dance, cinema, architecture, dress, self-decoration, agriculture, political and religious rituals and so on. Examples of the 90 per cent of culture of which we are unaware include all of the hidden aspects of our lives such as those listed below the water-line in the iceberg handout.

Culture is something a group of people have in common while still being individuals:

Culture consists of human characteristics that are learned by children and youth as they are socialized in a geographical area where they are born and raised, and that are shared by adult members of the population – but not necessarily in equal amounts. Thus, members of a given culture are more or less similar, but they are not identical to one another. Anyone may be 'typical' of his or her culture in terms of some characteristics, but more or less atypical in terms of other characteristics.

Shortest definition of culture:

Culture is the collective programming of the mind which distinguishes the members of one human group from another. (Geert Hofstede, 1980)

With this definition, Hofstede emphasizes that culture is not a property of individuals, but of groups. It is a collection of more or less shared characteristics possessed by people who have been conditioned by similar socialization practices, educational procedures and life experiences. Because of their similar backgrounds, the people in any given culture may be said to have similar 'mental programming'. Thus, one can speak of the culture of a family, a tribe, a region, a national minority or a nation. Culture is what differentiates people in a given collective from people in other collectives at the same level.

A pictorial representation of the nature of culture

Culture is like an iceberg in that only a small percentage is visible. The larger part of what makes up culture is beyond our consciousness. Above the waterline are such things as fine arts, literature, cooking, lifestyles, etc. Below the waterline are all those elements of culture that monitor and determine our daily behaviour, thinking and emotions, but are not primarily conscious.

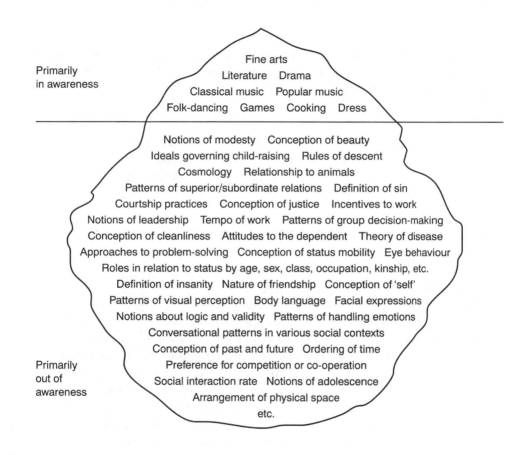

Primarily
in awareness

Fine arts
Literature   Drama
Classical music   Popular music
Folk-dancing   Games   Cooking   Dress

Notions of modesty   Conception of beauty
Ideals governing child-raising   Rules of descent
Cosmology   Relationship to animals
Patterns of superior/subordinate relations   Definition of sin
Courtship practices   Conception of justice   Incentives to work
Notions of leadership   Tempo of work   Patterns of group decision-making
Conception of cleanliness   Attitudes to the dependent   Theory of disease
Approaches to problem-solving   Conception of status mobility   Eye behaviour
Roles in relation to status by age, sex, class, occupation, kinship, etc.
Definition of insanity   Nature of friendship   Conception of 'self'
Patterns of visual perception   Body language   Facial expressions
Notions about logic and validity   Patterns of handling emotions
Conversational patterns in various social contexts
Conception of past and future   Ordering of time
Preference for competition or co-operation
Social interaction rate   Notions of adolescence
Arrangement of physical space
etc.

Primarily
out of
awareness

Cultural Differences   CU/CD 2

Category
- Cultural differences

Learning objectives
- To become aware of cultural differences.
- To understand own culture.
- To begin to identify the impact of culture on behaviour.

Duration
Between 2 and 2½ hours. This exercise is Part 3 of a series of three exercises and should only be done when Part 1 ('Personal maps', GS/IE 4) and Part 2 ('Concept of culture', CU/CD 1) have been done.

Group
Normal class size but can be taken with two classes that are linked. There are three variations so the composition of the class can vary – monocultural to multicultural – depending on the setting in which the exercise is being used.

Supplies/resources
Handouts of cultural dimensions, ranges of dimensions and scoring sheet, one copy each.

Description of exercise
Dr Geert Hofstede is a Dutch social science researcher who conducted a massive research project that began in 1966 and involved a large multinational company. During the project, 116,000 questionnaires were completed by company employees located in 50 countries. The questionnaires were administered in the language of the country; in total 20 languages were used. The main difference among respondents was 'culture', as all of them were otherwise similar in terms of age, sex and job category – and they all worked for the same company. As a result of the massive quantity of data acquired from the questionnaires, Hofstede was able to define four key elements or dimensions of culture. This meant that he specified four major dimensions along which the dominant value systems in the 50 countries could be ordered and described. Hofstede explains 'dimension' in the following manner:

> To understand the dimensions of national culture, we can compare it with the dimensions of personality we use when we describe individuals' behaviour. In recruiting, an organization often tries to get an impression of a candidate's dimensions of personality, such as intelligence (high–low), energy level (active–passive), and emotional stability (stable–unstable). These are sets of criteria whereby characteristics of individuals can be described. The dimensions of culture I use represent a corresponding set of criteria for describing national cultures.

Hofstede has updated his research more recently because it was felt that the original research instrument had been designed by Westerners and therefore might have had a cultural bias. As a result, a fifth dimension has been added and is included in this part of the workshop. Descriptions and tables of the five dimensions appear on pages 192 to 196. These can be adapted or photocopied for class use.

Instructions (setting for a class/group preparing to go abroad)
Distribute the handout that illustrates the first dimension of culture, power distance. Explain that this dimension is a continuum between the two extremes of large power distance and small power distance, and that very few national cultures, if any, will be wholly at one or the other extreme. Almost all cultures will be somewhere between the two extremes, though closer to one than to the other. Ask pupils to read through the power distance criteria. (10 minutes)

Distribute the handout that describes the second dimension, uncertainty avoidance. Again, explain that there is a range to the extent that people or society feel threatened by ambiguity or uncertainty and very few, if any, national cultures will be at one extreme or the other. Ask pupils to read. (10 minutes)

Distribute the individualism dimension handout. The same explanation as for individualism and collectivism holds true. Ask pupils to read. (10 minutes)

The masculinity handout requires an additional explanation. The values on the left-hand side of the list are labelled 'masculinity' because within nearly all the 50 countries men were more likely to score high on these values than were women. This was true even in societies that, as a whole, tended to be characterized by the set of values labelled 'femininity'. Hofstede found that the more a country is characterized by masculine values, the greater the gap between values espoused by men and women in that country. (10 minutes)

Power distance
Power distance indicates the extent to which a society accepts the fact that power in institutions and organizations is distributed unequally among individuals.

Large power distance	Small power distance
Superiors consider subordinates to be different kind of people.	Superiors consider subordinates to be 'people like me'.
Subordinates consider superiors to be different kind of people.	Subordinates consider superiors to be 'people like me'.
Power is a basic fact of society that has nothing to do with good and evil; questions about its legitimacy are irrelevant.	The use of power should be legitimate; it is subject to judgements as to whether it is good or evil.
Power-holders are entitled to special privileges.	All should have equal rights.
The way to change a social system is to dethrone those in power and then give power to another elite group.	The way to change a social system is to redistribute power among all members of society.

Uncertainty avoidance

Uncertainty avoidance indicates the extent to which a society feels threatened by ambiguous situations and tries to avoid them by providing rules, believing in absolute truths and refusing to tolerate deviance.

Strong uncertainty avoidance	Weak uncertainty avoidance
Conflict and competition can unleash aggression and therefore should be avoided among friends and colleagues.	Conflict and competition can be contained on the level of fair play and used constructively.
Deviant persons and ideas are dangerous: they are dealt with in an intolerant fashion.	Deviant persons are not necessarily danger-. ous: they are dealt with in a tolerant fashion.
There is great concern with security in life.	There is a willingness to take risks in life.
People feel a need for written rules and regulations.	People feel that there should be as few rules as possible.
Ordinary citizens are incompetent compared with the authorities.	The authorities exist to serve ordinary citizens.

Individualism

Individualism indicates the extent to which a society is a loosely knit social framework in which people are supposed to take care only of themselves and their immediate families, instead of a tight social framework in which people distinguish between in-groups and out-groups and expect their in-group to look after them.

Individualism	Collectivism
In society, each person is supposed to take care of himself/herself and his/her immediate family.	In society, people are born into extended families or clans who protect them in exchange for their absolute loyalty.
One's involvement with organizations is calculated in terms of individual goals and aspirations.	One's involvement with organizations is seen in terms of moral duty.
The emphasis is on individual initiative and achievement: leadership is the ideal.	The emphasis is on belonging to organizations or other in-groups; membership is the ideal.
Belief is placed in individual decision-making.	Belief is placed in group decision-making.
Organizations have a modest influence on a person's well-being.	Organizations have a great influence on a person's well-being.

Masculinity

Masculinity indicates the extent to which the dominant values in a society tend towards assertiveness and the acquisition of things, and away from concern for people and the quality of life.

Masculinity	Femininity
Sex roles in society are clearly differentiated.	Sex roles in society are more flexible and fluid.
Men should dominate in society.	Equality between sexes should prevail.
One lives to work.	One works in order to live.
The drive to get things done is provided by personal ambition.	The motivation to help others is provided by the ideal of service.
Some occupations are considered typically male, others female.	There is less occupational segregation on the basis of sex.

Time

The time dimension indicates the extent to which a society pursues a practical ethic, places importance on doing rather than in believing as a means of achieving greater virtue, and accepts persistence and perseverance as necessary in pursuit of whatever goals.

Long-term orientation	Short-term orientation
Acceptance of technological innovation.	Preference for doing things in time-honoured way.
Thrifty, being sparing with resources.	Social pressure to 'keep up with the Joneses', even if it means overspending.
Large savings, funds available for investment.	Small savings, little money for investment.
Perseverance towards slow results.	Quick results expected.
Willingness to subordinate oneself for a purpose.	Concern with 'saving face'.
Capacity for change considered necessary in environment.	Initiative or risk-taking considered threatening to stability.

Distribute the handout that illustrates the fifth dimension, called time. Again, explain about the continuum between two extremes. (10 minutes)

Distribute the handout of 'Range and average scores of 50 countries'. Ask pupils to read the explanation at the top of the figure; accept questions from those who are not clear about what is being represented by the five ranges.

Ask pupils, working individually, to rate themselves on each of the five ranges. For each self-rating, pupils should make an X at the appropriate point on each range. Stress that they are not to be overly concerned about arriving at some precise mathematical figure representing their personal degree of power distance, uncertainty avoidance, individualism, masculinity and time. The self-ratings should be done fairly quickly and intuitively, although in conjunction with the lists that appear in the handouts. Also stress that pupils are rating themselves as individuals, not with respect to their native cultures. If you are asked, say that it is theoretically possible, though practically unlikely, that an individual could realistically rate him or herself above the top or below the bottom of the ranges indicated. (10 minutes)

Divide into small groups of between four and eight. Within small groups, pupils should describe to each other why they rated themselves as they did on the ranges. Pupils may alter their self-ratings if they wish as a result of this discussion. (25 minutes)

Bring the class together again and quickly collect individual scores for each dimension. Add and find the class average, which can then be marked on the handout sheets by the pupils.

Distribute the handout 'Scores on four dimensions for 50 countries ...'. Accept questions from those who are not clear about how to interpret this table. Now ask pupils to find their own country on the chart. Ask pupils to make a tick at the location of their country on each range on the previous handout, and to think about the differences, if any, between the ratings they gave themselves, the class average and the ratings Hofstede found for their country. (10 minutes)

Read or paraphrase the following statement by Hofstede: 'Characterizing a national culture does not, of course, mean that every person in the nation has all the characteristics assigned to that culture. Therefore, in describing national cultures we refer to the common elements within each nation – the national norm – but we are not describing individuals.'

Now ask for a few volunteers to explain why one or two of the scores they assigned to themselves were different from the scores on the same dimensions found by Hofstede during his research. You may wish to ask for such explanations only from those pupils whose self-rating scores differ from Hofstede's scores by more than 15 or 20 points. (20 minutes)

Ask the pupils to find on the country chart (the last handout) the country to which they will be travelling or with which they will have contact through a school link. For the country selected, pupils should make a mark of some other kind at the appropriate locations on each range as before. Ask pupils to consider individually the following questions and to jot down answers for later discussion. (15 minutes)

Range and average scores of 50 countries on Hofstede's dimensions of culture★

Explanation. Look at the first continuum, for power distance. The country with the largest power distance scored 104; the country with the smallest power distance scored 11. The average of all 50 countries' scores on power distance was 56. The first continuum illustrates the range from 104 to 11, and the average of 56. The other three continua are organized and presented in identical fashion.

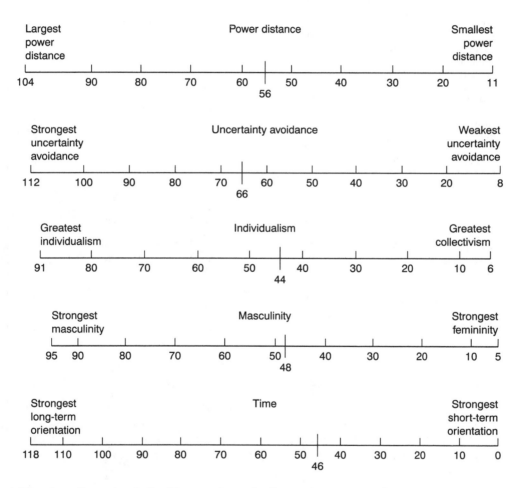

★ The time dimension is for 23 countries only, from separate research.

Scores on four dimensions for 50 countries and on the time dimension for 23 countries

Country	Power distance	Uncertainty avoidance	Individualism	Masculinity	Time
Argentina	49	86	46	56	
Australia	36	51	90	61	31
Austria	11	70	55	79	
Bangladesh					40
Belgium	65	94	75	54	
Brazil	69	76	38	49	65
Canada	39	48	80	52	23
Chile	63	86	23	28	
China					118
Colombia	67	80	13	64	
Costa Rica	35	86	15	21	
Denmark	18	23	74	16	
Ecuador	78	67	8	63	
El Salvador	66	94	19	40	
Finland	33	59	63	26	
France	68	86	71	43	
Germany (FR)	35	65	67	66	31
Great Britain	35	35	89	66	25
Greece	60	112	35	57	
Guatemala	95	101	6	37	
Hong Kong	68	29	25	57	96
India	77	40	48	56	61
Indonesia	78	48	14	46	
Iran	58	59	41	43	
Ireland	28	35	70	68	
Israel	13	81	54	47	
Italy	50	75	76	70	
Japan	54	92	46	95	80
Jamaica	45	13	39	68	
Korea, South	60	85	18	39	75
Malaysia	104	36	26	50	
Mexico	81	82	30	69	
Netherlands	38	53	80	14	44
New Zealand	22	49	79	58	30
Nigeria					16
Norway	31	50	69	8	
Pakistan	55	70	14	50	0
Panama	95	86	11	44	
Peru	64	87	16	42	
Philippines	94	44	32	64	19
Poland					32
Portugal	63	104	27	31	
Singapore	74	8	20	48	48
South Africa	49	49	65	63	
Spain	57	86	51	42	
Sweden	31	29	71	5	33
Switzerland	34	58	68	70	
Taiwan	58	69	17	45	87
Thailand	64	64	20	34	56
Turkey	66	85	37	45	
Uruguay	61	100	36	38	
USA	40	46	91	62	29
Venezuela	81	76	12	73	
Yugoslavia	76	88	27	21	
Zimbabwe					25

- What do the gaps between my own self-ratings, my native country's ratings (by Hofstede) and the other country's ratings (by Hofstede) suggest about possible misunderstandings on both sides when I am with people from the other country?
- In each case of possible misunderstanding, how can I prepare to cope with such situations when they happen?

Divide the class into groups of four to eight and ask each group to discuss the questions. Ask the pupils to try to arrive at some consensus regarding the types of preparations that can be made in order to cope successfully with value differences. Ask each group to prepare its own list. (25 minutes)

Groups should present short reports to the whole class. Summarize the exercise.

Variations

Before handing out 'Scores on four dimensions for 50 countries ...', ask the pupils to make 'assumptions' about where the country to be visited might be located on the ranges. Later, they could compare assumptions with the score on the chart. Discuss possible stereotypes underlying the assumptions.

Of course, the exercise can also be done with a class preparing for a visit by a class from another country. Similarly, it could be done during the exchange visit with both groups present. Compare scores in bicultural discussion groups. Discuss how this exercise might help them to understand each other better.

For multicultural classes, explain the dimensions as above and then ask pupils to find their country of origin on the chart. There will be differences in part because the pupils of 'different' origin will not be fully representative of their former culture/country. Ask pupils to consider the questions as above and to jot down their answers.

Another variation is simply to use the exercise for a monocultural class as a way of demonstrating research on cultural differences.

Comments

It has to be noted that the data used by Hofstede were collected on the basis of national cultures. Therefore the statistical data used in this exercise do not reflect possible differences, such as between French- and Flemish-speaking Belgium or between different cultural groups represented in many countries included in the research. The different dimensions could be dealt with one at a time in separate lessons. More information on the time dimension can be found in the book *Cultures and Organizations* by Geert Hofstede.

References
AFS Orientation Handbook, Vol. IV (New York: AFS Intercultural Programs, 1984). Copyright © AFS Intercultural Programs, Inc. Reproduced with permission.
Geert Hofstede, *Culture and Organizations* (Maidenhead: McGraw-Hill, 1991). Reproduced with permission of the publisher.

Field Exercise   CU/CD 3

Category
• Cultural differences

Learning objectives
• To understand intercultural learning in a practical sense.
• To try to communicate with people from a different culture.
• To experience communication with people from a different culture.
• To find out more about a different culture.

Duration
One half-day.

Group
Can be monocultural or multicultural but should be from one class or school. Can be involved in exchange (as preparation), project or any other activity relating to intercultural learning. Size of group is variable.

Description of exercise
Interview activity to research a specific topic or assumption, or simply to find out more about other people or a specific cultural group. If it is in own community, the field investigation describes what others in the community think. If done in another place, it can be a comparison with own community.

Instructions
1   Introduction to exercise; objectives, structure.
2   Interview exercise practice: groups of three; A interviews B and C observes (20 minutes interview, 10 minutes evaluation); take turns, so everyone has been in each of the three positions. (total 90 minutes)
3   Brainstorming. Who could be interviewed? Age, sex, cultural/ethnic, socio-economic factors to consider. (15 minutes)
4   Individual choice: what is my area of interest? Whom do I want to interview? (5 minutes)
5   Find one or two partners with the same interest. (15 minutes)
6   Plan an intercultural encounter/interview with partners; formulate questions to be asked during interview.
7   Go!
8   Produce a written record of results from the interview.
9   Share in plenary.

Guidelines for conducting interviews
• Tell the person being interviewed why you wish to make the interview and how long the interview will take.
• Be polite, show respect, dress appropriately.
• Use open questions (questions which require explanation for response) more than closed questions (questions which are answered with yes or no).

- Prepare core questions to be asked in all interviews.
- Practise interviewing.

Variations

One can skip the interview practice; one can also skip the brainstorming. Instead, the teacher could formulate the questions. It is preferable, though, to do the whole exercise as outlined above.

Comments

The people to be interviewed do not have to be 'exotic'. One can approach any group that is different from oneself. Be specific in your objectives rather than general. The interview should be realistic. The exercise is very useful as preparation for a later field study as part of a visit abroad.

Reference

Idea developed from H. Fennes *et al.*, *Projektunterricht 'Interkulturelles Lernen in der Schule'* (Vienna: Bundesministerium für Unterricht und Kunst, 1984). Used with permission.

Field Study   CU/CD 4

Categories
- Culture/cultural differences
- Lifestyles

Learning objectives
- To get to know a wide range of aspects of another culture: values, lifestyles, traditions, everyday life, rituals, patterns of relationships; but also geography, history, demography, economy, etc.
- To overcome barriers to getting in contact with people one does not know.
- To acquire information and knowledge independently as well as in teamwork.
- To encourage intensive encounter with another country and culture.

Duration

To ensure a significant learning process a full day is needed for this exercise: approximately 1 hour for introduction and preparation, half a day for the field exercise itself, and at least 2 hours for evaluation. Preparation, field exercise and evaluation can be done on different days.

Group

Can be used for group/class of any size. If the group is larger than 40 pupils one can divide into smaller groups for the evaluation, with one teacher/facilitator for each evaluation group. The exercise is best used for a class/group during a visit abroad. Pupils of the (native) partner class/school could serve as interpreters/guides but *must not* help to answer the questions or do the assignments.

Description of exercise

Pupils visiting another country are asked to do a number of assignments in small teams of three to five pupils each. Through interviews with local inhabitants, they should enquire about a wide range of aspects of life in the country they are visiting: values, lifestyles, traditions, everyday life, rituals, patterns of relationships; but also geography, history, demography, economy, etc. In an evaluation the pupils share their experiences and findings.

Supplies/resources

For each team the teacher(s) has/have to prepare a different list of assignments according to the attached guidelines. A greater balance and richness would be derived if the assignments were designed and developed by the teachers of both the receiving and the visiting class/school. In any case, detailed knowledge and experience of the country visited is necessary for the assignments. For practising the interview in a role-play, it is useful to prepare extra questions or assignments.

Instructions

1   Introduction of exercise: objectives, structure. (5 minutes)
2   Divide into small teams of three to five pupils each. The resources and skills of the class (for example, foreign language skills) should be spread equally over these teams; they should also have similar male–female ratios, etc. (5 minutes)
3   Hand out assignments for each team. Teams should not share their assignments or consult with each other. Teams should then look for a place where they can work independently without being disturbed (for example, different classrooms). Before the teams leave, advise them of the following tasks. Ask each team to develop plans and strategies. Ask teams to go through an interview role-play with one of their assignments or with assignments specifically prepared for this purpose. They should take turns within the teams, so that everyone has been in the role of the interviewer. (40 to 60 minutes)
4   Teams go out to do their assignments. (3 to 4 hours)
5   Lunch/dinner with guest from the visited country.
6   Teams prepare presentation for plenary. They should prepare a flip-chart as well as a sketch about their most impressive experience. (30 to 60 minutes)
7   Teams meet in plenary to share their experiences and findings: presentation of flip-charts and sketches; presentation of a piece of culture, including explanation of meaning and how it was acquired; short reports. (10 minutes per team)
8   Discussion in plenary:
    •   What has been learned about the visited country? What has been learned about one's own country?
    •   Did one become aware of any prejudices? What were they? Were they questioned or corrected?
    •   What has been learned about oneself? What has been learned about relating to other people?
    •   How did the people questioned react? Was the reaction expected/unexpected? Why?

- What were the most surprising experiences? What were the most impressive experiences?
- What experiences of overcoming barriers in relating to people did one not know of before? What communication problems were encountered? How were they solved? (60 minutes)

Guidelines for questions and assignments

Give pupils one or more names of persons who are or have been important in the country they are visiting: writers, painters, architects, politicians, scientists, etc. (do not take the most famous and therefore obvious ones). Ask pupils to enquire who these persons were (profession, meaning for the country, period they lived in, possible link to country where the pupils come from, etc.).

Confront pupils with various terms, expressions, words or names in the language of the country they are visiting that have a specific meaning with respect to history, tradition, politics, economy, everyday life, etc., and ask them to enquire about their meaning.

Ask pupils to make enquiries about the geography, demography and economy of the country: population, minorities, major political districts, regional capitals, business and economy, energy sources, etc.

Ask questions concerning the political and social system of the country: political institutions, distribution of power, political parties (goals, leaders, size), elections, other organizations or movements (e.g. Amnesty International, Greenpeace), social security, unemployment, retirement, private insurances, etc.

Ask pupils to buy at least three different daily newspapers and to find out the most important issues of the day. Is it possible to draw conclusions with respect to the political orientation of these newspapers?

Ask pupils to make enquiries about the media in the country they are visiting. How many newspapers, radio and television stations? Are they private or public? What is their political orientation? Can one receive radio/TV broadcasts from abroad?

Ask pupils to enquire about income and costs in the country they are visiting. How much do people in various jobs earn (for example, workers, nurses, teachers, doctors)? What are the costs of a loaf of bread, a pint of milk, a pint of beer in the pub, a pack of cigarettes, bus and train tickets, cars, rent for an apartment, etc.?

Ask pupils to find out the status of various occupations: workers, salespersons, civil servants, teachers, nurses, doctors, etc.

Ask pupils to enquire about the school system in the country they are visiting: general structure, types of school, structure within schools, teacher education, style of education, curricula, methods, funding of schools, school hours, etc.

Ask pupils to interview people in the street:

- about their opinion with respect to specific topics in the country that are relevant at the moment;
- about their attitude towards the country where the pupils come from;
- about people they know from the country the pupils come from;
- about their views on Europe, etc.

Ask pupils to enquire about specific links and relationships between their own country and the country they are visiting – historic, economic, cultural, etc.

Ask pupils to ask people in the street the following questions.

- Where would they want to go if they had won a one-month trip without a cost limit? Why would they want to go there?
- What would they do if they had won the equivalent of 100,000 ecu?
- What would one have to do to get married to a person in this country? What administrative steps are necessary? Would there be a difference for a foreigner, and if yes, what would it be? What would the marriage ceremony be like?
- How would one become acquainted with a girl or boy in this country?
- How would you start a new business in this country (for example, a restaurant)? Would there be a difference for a foreigner? If yes, what would it be?
- What would be typical dishes of this country and how would they be prepared (detailed recipes)?

Ask pupils to buy specific things for everyday use, such as bread, butter, cheese, soap, stamps, a pen, a battery, a film.

Advise pupils to perform certain tasks, such as mailing a letter, changing money, asking for a specific telephone number, taking a public bus to a certain stop, going for a cup of coffee (or the cultural equivalent).

Ask each small group to invite one or two 'locals' to lunch/dinner with the class/large group.

Ask each small group to get a 'piece of culture' of the country they are visiting – something that in their opinion is characteristic of this culture and in this culture has a special meaning and (non-material) value. It can be an object of everyday life or something special or symbolic.

Variation
The assignments can also be solely directed towards the community and the local surroundings, so that the pupils become familiar in detail with the community they are visiting. In a second field study, one could enquire about the visited country as a whole. The exercise can also be made into a competition between the different teams with the pupils of the partner class/school serving as a jury.

Evaluation
This exercise allows pupils to get to know another country on different levels: on a cognitive level by collecting information and acquiring knowledge; on an emotional level by experiencing barriers of communication and relating to people one does not know; on a personal level by developing relationships with people of the visited country.

Comments
The exercise can be done by the visiting class while the pupils of the partner class are following their regular lessons. Nevertheless, both groups/classes have to be involved in the evaluation. Of course, the host country teachers can design assign-

ments for their pupils at a different level and with a different content (see also the 'Field exercise', CU/CD 3, in this book). Another possibility would be to involve the host country pupils as interpreters or guides, but they must not help the visiting pupils to answer the questions or do the assignments.

Reference
Intercultural Centre, Vienna, 1991. Used with permission.

Piece of Culture   CU/CI 1

Categories
• Cultural identity/own culture
• Cultural differences, values

Learning objectives
• To become aware of own cultural identity.
• To get to know other cultures.
• To become aware of variety of identities within own culture/country.
• To become aware of connection/coherence between cultural identity and values.
• To become aware of differences between cultures.

Duration
From 60 to 80 minutes.

Group
Can be used for a group of any size. The exercise is most interesting in multicultural groups but can also be used in monocultural groups, as well as in a bicultural setting within a class exchange.

Supplies/resources
If possible, prepare a worksheet with the questions asked in step 2.

Description of exercise
Pupils/participants present an object that in their opinion is characteristic for their culture. They also describe why they have chosen this object and in what way it is meaningful to people in their country and to themselves.

Instructions
1 In a previous session (or in information to this session) pupils/participants are asked to bring a 'piece of their culture'. It should be an object that in their opinion is characteristic of their culture and has a special meaning and (non-material) value. It can be an object of everyday life or something special or symbolic. When using this exercise during an exchange one should ask the pupils to choose the 'piece of culture' before going on the trip. Advise

participants/pupils not to show their piece of culture to anyone else (which means they have to wrap it) and not to talk about it with their classmates.

2   Ask pupils to answer the following questions just for themselves on a piece of paper (it is useful to prepare a worksheet for this purpose).
  •   Why have you chosen this 'piece of culture'?
  •   What do you associate it with? What does it mean to you personally?
  •   What does it mean to other people in your country?
  •   Is it meaningful in everyday life or just for special occasions?
  •   What makes it so characteristic/typical of your country?
  •   Try to define the term 'culture'.
      (10 to 15 minutes)
3   Divide into small multicultural groups (mix groups culturally as much as possible) of approximately eight pupils each.
4   Ask small groups in a first round to guess which 'pieces of culture' all the other participants/pupils have brought and why they are making this guess/assumption. Make a list on a flip-chart. (5 minutes)
5   In a second round everyone shows his or her 'piece of culture' and explains it according to his or her answers to questions asked in step 2. (20 to 30 minutes)
6   Ask small groups to discuss the following questions.
  •   How would they define the term 'culture'?
  •   What is characteristic about the cultures represented in the group?
  •   What are the values underlying these characteristics?
  •   To what extent do pupils identify with the characteristics described in their 'piece of culture'? Why?
      Ask groups to summarize results on flip-charts. (15 minutes)
7   Meet in plenary and let groups share their results. Summarize and close session. (5 minutes)

Variations

If you have not asked the participants/pupils before leaving home to bring along a 'piece of culture' ask them to look for a piece in their luggage or any of the belongings they have with them. Many things from everyday life (such as clothes, things in a wallet or pocket) are quite characteristic of one's culture. If a pupil does not find anything appropriate, he or she can think of a 'piece of culture' and present it written on a piece of paper.

One can consider the 'piece of culture' as an event, a tradition, an institution, a symbol, etc. In this case, it is usually not possible to bring this 'piece of culture' along. So one has to ask the pupils to write a description of this symbolic or abstract 'piece of culture' and then to discuss it according to the instructions above. The assignment for the pupils is: 'Which tradition, event, institution, etc., do you think is so important to people of your country, cultural group or ethnic group that it would cause a riot or protest if it were taken away or prohibited?'

Evaluation

  •   What do I think is characteristic about the culture I am part of? What do others think?

- Do I identify personally with what I think is characteristic about the culture I come from?
- What is characteristic about other cultures? Do I feel attracted by it? Am I afraid of it?
- What are the values underlying all these characteristics?

Comments
Guessing about what the others have brought or described as their 'piece of culture' will actually reveal stereotypes and prejudices that can be discussed separately.

In a monocultural setting, the exercise serves simply to make one aware of one's own culture and of the different perceptions of one's own culture by different people of the same culture.

Reference
Idea and exercise developed by EFIL in cooperation with the European Youth Centre, Strasbourg, 1987. Further developed by the Intercultural Centre, Vienna, 1990. Used with permission.

Cultural Quotations   CU/CI 2

Categories
- Cultural identity/own culture
- Values

Learning objectives
- To become aware of own cultural identity.
- To become aware of the variety of identities within own culture/country.
- To become aware of the connection and coherence between cultural identity and values.
- To become aware of differences between cultures.

Duration
About 60 minutes. Can be expanded.

Group
Can be used for class/group of any size. The exercise was originally designed for a monocultural setting but can easily be modified to bicultural or multicultural settings.

Supplies/resources
Sufficient copies of a quotation list (about ten quotations) referring to culture, values, lifestyles, behaviour and traditions of own country. These quotations can come from literature, history, research, social science, newspapers, TV, radio, film, theatre, etc. An example is: 'The highest degree of recognition one can get in our country is jealousy' (André Heller, Austria).

Description of exercise
Participants/pupils identify with quotations from literature or well-known people from their country/culture and discuss in small groups why and how they identify with these quotations. Conclusions in plenary.

Instructions
1   Introduce the exercise – objectives, structure, schedule. (5 minutes)
2   Hand out list with quotations and ask pupils to choose:
    *   one which they personally identify most with;
    *   one which they think describes best the culture of their country. (10 minutes)
3   Divide the class into small groups of six to eight pupils each in such a way that pupils who choose the same quotations go into different groups, resulting in a diversity of chosen quotations in each group. Let groups discuss the following questions.
    *   Why and how do they identify with the first quotations (personal identification) they have chosen? Which values/lifestyles/behaviours relate to this identification? What makes my cultural identity? What are the consequences?
    *   Why have they chosen the second quotation (describing the culture)? Which values/lifestyles/behaviours relate to this identification?
    *   Are the two quotations different? If yes, how do they deal with the ambiguity resulting from this?
    *   What stereotypes they have about their own culture relate to one or both quotations?
    *   How do the quotations chosen relate to stereotypes and prejudices people from other countries have about their culture? (30 minutes)
4   Share results of group discussions in plenary. Reflect especially on stereotypes one has about one's own country/culture/people. Make sure that pupils become aware of the fact that the image of one's own culture is also stereotyped. (15 minutes)
5   It is also possible to ask pupils to write a short essay on 'My culture – our culture'. (optional, 30 to 40 minutes, can be a separate session or assigned as homework)
6   Summarize and close session.

Variations
One could additionally ask pupils to choose those quotations they identify least with and they think describe least the culture of their country.

A more lively method to choose quotations and form groups is the following. Put a sufficient number of copies (at least five) of each quotation (just one quotation per sheet) on a pin board or the like. Let pupils take those they choose off the board and have them marked 'personal identity', 'our culture', etc. They should form groups by pinning them on their shirt, jacket or sweater and walking around looking at the others' choices.

One can intensify the exercise by asking the pupils to find the quotations themselves, either as homework or from a set of books, newspapers, magazines, etc., in the classroom. It is also possible to interview parents, brothers or sisters, pupils from other classes, other teachers and people in the street about their 'cultural quotations'.

A very lively variation on this exercise is to use proverbs instead of quotations. Proverbs usually communicate attitudes, values and beliefs and thus serve as witnesses to the social, political, ethical and religious patterns of thinking and behaviour of a cultural group. For example, the proverb 'early to bed, early to rise' reflects the value of diligence and discipline. Ask the pupils to do a brainstorming on proverbs and list them on a flip-chart. Otherwise proceed as outlined in the instructions above.

The exercise could be used during a class exchange or within a school link not including an exchange. In this case, one needs to develop two different sets of quotations in the respective languages (possibly translations have to be provided to ensure full understanding of the quotations from the other country). The use of the exercise in this setting also allows pupils to discuss stereotypes and prejudices about each others' cultures and thus covers another learning area. This variation could also involve foreign language learning as well as touching on history, literature, media, etc., in the other country.

Of course, this exercise can also be used in a multicultural class: in which case, one needs a set of quotations for each cultural/ethnic group. For the rest see the variation for a class exchange/school link above.

Evaluation

What is my cultural identity? Where does it come from? What stereotypes do I have about my own culture? Where do they come from? Be careful to respond immediately to any nationalistic remarks made by the pupils since quotations also tend to refer to the nation. A nationalistic dynamic would be destructive to openness towards other cultures and possibly would enforce existing prejudices and the rejection resulting from them. Nationalistic attitudes are normally combined with a derogatory attitude towards other cultures. In this case, discuss the difference between culture and nation.

Comments

This exercise can easily be integrated in a language or literature class. It is very useful as preparation for a class exchange (visit abroad as well as receiving a class) to become aware of one's own cultural identity and to discuss and reflect on the concept of culture as such.

Reference

Idea developed jointly by Intercultural Centre and Österreichischer Informationsdienst für Entwicklungspolitik, Vienna, 1989. Used with permission.

Educational Paths and Occupational Options Questionnaire CU/CI 3

Categories
- Cultural identity/own culture
- Lifestyles/behaviour

Learning objectives
- To become aware of possible educational paths and occupational options in own country.
- To become aware of own future perspectives with respect to education and occupation.
- To compare own future perspectives with those of others in my class/school.
- To compare education and occupation options in own country with those in partner class/school/country.

Duration
First session 60 to 90 minutes. Second session (one or more days later) about 50 minutes. Sessions can be expanded, additional sessions can be added.

Group
Can be used for class of any size but also for a whole school – monocultural or multicultural. Best used for school link or class exchange.

Description of exercise
This exercise is very useful for a class exchange or for a school link. The two partner classes or groups of two partner schools (it can also be used for a multi-cultural exchange/link) complete a questionnaire on educational paths and occupational options and compare their results within their own class/school as well as with those of the partner class/school.

Supplies/resources
Enough copies of the questionnaire for all pupils participating in the exercise. If the exercise is used for a class exchange, the questionnaire should be either bilingual (to provide equal understanding of the questions for all) or in a third language which is foreign to both.

Instructions

FIRST SESSION

1 Introduce the exercise – objectives, structure, schedule – if possible in both
   languages. (5 minutes)
2 Hand out the questionnaire to pupils of both classes (receiving and visiting) and
   ask them to complete the questionnaire (15 to 20 minutes). Encourage pupils to
   answer spontaneously but leave enough time for everyone to finish.
3 Divide the two classes into bicultural groups of six to eight pupils each (three to
   four from each country represented) and let them share the results of their questionnaires individually. They should go through the questionnaire question by
   question and indicate why they answered it the way they did. (20 to 30 minutes)
4 Let the groups discuss what they have found to be significant for pupils from
   the two countries. What did they find they had in common, what was different? (10 minutes)
5 Meet in plenary and share the results from the small groups. Ask for conclusions
   and summarize. (10 to 20 minutes)
6 Ask for volunteers from both classes to evaluate the questionnaires statistically
   for the next meeting.
7 Close the first session.

SECOND SESSION

8 Ask volunteers to present results of evaluation. (10 minutes)
9 Let pupils discuss in bicultural groups of six to eight the result of the evaluation.
   (30 minutes)
   • Are the results from their own class typical for their country?
   • Are the results from the partner class what they would have expected or
     different? What would they have expected? Why?
   • How do the results reflect the values, lifestyles and behaviour of the two
     countries?
10 Share the results from the small groups in plenary, summarize, close session. (10
   minutes)

Variations
The results from the questionnaire could be evaluated statistically (possibly using
computers) during a mathematics lesson and be presented with visualization
through pie charts and bar graphs, etc.
   The enquiry can be expanded to the whole school and the class working on this
project could then make a statistical evaluation (see above). The same can be done
in the partner school before the visit and the results can be shared with all pupils of
both schools. The results could be picked up by teachers in other classes for similar
discussions, thus involving the whole school.
   The exercise can be used for a school link without exchange: the two
classes/schools complete and evaluate the questionnaires and share the results.
There is no direct discussion possible but the classes/schools can send each other a

Educational paths and occupational options questionnaire

(Please tick the boxes. Multiple answers are possible.)

1. Occupation
   1.1 If you had to decide now on an occupation, which one would you choose?

☐	skilled worker	☐	artist
☐	craftsman	☐	teacher
☐	athlete	☐	manager
☐	salesperson	☐	technician
☐	nurse	☐	scientist
☐	office worker	☐	journalist
☐	civil servant	☐	minister of religion
☐	medical doctor	☐	other: _____
☐	lawyer		

   1.2 What influences you in choosing an occupation?

☐	image and prestige	☐	talent
☐	interest	☐	challenge
☐	potential income	☐	social engagement/idealism
☐	labour market	☐	family tradition
☐	self-realization	☐	other: _____

   1.3 Who is giving you advice on your choice or on whose advice are you basing your decision?

   - ☐ parents
   - ☐ brother(s)/sister(s)
   - ☐ teachers
   - ☐ fellow pupils/colleagues
   - ☐ friends
   - ☐ vocational guidance counsellor/careers adviser
   - ☐ other: _____

2. Education
   2.1 What educational path must you pursue to reach your goals for your future occupation? How much time will it take?

   2.2 Indicate what skills you need for working in the Europe of tomorrow:

☐	ability to carry through	☐	ability to cooperate
☐	honesty	☐	ability to deal with conflict
☐	friendliness	☐	efficiency
☐	leadership skills	☐	political skills

☐ ability to work in teams   ☐ diplomacy
☐ idealism   ☐ technical skills
☐ communication skills   ☐ managerial skills
☐ foreign language skills   ☐ professional competence
☐ other: _____

2.3 Which of these skills are acquired through
family environment:

school:

university:

further education:

professional experience:

own initiative:

other:

3. Future options
3.1 Do you intend to work abroad sometimes?
☐ yes
☐ temporarily
☐ no

3.2 Estimate the job security and potential income of the occupation you are aiming at:
job security
☐ secure   ☐ insecure/risky
☐ rather secure   ☐ do not know
☐ rather insecure

income
☐ high   ☐ below average
☐ above average   ☐ low
☐ average   ☐ do not know

3.3 What monthly net income do you think you will receive at the age of 35 (based on incomes and currency value of today)?
☐ less than 1,000 ecu (or equivalent in respective currency)
☐ between 1,000 and 1,500 ecu
☐ between 1,500 and 2,000 ecu
☐ between 2,000 and 2,500 ecu
☐ between 2,500 and 3,000 ecu
☐ above 3,000 ecu

set of questions to find out more about educational and professional careers in each other's countries.

A similar questionnaire could be developed for another theme or topic.

Evaluation
This exercise should allow pupils to become aware of their own educational and professional perspectives as well as of those of pupils from another country.

Comments
This exercise is a typical example of a project as part of a school link or class exchange: two classes/schools work simultaneously on the same topic and thus learn about their own and the other country and culture. The exercise can also be used for cross-curricular work: it can involve social sciences, mathematics, etc.

Reference
The questionnaire was developed by the Intercultural Centre, Vienna, 1992, and is used with permission.

Playing Regions   CU/CI 4

Categories
• Cultural identity
• Prejudices and stereotypes

Learning objectives
• To become aware of (cultural) diversity within one's own country.
• To become aware of prejudices about one's own culture and about regions in one's own country.

Duration
From 50 to 60 minutes.

Group
Between 10 and 30 participants. Good beginning for monocultural class.

Supplies/resources
Enough space (small rooms) for all small groups.

Description of exercise
A group activity that enables the expression and sharing of ideas about cultural diversity within own country through dramatic representation and discussion.

Instructions
1 Introduction to exercise; objectives, structure. (5 minutes)
2 Split up into small groups of six to eight participants each. Allow each group 20 minutes to think up and rehearse in separate rooms a short sketch to be performed in front of the others, which they think is typical of a specific region of their country. (15 minutes)

3   Each group performs its sketch in front of the others (should not last more than 5 minutes per small group).
4   Plenary discussion. (20 minutes)
   •   What was considered to be typical of the different regions of the country?
   •   Is this correct or not? Do we really know?
   •   What are the differences between the various regions of the country?
   •   What do they have in common?
   •   What is typical of the country as a whole?

Variations
Rehearsing can be given as an assignment in one class and the performance and discussion carried out in another class period.

Evaluation
This exercise should allow the participants to realize that there is no uniform picture of their country, but that there are similarities in the way other groups of inhabitants of the country are perceived.

Comments
This exercise is useful for monocultural groups, especially if the participants come from different regions within the same country. In this case, form small groups according to regions of origin and let them perform a sketch they think is typical of another region of the country.

Reference
Idea developed from H. Fennes *et al.*, *Projektunterricht 'Interkulturelles Lernen in der Schule'* (Vienna: Bundesministerium für Unterricht und Kunst, 1984). Used with permission.

Associative Drawing   CU/CI 5

Categories
• Cultural identity/own culture
• Stereotypes/prejudices

Learning objectives
• To become aware of and to learn about one's own culture.
• To become aware of stereotypes and prejudices about one's own culture and possible reasons for them.
• To become aware of ethnocentrism and a 'we' consciousness.
• To become aware of cultural differences.

Duration
One to two hours.

Group
Can be monocultural, multicultural, two classes/groups from different schools. If

larger than 25 to 30, you will need to form smaller groups for discussion.

Supplies
Blu-tack, sticky tape, large sheets of paper (newsprint, butcher or flip-chart paper), felt-tip pens, magazines, newspapers, etc.

Description of exercise
A group activity that permits the expression and sharing of ideas about factors of own culture through drawing and discussion.

Instructions
1 Introduction to exercise; objectives, structure.
2 Ask the group to produce a series of associative drawings and/or collages on the theme 'our country'. The titles of these drawings could be:
   • What is typical of people of our country?
   • What is typical of my country in comparison with other countries?
   • How do foreigners see my country?
   • How do the people of my country want to be seen abroad?
3 Present drawings in plenary and discuss results.
4 Drawing contrasts. The participants should first draw a 'typical' situation for their own country (taken from family life, school, community life, leisure, etc.) and then imagine and draw a similar situation from another culture (in the case of an exchange visit, the culture of the partner school/country).
5 Present drawings in plenary and discuss results.
   • What do the different cultures presented have in common? What makes them different?
   • What is characteristic for my country? What about me and my country is specifically cultural?

Variations
The drawings or collages can also be done in small groups of two or three participants. Role-plays or sketches could be used, depicting everyday scenes.

Evaluation
Discuss how the drawings produced reflect stereotypes about one's own country. Also explain that stereotypes and prejudices about a country can be caused by the way representatives of this country present it to others.

Comments
If the group is multicultural, let everybody in step 2 draw associations to his or her own country. In step 4 the contrasts drawn should involve the cultures of the pupils present.

Reference
Idea developed from H. Fennes *et al.*, *Projektunterricht 'Interkulturelles Lernen in der Schule'* (Vienna: Bundesministerium für Unterricht und Kunst, 1984). Used with permission.

Sunshine and Rain   CU/CI 6

Categories
- Cultural identity/own culture
- Cultural differences

Learning objectives
- To understand that geography, including climate, is a part of culture.
- To be aware that other cultures respond to or think about sunshine and rain (or mountains and plains) differently.

Duration
One class period. Could be extended as a theme for an exchange or correspondence link.

Group
Any size. Could be monocultural, bicultural or multicultural composition. It is probably most interesting to have a bicultural or multicultural group representing different climatic conditions, e.g. Italy and Finland.

Description
Research (homework) and general discussion on two climatic/geographical features to enable awareness of these being part of our culture.

Instructions
1 Introduce topic, objectives, structure of exercise. (10 minutes)
2 Let all express themselves on the subjects of sunshine and rain (verbally, in writing, drawing pictures). When ideas seem to have been exhausted, ask participants whether they think people in different parts of the world might say different things on the subjects. You could begin with examples like: What would a desert-dweller say about rain if it had not rained for years? What would an umbrella salesperson have to say? A flood victim? Someone who lives above the Arctic Circle?
3 Suggest the following areas of research and ask for volunteers for each area. It is a matter of choice how many are covered. Participants will feel more involved if they are able to identify their own areas.
   - Sayings, proverbs and popular lore about weather.
   - Sunshine and rain in photographs, engravings, postcards, the arts.
   - Rain-making: rites, prayers, and modern techniques.
   - Protection from sun and rain: clothes, oils or other chemical preparations, adaptation of architecture, lifestyles.
   - Benefits of sun and rain: solar energy, reservoirs, water storage tanks (for the community, for individual homes).
   - Jobs. Are there jobs connected with sun and rain or jobs for which sun and rain are very important?
   - What do people do when it rains? When the sun shines?

- Observe sun and rain in the media and advertising.
- Observe sun in religion.

4 Based on the research findings (presentation to group on each area in whatever way deemed appropriate; could be small group reports, assembled projects of photographs, newspaper/magazine clippings, etc.), ask the group to discuss in small groups of about eight persons:
   - What is the impact of sunshine and rain on our culture?
   - How is it different from other world regions or even regions within our country with different climatic conditions?
   - Why do people from, for example, rainy climates opt to go on holiday to the Mediterranean?
   - Why is literature full of references to mist and fog?

5 If sunshine and rain are taken as a topic for a correspondence link, what are the differences between the two groups of correspondents?

Variations
Could be extended to other natural elements or geographical conditions, such as hail, wind, snow, hills, valleys, mountains, plains, woods, desert, etc.

Evaluation
Make sure that participants realize that the geography and climate in which they grow up has a bearing on how they think and feel about the world and how they relate to their natural environment.

Comments
This exercise makes the point that intercultural learning is not limited to the traditional purview of languages, history and the arts. A geography class in this instance could show a wider importance of the academic subject. The findings of the research and discussion would make interesting reading in local or school newspapers.

Reference
Idea developed from *Experiments in Intercultural Education, Guides for Intercultural Activities* (Strasbourg: Council for Cultural Co-operation, School Education Division, 1989). Used with permission.

Maps and Atlases   CU/CI 7

Categories
- Cultural identity/own culture
- Cultural differences

Learning objectives
- To become aware that a world view is often understood from a single cultural viewpoint.
- To understand that other cultures express different viewpoints in their drawing of maps and atlases.

Duration
One class period (with homework).

Group
Any size. Interesting for bicultural or multicultural groups but not necessary.

Description
Through the use of maps and atlases, participants gain understanding of how their world view is culturally (nationally) influenced and determined.

Supplies/resources
Variety of maps and atlases, preferably from a range of countries. (Securing these resources could be part of the homework. In the case of a class exchange or school link, obtain maps from the partner school.) Look for maps with an unusual perspective, e.g. north is not at the top of the page.

Instructions
1 Introduce topic, objectives and structure. We see the world egocentrically and know it from our own point of view. When nations represent the world by geographic maps, they also do it from their own perspective. These self-centred presentations of the world are politically and technically inevitable.
2 Ask pupils as homework to look at maps of their country in as many sources as possible: maps, atlases, dictionaries, advertising, newspapers. Pupils should be asked to reflect on the position of their country in relation to other countries and to the whole world in the map sources.
3 In small discussion groups. What is the meaning of this central position in terms of symbolism, value, political situation (centre of a former empire), cultural situation (language, modern history, Western orientation)? Look at the toponymy used: English names in the United Kingdom but also in non-English-speaking countries (Rome/Roma, Athens/Athina, Vienna/Wien). How are atlases organized? Why? What does this say about our cultural identity? What would someone from a small island country in the Caribbean feel about his or her 'place' in the world when looking at a British, or any European, atlas? What would a Brazilian atlas look like to a European?
4 Ask pupils to draw a map of their community or town. How does the community or town relate to the rest of the country, to towns nearby? Draw own country 'upside down'; how does Europe look if drawn from the North Pole? Discuss in small groups.

Variations
Can be used as an activity in a class link/exchange, which gives the possibility of a bicultural or binational perspective and comparison.

Evaluation
The centre of everyone's world is always where they are and this is natural. Cultural

identity can be translated into the extreme negativism of nationalism. By understanding the positioning of maps and atlases, the notion of single perspective is recognized.

Comments
Stating the obvious, this exercise fits well in the geography class.

Reference
Idea developed from *Experiments in Intercultural Education, Guides for Intercultural Activities* (Strasbourg: Council for Cultural Co-operation, School Education Division, 1989). Used with permission.

Lifestyles   LB 1

Categories
- Lifestyles and behaviour
- Values, cultural identity/own culture

Learning objectives
- To become aware of own and others' lifestyles.
- To become aware that one's own lifestyle can reflect one's own culture.
- To become aware that values influence one's lifestyle.
- To become aware of own culture.

Duration
Minimum 90 minutes.

Group
From 10 to 30 participants. Useful in a monocultural setting to demonstrate range of lifestyles. A multicultural class is also possible but requires sensitivity to values behind lifestyles.

Supplies
Copies of 'ways to live' lists, one for each participant.

Description of exercise
Brief descriptions (13) of 'ways to live' are rated by participants, followed by a discussion. The exercise enables pupils to acknowledge different lifestyles, perhaps to learn about some new ones, and to recognize that different lifestyles mean both synergy and conflict.

Instructions
1 Introduction to exercise; objectives, structure. Hand out 'ways to live' sheet. Allow participants 15 minutes to read it and clarify content if necessary.
2 Allow participants another 5 to 10 minutes to rate the different lifestyles individually according to the explanation.
3 Each participant should find a partner with a rating contrary to his or her own and the two should discuss their reasoning for their respective ratings.

4 Discussion in small groups (maximum seven participants):
- Which attitudes does the group have in common? How are they different?
- Which lifestyles are positively valued and/or practised in everyone's social environment? Which lifestyles are negatively valued and/or rejected?
- Which lifestyles are supported or represented by the various groups in one's social environment? Why?
- Which lifestyles conflict and which agree or complement one another?
- Which lifestyles could guarantee a peaceful life for everyone?

Summarize the results of the group's work on a flip-chart.
5 Share the results of the group's work in plenary and discuss similarities and differences.

Evaluation
This exercise allows participants to realize that lifestyles can be very different, even within a rather limited region.

Comments
This exercise is about lifestyles, not culture. It should therefore be used in tandem with activities that require or benefit from the difference between the two being made clear.

Reference
'Ways to live' adapted from Charles Morris, *Varieties of Human Value* (Chicago: University of Chicago Press, 1956), pp. 15–19. Reproduced with permission.

Ways to live

1 The individual actively participates in the social life of the community in order to understand, appreciate and preserve the best that people have attained. In this lifestyle, one wants the good things of life but in an orderly way. Life should have clarity, balance, refinement and control. Life is marked by discipline, intelligibility, good manners and predictability. Friendship is to be esteemed. Social change is to be made slowly and carefully so that what has been achieved in human culture is not lost. Restraint and intelligence should give order to an active life.

2 The individual for the most part goes it alone. Self-sufficiency, reflection, meditation and knowledge of the self are emphasized. One should aim to simplify one's external life, to moderate desires that depend upon physical and social forces outside of oneself. The centre of life should be found within oneself.

3 A sympathetic concern for others is central to life. Affection is the main thing. One should purify oneself, restrain one's self-assertiveness and become receptive, appreciative and helpful in relating to other persons.

4 The aim in life is to be open and receptive to things and persons and to delight in them. Such enjoyment requires that one be self-centred enough to be keenly aware of what is happening within oneself in order to be free for new happiness. Both solitude and sociability are necessary for the good life.

5 The social group rather than the individual is stressed. Persons are social, and persons are active; life should merge energetic group activity and cooperative group enjoyment. One should live outwardly with gusto, working with others to secure a pleasant and energetic social life.

6 Life is seen as dynamic and the individual as an active participant. The future depends primarily on what we do, not on what we feel or on our speculations. Improvement must always be made if there is to be progress. We should rely on technical advances made possible by scientific knowledge. The goal is in the solution of problems.

7 Life is about enjoyment, action and contemplation in about equal amounts. We should cultivate flexibility and be willing to accept things from all paths of life, giving no one thing exclusive allegiance. The goal of life is found in the dynamic integration of enjoyment, action and contemplation and in the interaction of various paths of life. We should use all possibilities as appropriate.

8 Enjoyment is the keynote of life: existing, savouring food and comfortable surroundings, talking with friends, rest and relaxation. Body at ease, calm in its movements, a willingness to nod and rest, gratitude to the world that feeds the body – so it should be.

9 Receptivity is the keynote of life. The good things of life come of their own accord. Sitting alone under the trees and the sky, open to nature's voices, calm and receptive, then can the wisdom from without enter within.

10 The good life is rationally directed and firmly pursues high ideals. Self-control is emphasized. One can with vigilance hold firm the reins of self-control, understand one's place in the world, guide one's actions by reason, maintain independence. In this way we can keep our human dignity and respect.

11 The contemplative life is the good life. The rich internal world of ideals, sensitive feelings, reverie, self-knowledge – this is our home. In giving up the world, we find the larger and finer sea of the inner self.

12 The use of the body's energy is the secret of a rewarding life. It is the active deed that is satisfying, the deed that meets the challenge of the present, the daring and adventurous. Outward energetic action, the excitement of power in the tangible present, is the way to live.

13 We should let ourselves be used by other persons in their growth, by the great objectives in the universe, for these purposes are dependable. We should be humble, constant, faithful, grateful for affection and protection but not demanding. We should be a serene, confident and quiet vessel of the great dependable powers that move to fulfil themselves.

Instructions (may be prepared as separate handout)
This list describes 13 different lifestyles that have been represented and put into action by different people at different times. The question is not which kind of life you now lead or which lifestyle is accepted in society or which lifestyle you would approve for others. The question is: how would you personally like to live?

Rate each of the attitudes to life given in the list using the numbers 0 to 3 and note them down on a piece of paper.

3 I am in favour of it.
2 I agree with it a little.
1 I have neither a negative nor positive attitude towards it.
0 I am against it.

Eating Rituals

LB 2

Categories
- Lifestyles/behaviour
- Cultural differences

Learning objectives
- To become aware that what seems obvious (eating rituals) is a matter of convention or lifestyle.
- To understand that the roots of rituals or daily habits can be found in cultural values and norms.

Duration
This can vary depending on interest and how used: one class period or extended as a theme for class exchange or correspondence with a school link in another country.

Group
Any size, but would work best with a bicultural/multicultural composition or component.

Description
Through use of a questionnaire, analysis of the findings and discussion, participants become aware that daily eating habits are influenced by their lifestyles and culture.

Supplies/resources
Copies of questionnaire.

Instructions
1 Introduce topic with objectives and structure of the exercise. (10 minutes)
2 Distribute questionnaire or ask the group to generate their own.
3 Possible target groups: the class itself, two classes engaged in an exchange, two or more schools engaged in a correspondence link, community-based interviews, others that you think of.
4 Assemble and sort the findings, making the point that the questionnaires are not to be graded, that there are no right or wrong answers, that the results will be used for discussion only. (The analysis of the questionnaires could be a good project for a small group of pupils who have a keen interest in computers.)
5 Discussion.
   - For a single class, divide into small groups of six to eight. Where were there common responses, where different? Why common or diverse?
   - For a class exchange divide into bicultural groups and discuss which questions produced the greatest diversity of response? Is this to do with more than lifestyle and how are the responses influenced by the culture?
   - For a community-based questionnaire, does the age of the respondents make a difference? If the community-based target group was multicultural, does this influence the response?

Questionnaire: Everyday meals

1   How many meals are eaten in the day?

2   For each meal:

- Where is it eaten?
- At what time?
- By whom?
- Who prepares it, serves it, clears the table?
- Are there any particular rituals connected to the meal, e.g. saying 'Bon appétit' before the meal?
- Where does everyone sit? Are there specific places for everyone? How do you choose your place?
- Does everyone begin and finish together?
- Do the children leave the table before the end of the meal?
- Is there an order for eating the food?
- What order do the courses come in?
- Do any of the eaters have particular roles at or during the meal?
- Do the eaters watch television during the meal? Listen to the radio?
- Do the eaters converse? About what? Is any subject 'forbidden' or taboo?
- Are there any other rules?

3   Which is the main meal?

4   Are there days of the week when meals (or some meals) are different? Which ones? How are they different? Is there a reason for the differences?

5   During the year or a lifetime are there special meals for celebrations or ceremonies? What are they? Describe them.

6   Ask a grandparent or other older person how meals were when he or she was your age. What are the differences? If eating habits have changed, why do you think this is?

- For all groups, what is the convention or lifestyle and what is rooted in the culture? What are the underlying values?

Variations
Not only could this exercise be used in a variety of settings but the topic could vary. What about celebrations, holidays, reading, playing games, etc.?

Evaluation
After a class has returned from an exchange, the discussion could be revisited, since the participants will undoubtedly have encountered differences in eating rituals while abroad. Did these differences 'make sense' in the family, community, environment abroad? If there were differences, what were the reasons and meanings?

Reference
Idea developed from *Experiments in Intercultural Education, Guides for Intercultural Activities* (Strasbourg: Council for Cultural Co-operation, School Education Division, 1989). Used with permission.

Time in Europe   LB 3

Categories
- Lifestyle/behaviour
- Cultural differences, values

Learning objectives
- To become aware of one's own use of time and what effect this has on one's lifestyle.
- To find out how time is used in another country (when using the exercise during a visit abroad).
- To become aware that time is used differently in different countries and that there are different concepts of time.
- To understand that the use of time is based on values.

Duration
From 60 to 120 minutes depending on group composition. Can be expanded to half a day. Can be done in two or more sessions.

Group
Can be used for a group/class of any size. If the group is larger than 40 pupils one can divide into smaller groups for the evaluation, with one teacher/facilitator for each evaluation group. The exercise is best used with a multicultural group or with a bicultural group within a class exchange. The exercise can also be used with a monocultural group as part of an intercultural learning project or as preparation for a trip abroad.

Description of exercise
Pupils look at their own use of time as well as at their estimate of the use of time by other people in their country and compare it with the use of time by pupils/people in other countries as well as with statistical data. They discuss differences as well as similarities, and what lifestyles and values are underlying the use of time.

Supplies/resources
A sufficient number of copies of the worksheet, which has to be adapted to the respective working situation. When the exercise is used for a class exchange the worksheet should be bilingual (to provide equal understanding of the questions for all). For each country represented in the group doing the exercise prepare a worksheet with the respective data from the tables with data from 21 European countries. Prepare enough copies for each country group. A sufficient number of copies of the complete tables with data from 21 European countries.

Instructions
This instruction is for the use of the exercise with a bicultural group during a class exchange. For other settings it has to be modified accordingly.

1 Introduce the exercise – objectives, structure, schedule – if possible in both languages. (5 minutes)
2 Hand out worksheets to pupils of both classes (receiving and visiting) and have them filled out individually. (15 minutes – encourage pupils to answer spontaneously but leave enough time for everyone to finish)
3 Divide the two classes into monocultural groups of three to four pupils each and let them share their answers to the questions in the worksheet. They should go through the worksheet question by question, quickly calculating average times for each small group (add times and divide by number of pupils in small group). No discussion should take place yet; clarification is possible. (15 to 20 minutes)
4 Hand out a worksheet with statistical data for the respective country group. Ask groups to compare these data with their group averages and to discuss significant differences and possible reasons for them. (10 minutes)
5 Form bicultural groups of six to eight pupils each by asking the monocultural groups from steps 3 and 4 to join a group from the other class. Ask groups to compare their respective average times as well as the statistical data and to discuss the following questions.
    • What are the major differences? What are possible reasons for these differences? How is the use of time reflected in lifestyles? What are the underlying values for the use of time?
    • Are the results of the partner class what they would have expected or different? What would they have expected? Why?
    • Have the differences of use of time resulted in misunderstanding or conflict during the exchange? If yes, what would be possible solutions for a constructive cooperation and relationship? (20 to 30 minutes)
6 Meet in plenary and share the results from the bicultural groups. Ask for conclusions and summarize. (10 to 20 minutes)

Worksheet

Indicate average times for getting up, starting work/school and going to bed (weekdays only; use a separate worksheet for Sundays/weekends/holidays):

_____ I get up
_____ my parents get up
_____ most people in my country get up

_____ my school starts
_____ most schools start
_____ my parents start working
_____ most people in my country start working

_____ I go to bed
_____ my parents go to bed
_____ most people in my country go to bed

_____ I have breakfast
_____ my parents have breakfast
_____ most people in my country have breakfast

_____ I have the midday meal
_____ my parents have the midday meal
_____ most people in my country have the midday meal

_____ I have the evening meal
_____ my parents have the evening meal
_____ most people in my country have the evening meal

Estimate how much time per day you use for the following activities (in hours/half-hours/quarter-hours):

Average time I use for	Average time most people in my country use for
_____ sleep	_____
_____ personal hygiene	_____
_____ housework	_____
_____ television	_____
_____ other media	_____
_____ recreation	_____
_____ trip to school	_____
_____ leisure/spare time	_____
_____ school/work	_____
_____ homework	_____
_____ socializing	_____
_____ being with my family	_____
_____ other	_____

When does the alarm go off?

	Getting up	Starting work	Going to bed
Austria	6:15	7:30	22:50
Belgium	7:15	8:30	23:00
Czechoslovakia[a]	5:45	7:00	23:00
Denmark	6:45	8:15	23:35
Finland	6:30	8:00	23:15
France	7:00	8:30	23:30
West Germany[a]	6:45	7:45	23:10
East Germany[a]	6:15	7:00	22:50
Greece	7:00	8:00	00:40
Hungary	5:45	7:15	23:05
Ireland	8:00	9:00	23:45
Italy	7:00	8:15	23:20
Luxembourg	7:00	8:00	23:20
Netherlands	7:00	8:15	00:00
Norway	7:00	8:00	23:30
Poland	6:00	7:00	23:10
Portugal	7:00	8:30	23:30
Spain	8:00	9:00	00:15
Sweden	6:15	8:00	23:15
Switzerland	6:45	7:45	23:15
United Kingdom	7:00	9:00	23:30

When do they eat?

	Breakfast	Lunch	Dinner
Austria	7:00	12:30	18:30
Belgium	7:30	12:30	18:15
Czechoslovakia[a]	7:15	12:30	19:00
Denmark	7:30	12:00	18:00
Finland	7:30	12:00	18:00
France	7:30	12:30	20:00
West Germany[a]	8:00	12:30	18:45
East Germany[a]	8:00	12:30	18:45
Greece	7:45	13:30	21:00
Hungary	7:00	12:30	19:00
Ireland	8:30	13:30	18:30
Italy	7:45	13:30	20:00
Luxembourg	7:30	12:30	18:45
Netherlands	7:45	12:30	18:00
Norway	7:30	11:30	16:30
Poland	6:30	13:30	19:10
Portugal	8:00	13:00	20:00
Spain	8:30	13:30	21:30
Sweden	7:30	12.00	17:00
Switzerland	7:45	12:30	18:45
United Kingdom	8:15	13:00	18:00

[a] Study done before 1992.

How much time for what?

	Sleep	Personal hygiene	Housework	Television	Other media	Recreation	Trip to work	Leisure/ spare time	Work	Socializing
Austria	7:54	0:48	4:05	2:27	3:28	1:30	0:36	1:12	4:53	1:47
Belgium	8:27	0:39	3:58	2:52	3:20	1:19	0:40	0:44	4:45	1:33
Czechoslovakia[a]	7:25	0:52	4:10	2:02	4:22	1:45	0:46	1:03	5:31	1:35
Denmark	7:28	0:50	4:21	2:17	4:16	1:45	0:37	1:36	4:54	2:00
Finland	7:56	0:31	3:22	2:21	3:09	1:45	0:28	1:19	4:24	2:09
France	8:11	0:37	4:08	3:04	1:57	1:03	0:38	1:10	4:29	1:56
West Germany[a]	8:22	1:10	5:13	3:10	3:48	1:50	0:44	0:57	4:29	1:42
East Germany[a]	8:06	1:14	5:21	3:21	3:55	1:37	0:42	1:12	4:52	1:23
Greece	7:21	0:34	4:18	2:58	1:40	2:39	0:21	1:10	3:12	2:24
Hungary	7:46	0:48	4:24	2:43	3:16	1:45	0:40	0:55	5:04	0:59
Ireland	8:22	0:37	4:48	2:59	2:56	1:40	0:26	0:56	3:24	2:35
Italy	8:02	0:46	4:10	3:16	1:05	1:18	0:40	0:51	4:21	1:57
Luxembourg	8:21	0:41	4:23	2:09	1:36	2:06	0:37	1:16	3:59	1:43
Netherlands	7:52	0:41	3:51	2:40	2:23	1:01	0:39	1:37	4:31	2:06
Norway	7:42	0:42	3:55	2:22	2:45	1:53	0:37	1:26	5:10	1:51
Poland	7:34	0:52	4:08	2:37	4:22	1:46	0:47	1:04	5:16	1:27
Portugal	8:23	0:46	4:24	3:22	2:02	1:29	0:40	0:28	4:58	1:40
Spain	8:17	0:48	4:27	3:18	1:18	1:54	0:39	0:58	3:45	2:29
Sweden	7:34	0:39	4:14	2:37	5:12	0:43	0:45	1:27	4:42	2:44
Switzerland	8:03	0:44	4:28	2:06	3:06	1:23	0:36	1:23	4:33	1:58
United Kingdom	8:09	0:50	4:58	3:50	2:09	1:36	0:35	1:07	3:00	1:54

[a] Study done before 1992.

Variations

In an extra step between steps 4 and 5 the monocultural groups could make assumptions about the use of time in the countries of the partner class. Additional question for discussion in bicultural groups: What prejudices and stereotypes are underlying these assumptions?

The worksheets could be evaluated statistically (possibly using computers) for both classes during a mathematics lesson and be presented with visualization through pies and bars, etc.

The enquiry can be expanded to the whole school. The same can be done in the partner school before the visit and the results can be shared with all pupils of both schools.

The exercise can be used for a school link without exchange: the two classes/schools complete and evaluate the worksheets and share the results. There is no direct discussion possible but the classes/schools can send each other a set of questions to find out more about the use of time in each other's countries.

A similar exercise can be used for a field study abroad: pupils visiting another country could ask about the use of time there. In this case a modified worksheet would have to be prepared

Evaluation

How do I use my time? How does this compare to other pupils in my class? How does this compare with the average use of time in my country? What is the effect of the differences between my personal use of time and that of other people in my class/country? How does the use of time relate to lifestyles and values? How do people in other countries use their time? How do differences between the use of time affect personal encounters between people from different countries?

Comments

One has to be aware that the data on pages 227 and 228 show times indicated by people in interviews – they have not been verified through actual measurements. One also has to be aware that although the questions for the interviews in different countries were identical it is possible that the same activity could be perceived or interpreted in a different way in different countries. For example, something could be perceived as 'recreation' in one country and as 'leisure' in another country.

Reference

Intercultural Centre, Vienna, 1993. Used with permission. The data in the attached tables were published by World-Media-Network, based on an enquiry by Information et Publicité in 1991. In total 9,774 persons were asked identical questions about their use of time.

Where Do I Come From? LB 4

Categories
- Lifestyles/behaviour
- Cultural identity/own culture, values

Learning objectives
- To become aware of own social and cultural background, values, lifestyle.
- To become aware of assumptions, expectations, prejudices and stereotypes about life in the country to be visited during an exchange.

Duration
Variable. Depends on how much of the questionnaire is used and for what purposes, but at least one class period with outside preparation of answers to the questionnaire.

Group
Can be done with a monocultural class to achieve awareness of own culture, values, lifestyles, or a multicultural class to compare differences in the classroom. Both a class going abroad and a class receiving could do the questionnaire as preparation for the exchange, then compare results together. Do the questionnaire again after the exchange and compare the results with those from before the exchange.

Supplies/resources
Copies of questionnaire for each participant.

Description of exercise
The questionnaire is made up of five parts: my community/country, my family, my life in my community/country, me, the country I am going to visit. The questionnaire helps pupils to prepare factually for an exchange, become aware of their own social, cultural, economic and political background, recognize and compare values and lifestyles.

Instructions
1 Introduce questionnaire (see pages 232–5) with objectives, structure and schedule.
2 Distribute questionnaire, one copy per participant, asking for it to be completed outside of classtime and as individuals. Make the point that the answers are not to be graded, that the questionnaire will be used as a basis for discussion only.
3 Using the setting of a class going abroad, divide the class into discussion groups and ask them to discuss and compare their thoughts and responses to the questionnaire. Which questions brought a common or similar response? Which ones had greatest diversity of response? Why common or diverse?
4 The fifth part of the questionnaire, about 'The country I am going to visit', should be discussed in terms of expectations. Suggest that pupils put this page in their 'journal' so that their expectation responses can be checked with reality during the visit. The partner school could also complete the questionnaire but it

would require translation. A discussion session involving both classes in small bicultural groups of about eight pupils each would provide the opportunity for a comparison of lifestyle and value differences.

Variations

A variation within a single school setting would be to apply the tables in parts 2 and 4 to an interview sample, within the larger school and/or community. What happens if a different age group is asked to complete the questionnaire? The results could be statistically calculated and reported on in an article in the school or local newspaper. Writing about what is being learned and how gives confidence and validation to the learners and is good public relations for the school.

A multicultural class could also prepare the questionnaire. The discussion could take place in bicultural or multicultural groups, the purpose of which would be to enable understanding and acceptance of differences, not better or worse ways of doing things but different, with a cultural reasoning for that difference.

Evaluation

After the class has returned from the visit abroad, the questionnaire, particularly the last part, could be revisited. Can pupils answer questions about the partner country now with greater confidence and clarity of ideas? Has anything changed in their responses to the other parts of the questionnaire?

Questionnaire

My community/my country

1.1   How many inhabitants does your community/country have?

1.2   How do people live in your community/country? Flats, semi-detached, one-family houses? Are the houses big or small? Are they close together or far apart? Are gardens a feature? How old are the houses? In what condition are the houses?

1.3   What is the main source of employment in your community? Is this kind of employment also important for the whole country?

1.4   Who is the owner of industry and big/medium/small businesses in your country? Private? Government? What is the difference? What are the consequences? Who takes the decisions? What possibilities exist for employees to take part in the decision-making process?

1.5   What is the level of unemployment in your community/country? What support do unemployed people get?

1.6   What political system does your country have? What are the most important parties?

1.7   What parties are represented in the local council/government? Which one does the mayor/prime minister represent? For how long is the local council/government elected?

1.8   What is your opinion about political decision-making in your community/country? Are you satisfied with it? Why or why not?

1.9   Are there different cultural/ethnic groups in your community/country? Which ones? What percentage of the total population does each one represent?

1.10 Are there special traditions, customs, food or clothes for your community? What are they?

1.11 What are the most popular free-time activities in your country? Which sports are the most popular?

1.12 Is it expensive to live in your community/country?

1.13 What event would really cause emotion in your country? What tradition, custom or things would one have to take away to really cause an uprising in your country?

1.14 What is considered most important for a happy and contented life in your country?

My family

2.1 Describe three to five activities you do together with your family. Describe three to five activities you never do together with your family.

2.2 Indicate with a tick the importance of the following in your family.

	Important	Not important
Cleanliness		
Orderliness		
Punctuality		
Spontaneity		
Intellectualism		
Sports		
Outdoor activities		
Cultural activities		
Work		
Educational activities		
Television		
Eating		
Reliability		
Flexibility		

2.3 Describe your family. With whom do you live in one household? How many of your family (parents, brothers, sisters) live outside the home? Where do they live? Do your aunts, uncles and cousins live in the same community? If not, where do they live? Far away, near by?

2.4 How have divorce, separation or death affected your family?

My life in my community/country

3.1 What are your favourite places in your community/country?

3.2 Are there any traditions or customs in your community in which you participate? Which ones? Why? What do they mean to you?

3.3 Which school do you attend? Why did you choose this school? Did you have a free choice of which school to attend? Who influenced you in this choice?

3.4 Describe a typical day at school.

3.5 What do you do on a typical evening or weekend?

3.6   What are your favourite free-time activities?

3.7   With whom do you spend your free time?

3.8   Do you like to watch TV/go to the cinema?

3.9   What are your favourite films/programmes? What was the last film you saw?

3.10 What do you like to eat/drink?

3.11 In what sports do you participate? What sports do you watch?

3.12 Which media do you use (newspaper, radio, TV, etc.)?

3.13 Which parts of the newspaper do you read?

3.14 How many weeks of holiday do you have? How do you spend your holiday?

3.15 What are your monthly expenses for?
      Food
      Clothes
      Travel
      Free-time activities
      Other (please indicate)
      Total

3.16 Where do you get this money? (Mark and indicate approximate percentage.)
      Parents
      Part-time job
      Other (please indicate)

Me

4.1   What does religion mean to you? How do you perceive God?

4.2   How important is politics for you?

4.3   What is most important for you for a happy/contented life?

4.4   Indicate on the following list how important these things are for you/your community/the country you are going to (if appropriate) (1 means important, 2 means not so important, 3 means not important).

	For me			For my community			For the visited country		
	1	2	3	1	2	3	1	2	3
Family									
Friends									
Religion									
Cinema									
TV									
Music									
Theatre									
Politics									
Humour									
Clothes									
Cars									
Money									
Work									
Education									
Drinking									
Eating									
Sports									
Nature									
Love									
Sex									
Socializing									
My town									
My neighbourhood									
My country									
The army									
Europe									

The country I am going to visit

5.1   What do you know about this country with respect to politics, economy, lifestyle, habits?

5.2   List at least five things you want to know about this country.

5.3   Collect newspaper articles about this country.
5.4   Do you believe that school would be different in this country? How?

5.5   List some things you want to spend money on and estimate how much they cost in this country.

5.6   How do you think pupils of your age in this country would answer the questions outlined in this questionnaire about their own country? Look especially at questions 1.13, 1.14 and 3.5 to 3.16.

Community Project   GP 1

Category
• Global perspectives

Learning objectives
• To become aware of and understand the interrelationship between local, regional, national and international issues.
• To gain commitment to and to search for solutions.
• To design and implement a concrete project.
• To apply knowledge and skills acquired during the project.

Duration
Between $1\frac{1}{2}$ and 2 hours for design of the project. Duration of project depends on type of project. Evaluation 45 to 60 minutes.

Group
From 10 to 30 participants. Can be monocultural or multicultural but focus of exercise is on local community. Visiting group (if there is one) would have to be able to take the project home.

Supplies/resources
Newspapers, magazines.

Description of exercise
Identification of issues affecting own community/region, followed by individual reflection, followed by the design of a project to make a positive contribution to the resolution or understanding of the issue.

Instructions
1 Introduction to exercise; objectives, structure.
2 Brainstorming. What are some of the present issues/conflicts/problems in our community/region? The class should come up with at least 20 such issues.
3 Review this list together with the group. Which issues have a cultural/cross-cultural dimension? Which are caused by a multicultural setting? Which have a national or international aspect or dimension? Mark them accordingly.
4 Split up into interest groups according to the marked issues (one issue per group; a maximum of five participants per group).
5 Allow participants 15 minutes to note down the following individually.
   • What is my point of view on the issue of my group?
   • What role do I play in relation to this issue? Am I personally involved in some way? What is my behaviour in relation to this issue?
   • What roles do others play?
   • Am I satisfied with my role/behaviour?
   • What role do I want to play?
   • What could I do?

6 Interest groups should share results and try to analyse the situation. Then they should discuss how they could individually or as a group contribute in a constructive way to this issue.
   • What are the possible approaches or actions?
   • Design and plan in detail one concrete action or project to be implemented by the group.
7 Share action plans or projects in plenary session.
8 Implement the project.
9 Evaluate the project in plenary session. Reports by the groups to answer following questions.
   • What was the result of the actions taken?
   • Were the projects successful? How and why?
   • What did everyone learn from the project? What will everyone do about these issues in the future?

Variations
It is possible to do a second exercise with the same structure starting out from national, international or global issues (migration, development issues, disarmament, unemployment, etc.). The class should then discuss how these issues affect their lives and design projects to respond to these issues at the local level. This approach could also be taken if there are no local/regional issues with a cultural/cross-cultural dimension.

Evaluation
It is important that the participants realize that it makes a difference how they act and behave, though the consequences of their actions are not measurable or visible globally.

Comments
It is important that the projects designed can realistically be implemented by the groups at the community level. Groups should be specific and to the point when deciding on a project.

Where Is It From? Where Is It Going?   GP 2

Category
• Global perspectives

Learning objectives
• To become aware of the global nature of material things.
• To understand the interrelatedness of local and global.

Duration
One class period with assigned research ahead of class.

Group
Any size but small groups of 10 to 15 for discussion. Can be done with either monocultural or multicultural groups. Can be easily adapted for younger age group.

Description of exercise
Informal research to determine where everyday household items, clothes, food, etc., come from. Products we use and wear and eat every day demonstrate a degree of global interdependence and interrelatedness.

Instructions
1 For homework (research), ask pupils to examine a group of products that they use everyday for the purpose of finding out where the products come from. This can be: furniture at home; food they eat; their clothing; the supplies they use at school, at play, at work; vehicles, such as cars, bicycles, motorbikes or buses. Depending on how large the investigation is, the products can be limited to one thing (e.g. clothing) or pupils can choose a product type they wish to research (e.g. one group of pupils to look at food, one group at household furnishings, one group at vehicles). Ask the pupils to identify ten items within a product group and to make a list of the items and their findings about where the items come from.
2 If it is appropriate and you want to know where the products go from your local community, similar research can be done for goods leaving the community. Ask the pupils to develop a list of products or services that are made in the local community. Then agree with the pupils on a way to find out where the goods and services go. (Remember parts suppliers as well as finished products, agricultural products, services, cottage industries.)
3 In school in small groups, which can be defined either by product or randomly, discuss the findings of the research investigation. It usually happens that people are surprised by the 'global' nature of their findings. Where do products come from (go to)? How great are the distances and what is the effect on transport and therefore on the environment? What is the reason for importing products and not producing them within the country? Do the places products come from represent other relationships, such as colonial history, the European Union, traditional partner, economic costs, individual (or family or national) preference? Are the product items known or promoted as being 'international' or 'other national'? Are the products 'new' in the sense of being a new food, like tacos or taramasalata, or are they products like tables, shirts and cars that are simply made elsewhere for sale in the local market? Given the findings, what is the impact of the EU on the local community, either for goods and services shipped into the local markets or for goods and services produced locally and distributed elsewhere?

Variations
As has been suggested, this exercise can be used for material goods and services available for sale in the community or for goods and services being produced and

distributed from the community. Instead of material things, a science class might look at the development of scientific research. Where does it happen? How is it communicated? Medicine, alternative medicine and medical treatment can be used, for example. Political decisions, social affairs, parliamentary decisions, movements such as Greenpeace and Amnesty International, environmental disasters such as Chernobyl, etc. – these could be looked at in terms of impact on or implications for the local community. Turned around, what is the effect of a town being twinned with a town in another country? Of passing local legislation declaring the community to be a nuclear-free zone? It would be possible in some schools to look at the international relationships of the school and ask the question: What is the effect of those relationships? How developed is the school's global awareness?

Evaluation
It is important for pupils to realize that their purchasing power, and how they feel about and act towards local initiatives with an international component, is of consequence even if their actions are not individually measurable or visible globally.

Comments
For this exercise, it is important to start from the local perspective, particularly with goods and services, as this is where pupils define 'their' world.

ABA–ZAK: A World View   GP 3

Categories
• Global perspectives
• Communication

Learning objectives
• To gain insight about 'world view', i.e. the interrelationships of speakers, language and meaning.
• To become aware of the complexity of communication.
• To develop communication skills and strategies.

Duration
Approximately 2 hours.

Supplies/resources
Envelope sets (as many as you will have teams) containing coloured pieces of paper of varying sizes and shapes (squares, triangles, circles, etc.). Objects are held together by a paper clip, folded inside a sheet of paper containing loose tea and inserted in the envelope.

Group
A minimum of six but size is not a limiting factor. Monocultural or multicultural groups, or bicultural as in a class exchange context, are fine for this exercise.

Description of exercise
A team-focused exercise that enables participants to develop their understanding of a 'world view', how that 'view' is made up of individuals, their language and the meanings ascribed to the language.

Instructions
Divide the group into teams of about six people each, depending on the size of the total group.

PREPARATION
1   Teams organize themselves in terms of how they wish to work together, e.g. how decisions will be made, who will do what, etc.
2   Give each team an envelope containing the objects of their 'world'. After examining the contents, each team should determine which characteristics of the enclosed items are of importance or interest (colour, shape, size etc.) and then proceed to categorize the items accordingly. Each category should be given an invented name. The items may be sub-categorized on the basis of secondary characteristics, each group being labelled. Example: 'zak' could stand for a category of squares; 'aba' or 'baba' could represent red and blue; so 'aba–zak' and 'baba–zak' stand for red squares and blue squares, etc.
3   Each team should decide whether all its members will use the same words for categories or whether different members of the 'society' will use different expressions. Example: boys could use different expressions from girls etc.

INTERACTION
4   One member of each team should visit another group. Visitors should explore the new society and try to learn as much as possible about the different culture. However, visitors must use only the language of their own team and hosts must use only their own tongue.
5   Visitors should try to find out whether there are equivalents in the new culture for words in their own language. If words in the host language do not easily translate, try to determine why and what words in the host language 'mean'.
6   After about 15 minutes, visitors should return 'home' to their original team and recount what they have learned about the host culture and language (from their own perspective).

ASSESSMENT
7   Discuss the following questions with the whole group.
   • How successful were you in being accepted by your hosts? How important was language to the process?
   • Was it difficult to find word equivalents? Why or why not?
   • How did the host culture (and organization of their world) influence what they perceived and paid attention to? How did language not only reflect their perception and organization of their world view but also reinforce and give them shape?

- How did the way teams were organized (societally) affect how different members of the same culture referred to the same thing? How did differentiated speech reflect and reinforce any sub-groups?

Evaluation
Discuss 'world view'. How are speakers, their language and what they mean inter-related? If this is a group that has been on a class exchange or if pupils have had other intercultural experiences, ask them to relate their experience to 'world view'.

Comments
This exercise is also very useful for developing communication skills and strategies.

Reference
A. E. Fantini, *Exploring Language and Culture* (Brattleboro, VT: The Experiment Press, 1985). Copyright © A.E. Fantini. Used with permission.

Personal Values   V1

Category
- Values

Learning objectives
- To become aware of own values.
- To compare own values with values of others.
- To realize social and cultural limitations to the ability to change values.

Duration
From 60 to 90 minutes.

Group size, composition and setting
Can be used for a class/group of any size. Can be used in a monocultural setting or as part of a class exchange/school link.

Description of exercise
Participants develop a list of values and rank them individually. They decide individually which ones are most/least important to them and discuss their individual results in small groups.

Supplies/resources
Copies of value lists for each pupil. Cards in two different colours, felt-tip pens/markers for all pupils, flip-chart paper and scotch tape, or pin boards (one per small group) and pins.

Instructions

1 Introduce the exercise – objectives, structure, schedule. (5 minutes)
2 Brainstorming with class about values that exist and values that determine our lives. If necessary, complete the list from the worksheet. (10 minutes)
3 Ask pupils to decide individually which two values are most important to them personally and which two values are least important. Ask them to write these values on cards (one value per card, different colours for important and unimportant values). (5 minutes)
4 Divide the group into small groups of six to eight pupils each. Ask them to pin cards on the board (stick them on flip-chart paper) in a logical order and to discuss the result. Which values do they have in common? Which ones are different? Why is it like this? Where did these personal values come from? How do these values influence lifestyle and behaviour? Ask pupils to summarize results on a flip-chart. (30 minutes)
5 Share results in plenary and discuss the following. Which values would pupils expect to be shared by other people in their community/country? Which values would they expect to be different or not shared? How have their values been influenced by their social and cultural background? Do values change? If yes, why and how? Hand out the sheet with rankings for West Germany and USA (study done before 1990). Compare with your own results. What is there in common/different? (20 minutes)
6 Summarize and close session.

Variations

Instead of or as well as developing one's own list of values one can use the following list and ask pupils to rank it. Then one could evaluate the result for the class statistically and produce a ranking for the whole class.

It can be interesting to have a larger group rank the attached list: it could be the whole school or people outside the school. The latter would allow the enquiry to be made according to different age groups. The result could be made available to the whole school.

The exercise can be used as a preparation for a class exchange. In this case, the pupils could make a second ranking indicating their assumptions about the value system in the country of the partner school, thus increasing their awareness of their stereotypes and prejudices. They could then discuss how the anticipated differences in specific values would affect their relationship and how they would deal with this. After the exchange, the pupils could look at their original ranking and discuss how the experience has changed their view of the value system of the other country.

The exercise can also be used during a class exchange or within a school link not involving an exchange. When it is done during an exchange, the small groups should not be mixed. Another session with mixed/bicultural groups should then be added after the plenary. The statistical evaluation should be made separately for each class. Of course, in this case the enquiry could be made in both countries with the whole school and/or people from outside school, and the results could be compared.

Value scale

Please rank the following values according to how important they are to you personally:

A world at peace
  free of war and conflict

Happiness
  contentedness

Inner harmony
  freedom from inner conflict

Family unity and security
  maintaining kinship bonds
  taking care of loved ones

True friendship
  close companionship

Freedom
  independence, free choice

A sense of accomplishment
  a lasting contribution

Self-respect
  self-esteem

A comfortable life
  a prosperous life

A world of beauty
  beauty of nature for all

Equality
  brotherhood
  equal opportunity for all

Mature love
  sexual and spiritual intimacy

National security
  protection from attack

An exciting life
  a stimulating, active life

Wisdom
  a mature understanding of life

Social recognition
  respect, admiration

Pleasure
  an enjoyable, leisurely life

Religious harmony
  living in harmony with religious
  principles

Value scale according to Rokeach

Value	Ranking	
	West Germany	USA
A world at peace	1	1
Happiness	2	4
Inner harmony	3	13
Family unity and security	4	2
True friendship	5	11
Freedom	6	3
A sense of accomplishment	7	8
Self-respect	8	5
A comfortable life	9	9
A world of beauty	10	15
Equality	11	7
Mature love	12	14
National security	13	12
An exciting life	14	18
Wisdom	15	6
Social recognition	16	16
Pleasure	17	17
Religious harmony	18	10

Source: S. Lang, *Werte und Veränderung von Werten* (Frankfurt, 1979).

This exercise can also be used in a multicultural class. Again, small-group discussions should be done first in monocultural groups and only later in multicultural groups.

Evaluation
How have my own values changed in the past? How were these changes influenced? How do values determine our lifestyle and behaviour? How can differences between values of people in different countries be explained? How can differences in values between men and women, between different age groups and between different social groups be explained?

Reference
Idea developed from H. Fennes *et al.*, *Projektunterricht 'Interkulturelles Lernen in der Schule'* (Vienna: Bundesministerium für Unterricht und Kunst, 1984). Used with permission.

Cultural Values Checklist   V 2

Category
• Values

Learning objectives
• To become aware of own and others' values.
• To realize a range of values in own culture.

Duration
One class period (40 to 60 minutes).

Group
Unlimited in size but discussion groups should be no larger than six to eight pupils. Probably best in a monocultural setting, but could be used with a multicultural group as well.

Supplies/resources
Copies of checklist, one per participant.

Description of exercise
Checklist of value ranges is completed individually, then discussed in small groups.

Instructions
1 Introduce the exercise, explaining that there are no right or wrong answers. As individuals we develop our values based on our background and how we have learned to relate to the environment.

2 Ask the pupils to complete the checklist by placing a mark on each range where they feel the mark describes their value on that issue. (15 minutes)

3 Divide into small discussion groups (if necessary). Ask the pupils to identify three or four issues to be discussed. The selection of these issues might differ depending on age, social or economic background of pupils, etc. It is important that the issues that the pupils are most interested in are discussed. Ask pupils to explain their marks and to discuss the meaning and the effect of similarities and differences.

4 Possible questions:
   • Are there issues on which there is common agreement within the group? Are there issues where there are significant differences? Why might this be the case?
   • How do they think parents might have marked the range? How does this affect the relationship with the parents?
   • How would the pupils in the country with whom you are doing an exchange, carrying out a project or engaging in correspondence mark the ranges? How might this affect the relationship with these pupils? How are the pupils going to deal with this?

5 Conclude, making certain that pupils feel their views have been heard by each other. Point out again that there are no correct answers, that it is possible to change one's values, and that this happens not by values being imposed but by individuals making conscious decisions.

Variations
This exercise could be tabulated statistically for a class, for the school, for a sample of the community, etc. It depends on the availability of and interest in statistical methods and technology.

Evaluation
See item 5 of instructions.

Reference
Centre for International Briefing, Farnham Castle, Farnham, Surrey, 1990. Used with permission.

Cultural Values Checklist

1 *Status, title, degrees*
Reasons other than merit   Earned by merit
(e.g. hereditary)

| 1 | 2 | 3 | 4 | 5 | 6 | 7 | 8 | 9 |

2 *Use of time*
Live from day to day   Time lost can never
be regained

| 1 | 2 | 3 | 4 | 5 | 6 | 7 | 8 | 9 |

3 *Child-rearing*
Strict reliance on control   Permissive reliance on
(rewards/punishment)   child responsibility

| 1 | 2 | 3 | 4 | 5 | 6 | 7 | 8 | 9 |

4 *Problem-solving*
Rational, logical   Instinctive, impulsive

| 1 | 2 | 3 | 4 | 5 | 6 | 7 | 8 | 9 |

5 *Life*
All life highly valued   Individual life less
and spared at all cost   important than group

| 1 | 2 | 3 | 4 | 5 | 6 | 7 | 8 | 9 |

6 *Sciences, technology, machines*
Servant of man   Enemy of man

| 1 | 2 | 3 | 4 | 5 | 6 | 7 | 8 | 9 |

7 *Family*
Other relations as valued   Strong, first loyalty
or more important

| 1 | 2 | 3 | 4 | 5 | 6 | 7 | 8 | 9 |

8 *Relation to others*
Privacy valued   Company valued

| 1 | 2 | 3 | 4 | 5 | 6 | 7 | 8 | 9 |

9 *Influence of others*
Independence valued   Group valued over
individual

| 1 | 2 | 3 | 4 | 5 | 6 | 7 | 8 | 9 |

10 *Women*
Inferior to men   Superior to men

| 1 | 2 | 3 | 4 | 5 | 6 | 7 | 8 | 9 |

11 *Work*
A necessary evil   People's highest
                                                             expression

| 1 | 2 | 3 | 4 | 5 | 6 | 7 | 8 | 9 |

12 *Death*
Predetermined and   Accidental and
inevitable   haphazard

| 1 | 2 | 3 | 4 | 5 | 6 | 7 | 8 | 9 |

13 *Material objects*
Of utmost value   Of little value

| 1 | 2 | 3 | 4 | 5 | 6 | 7 | 8 | 9 |

14 *Relationships with elders*
Honour, respect, deference   Of little importance,
                                                             disregarded

| 1 | 2 | 3 | 4 | 5 | 6 | 7 | 8 | 9 |

15 *The past*
Respect of rediscovery   Ways have to be found
of past traditions   to break away from the past

| 1 | 2 | 3 | 4 | 5 | 6 | 7 | 8 | 9 |

16 *Relationships between sexes*
Platonic relationships possible   Sexual relationships
                                                             always exist

| 1 | 2 | 3 | 4 | 5 | 6 | 7 | 8 | 9 |

17 *One's environment*
Can be controlled by people   Beyond people's control

| 1 | 2 | 3 | 4 | 5 | 6 | 7 | 8 | 9 |

18 *Authority*
Resentment, rebellion   Valued, respected

| 1 | 2 | 3 | 4 | 5 | 6 | 7 | 8 | 9 |

19 *Style of communication*
Polite, vague, indirect   Frank, open, direct

| 1 | 2 | 3 | 4 | 5 | 6 | 7 | 8 | 9 |

20 *Strangers*
Complete distrust   Great hospitality

| 1 | 2 | 3 | 4 | 5 | 6 | 7 | 8 | 9 |

21 *Time*
Only the present is important   Planning for future valued

| 1 | 2 | 3 | 4 | 5 | 6 | 7 | 8 | 9 |

Cave Rescue   V 3

Category
• Values

Learning objective
• To become aware of own/others' values.

Duration
At least one class period or 40 to 50 minutes; discussion may require additional time.

Group size
Six to eight participants is the basic group but multiples of this group size can be accommodated.

Supplies/resources
Sufficient copies of the briefing sheet.

Description of exercise
A simulated problem-solving exercise that raises various values issues. The exercise makes evident how values differ, how difficult it is to determine 'best' values or how difficult it is to listen to others whose beliefs are different.

Instructions
1 Introduce exercise (objectives, structure, schedule).
2 Divide large group/class into smaller groups of six to eight pupils each. Before splitting into the small groups, give briefing to large group/class as outlined in the following handout.
3 Distribute the handout, which includes the briefing and rules for the small-group discussions as well as the 'descriptions of volunteers to be rescued'. Ask the whole group to read the briefing individually and rank the volunteers in the order in which they should be rescued from the cave. (15 minutes) In small groups, ask each group to assume the role of the police and come to an agreement about the order of rescue. A rule for the small-group discussion is that there can be no votes taken. The group must talk through the sequence order until everyone agrees unanimously. This can be very difficult, but be firm. The timing must be very tightly controlled. Allow no more than 45 minutes for the group ranking/discussion. This can be very realistic; no emergency has the luxury of too much time. Warn the groups at 15-minute intervals about the time. The total group can review the process. Ask questions like: How well did you listen? Did you feel pressured into changing your mind? Did you feel that you had the right answer? What do your own selections say about your values?

Cave rescue

Your group is asked to take the role of the police force that is responsible for emergency decisions in your area. You have been called to an emergency meeting because there has been radio contact with a group of volunteers who are trapped in a cave by falling rocks and rising water. The only rescue team available tells you that the rescue will be extremely difficult and that only one person can be brought out each hour with the equipment at their disposal. It is likely that the rapidly rising water will drown some of the volunteers before rescue can be effected.

The trapped volunteers are aware of the dangers and have said that they are unwilling to take a decision as to the sequence in which they will be rescued. Your department must therefore take the responsibility for making this decision.

Life-saving equipment will arrive in 30 minutes at the cave entrance and you will need to advise the rescue team of the order of rescue by completing the ranking sheet. The only information available is drawn from the volunteer organization's files. You may use any criteria you think fit to help you make a decision.

There can be no votes taken. The group must talk through the sequence order until everyone agrees.

Descriptions of volunteers to be rescued

Helen is 34 years old, a housewife and has four children between 7 months and 8 years old. Her hobbies are ice-skating and cooking. She lives in a pleasant house in Gloucester and was born in England. Helen is known to have developed a secret romantic and sexual relationship with another volunteer (Owen).

Yoko is 19 years old, a sociology student at Keele University. She is the daughter of wealthy Japanese parents who live in Tokyo. Her father is a businessman and a national authority on traditional Japanese mime theatre. Yoko is unmarried but has several 'high-born' suitors as she is outstandingly attractive. She has recently been the subject of a TV documentary on the role of women in Japan and flower-arranging.

Jobe is a 41-year-old man, born in Central Africa. As a religious minister, he has been devoted to the social and political evolution of African people. Jobe has been a member of the Communist Party, and visited the former USSR several times. He is married with eleven children, whose ages range from 6 to 19 years. His hobby is playing in a jazz band.

Owen is unmarried and 27 years old. As a short-commission officer he spent part of his service in Northern Ireland where, as an undercover agent, he broke up an IRA cell, for which he received a commendation. Since returning to civilian life, he has been unsettled; drinking has become a persistent problem. At present, he is a youth adventure leader, giving much energy to helping young people and leading caving groups. He enjoys fixing and driving stock cars. He lives in Brecon, Wales.

Paul is 42 and has been divorced for six years. He was born in Scotland but now lives in Richmond, Surrey. Paul works at the Hammersmith Hospital as a medical research scientist and is recognized as a world authority on the treatment of rabies. Recently, he developed a low-cost treatment which could be self-administered. Much of the research data is still in his notebooks. Unfortunately, Paul has experienced emotional difficulties in recent years and has twice been convicted of indecent exposure, the last occasion being 11 months ago. He likes classical music, opera and sailing.

Edward is 59 and has lived and worked in Barnsley for most of his life. As general manager of a factory producing rubber belts for machines, he employs 71 persons. Prominent in the local community, he is a Freemason and a Conservative councillor. He is married with two children, who have their own families and live away from Barnsley. Edward recently returned from Poland, where he was responsible for securing a contract to supply large numbers of industrial belts over a five-year period. The contract when signed will mean work for another 25 people. Edward's hobbies include collecting antique guns. He intends to write a book about the Civil War when he retires. He is also a strong cricket supporter.

Ranking sheet

Order of rescue	Name
1	
2	
3	
4	
5	
6	

Variations
There are numerous variations both to the setting and to the characters who need to be rescued. Design the exercise as appropriate, keeping in mind that you want to appeal to a range of values in order to have a spirited discussion.

Comments
Use this exercise only after a level of trust has been built in the group. Strong emotions are possible and likely. Members of the group may identify with one of the volunteers stranded in the cave, others may feel strongly that they cannot take on the responsibility of making such judgements. Participants who feel this way should be allowed to opt out.

Reference
Centre for International Briefing, Farnham Castle, Farnham, Surrey. Used with permission.

Who Am I?   V 4

Categories
• Values
• Getting started/getting to know each other/warm up

Learning objectives
• To become aware of the influence of education and circumstances during child-hood on personal values.
• To get to know other people in the group.
• To prepare for more intensive group work.

Duration
Approximately 90 minutes.

Group
Any size is possible as long as the small groups do not become unmanageable, i.e. more than 12 to 15. Can be used with either monocultural or multicultural groups.

Description of exercise
Pupils group according to various criteria (socialization, characteristics, habits, pre-ferences, etc.) and thus find out about differences and similarities with other pupils in the group/class. The exercise can become very lively and is a good tool to wake up a group. It also helps the members of the group to get to know each other better.

Instructions

1   Group splits up according to the following criteria:
    In my childhood family, I was the
    * youngest child
    * oldest child
    * in between
    * only child

    If one of these groups is larger than ten people, it splits into smaller groups. The small groups should not leave the room but just move into the corners or find a place where they can discuss as a group without disturbing the other groups.

2   Ask pupils to perceive visually and without talking how the large group has split up and thus who is in which small group. Then ask pupils to exchange their experiences within the small groups, how the common criterion has influenced their personal development, their attitudes and values, etc. (20 minutes)

3   Repeat steps 1 and 2 with the following question:
    In my childhood family, there was
    * sufficient money
    * not enough money
    * too much money

4   Repeat steps 1 and 2 with the following question:
    In my childhood family,
    * religion played an important role;
    * religion was a formality;
    * religion was no issue;
    * we were atheist/agnostic.

5   Meet in plenary and let pupils reflect on the exercise. Summarize and close the meeting.

Variations

Groupings could also be done according to the following issues or criteria:

* education in my childhood family (dominated by father/dominated by mother/ determined by parents as real partners/characterized by a *laissez-faire* attitude of parents)
* male/female
* smokers/non-smokers
* morning persons/evening persons
* quiet/active
* having been in the country of partner school or not

It is also possible to imagine the room to represent the geographical area where the pupils come from (depending on the class composition this would be the town, the province, the country or even Europe or larger). Indicate which side of the room is north, etc. Ask pupils to take the position where they originally come from. Continue as step 2.

Abigale

Category
• Values

Learning objectives
• To become aware of own values.
• To become aware that not everyone agrees with one's own values.
• To understand how values influence judgement, decisions, behaviour, etc.
• To understand that values can change.

Duration
One hour.

Group
From 10 to 30 participants. Can be used in monocultural or multicultural settings.

Supplies
Paper and pencils for each participant.

Description of exercise
By way of a story, pupils reveal their values in the way they relate to the various characters. The discussion phase of the exercise enables pupils to become aware of their own attitudes and values, and how these might influence behaviour.

Instructions
1 Introduction to exercise: objectives, structure.
2 Read aloud the story of Abigale (two versions given).
3 Ask the pupils to rank the five characters according to their personal preferences from best to worst. Participants have five minutes to rank individually and note on paper.
4 Split into small (culturally homogeneous) groups of five to seven participants. Each group takes 15 minutes to share the individual lists and to agree on a common ranking. The final list has to be agreed on by consensus and not by a majority vote.
5 Small groups present their results in plenary, compare the lists and discuss the results. Which rankings are similar, which rankings are different? What is the reason for this? Why have participants ranked the way they did? What are the values underlying the various rankings? (15 minutes)
6 Give a short presentation, emphasizing how this little story touches very deep values in all of us (love, relationship with parents, sexual relationship, violence, materialism), and how even in relatively homogeneous groups – with people of more or less the same age, education, place of residence, etc. – views on these values are found to be different.

7 Ask the pupils to think of situations they have experienced where differences of values have resulted in confrontation and conflicts and how they have been dealt with. Ask them to discuss how differences in values within the group are dealt with and what other possibilities could exist.

8 This should be followed by reflection and discussion on the fact that we find ourselves in a period of transition with very fast changes, and on the fact that greater differences in values could be found when moving on to other parts of the country or world.

Variations

Discuss how representatives of another (cultural) group might rank these characters and why. The group leader has to emphasize that these are only assumptions – thus the result of this discussion is a number of questions.

When the exercise is done with a bicultural or multicultural group the small groups have to be monocultural or culturally homogeneous. In plenary, ask the pupils to discuss how the different values underlying their respective rankings affect the relationship between people of the different cultural groups present. Ask the pupils to try to develop approaches to cope with differences of values within the larger group.

Comments

This exercise is well suited to multicultural groups. In any case it is useful to split up into monocultural or homogeneous sub-groups in step 4.

Abigale (version 1)

Abigale is in love with Gregory, who lives on the other side of the river. A flood has destroyed all bridges. Abigale therefore turns to Sinbad, the boat man, begging him to take her to the other side of the river so that she can embrace Gregory. Sinbad agrees to take her over but on the condition that Abigale must first make love to him. Abigale, not knowing what to do, turns to her mother for advice, who responds by saying that she does not want to interfere with her personal affairs.

Abigale in despair agrees to make love to Sinbad. She is then taken over the river. When she arrives on the other side, she runs to Gregory and tells him all that has happened. Gregory is shocked, and rudely sends her away. Coming out of Gregory's house Abigale meets John, Gregory's good friend. She tells John the story. John then slaps Gregory under the pleased glance of Abigale and leaves with her.

Abigale (version 2)

Abigale was in love with a boy named Gregory. Gregory had an unfortunate accident and broke his glasses. Abigale, being a real friend, volunteered to take them to be repaired. The repair shop was across the river and, during a flash flood, the bridge was washed away. Poor Gregory could see nothing without his glasses so Abigale was desperate to get across the river to the repair shop. While she was standing forlornly on the bank of the river, clutching the glasses in her hands, a boy named Sinbad glided by in a rowing boat.

Abigale asked Sinbad if he would take her across the river. He agreed to on the condition that while the glasses were being repaired, she would go to a nearby store and steal a transistor radio that he had been wanting. Abigale refused to do this and went to a friend named Ivan who had a boat.

When Abigale told Ivan her problem, he said that he was too busy to be of help and didn't want to be involved. Abigale, feeling that she had no other choice, returned to Sinbad and told him that she would agree to his plan.

When Abigale returned the repaired glasses to Gregory, she told him what she had had to do. Gregory was appalled at what she had done and told her that he never wanted to see her again.

Abigale, upset, turned to Steve with her tale of woe. Steve was so sorry for Abigale that he promised her he would get even with Gregory. They went to the school playing field, where Gregory was playing football. Abigale watched while Steve beat up Gregory and broke his glasses again.

Albatross   CO 1

Categories
- Communication
- Cultural differences

Learning objective
- To become aware of the importance and role of non-verbal communication in experiencing another culture.

Duration
One and a half to two hours.

Group
Best done in groups of 12 to 15 participants. If possible, participants should be represented by both sexes more or less equally. Can be a monocultural or multicultural group.

Supplies/resources
Dishes or bowls for (a) hand washing, (b) liquid to drink, (c) food to eat. Water and some type of food (biscuits, crisps, etc.). Sheets or other cloth for Albatrossian man and woman, chairs, candles, incense or other 'extras' as desired.

Description of exercise
There are two parts to the exercise. The first part consists of performing a ceremonial greeting between members of an imaginary culture (Albatrossian) and foreigners (the group of participants). There should be no observers.

The second part consists of an extended discussion. 'Albatross' is an experiential learning tool, but is relatively useless unless the discussion following the ceremony is treated with particular thoughtfulness and attention.

Instructions

There is no set sequence to follow. What is described here is the standard outline for running Albatross. Clear objectives and valid reasons for what is done are important.

1 A male and female Albatrossian are in their places, the man on the chair, the woman kneeling beside him. (These two persons should know their parts ahead of time as it will be their portrayal of the Albatrossian culture that forms the basis of the exercise.) Participants (the rest of the group) are brought into the circle of chairs, females with shoes off and males with shoes on. The Albatrossian couple are dressed in their sheets, the woman without shoes, the man with shoes.

2 The first activity is for the Albatrossian man to attempt to induce female participants off any chairs they may happen to be sitting on, and down on to the floor, and for any male participants the reverse (from the floor on to chairs.) This effort and all other communication during the exercise is in a 'special' Albatrossian language. Albatrossians are sedate, reserved, gentle and loving people who do not manhandle their guests. Touching is only done in ceremonial ways, such as in greetings. The effort to get participants into their proper place is done principally through:

- a hiss, which indicates disapproval;
- an appreciative hum, which indicates approval;
- a clicking of the tongue, which serves for all sorts of attention-getting, transfer of factual information, etc.

3 The next activity is the circle of greetings. The Albatrossian man gets up and greets each male participant in turn around the circle by holding by the shoulders and waist and rubbing right legs together. After the greeting, the participant should sit back down in a chair. Then the Albatrossian woman greets each female participant in turn around the circle. She kneels in front of a standing female guest and runs both hands down her lower legs and feet in a ceremonious way. The women resume a kneeling position.

4 After the greetings, a pause ensues during which everyone simply waits. The Albatrossions always maintain unsmiling but serene and pleasant expressions, and do not register in their facial reactions any of their feelings or responses to what is going on in the circle. Participants (guests) who giggle or talk or otherwise disturb the ritual are hissed at but not with anger.

5 A bowl of water is brought around the circle by the Albatrossian woman. Beginning with the Albatrossian man, each male in the circle dips the fingers of his right hand into the bowl and lifts or gracefully waves the hand about to dry. The women's hands are not washed. The Albatrossian woman returns to her kneeling position next to the Albatrossian man for a few minutes before beginning the next activity.

6 She then, upon a clicking cue from the man, rises and offers food to each male in turn, beginning with the Albatrossian man. She sticks her hands into the food and stuffs a little into each mouth. Upon being fed the Albatrossian man

indicates his appreciation by a loud hum or moan (which can be accompanied by a rubbing of the stomach). After the men are fed, the Albatrossian woman next feeds each woman in turn. After this, she returns to her position next to the Albatrossian man.

7   During the pauses, which should be prolonged for effect, the Albatrossian man gently pushes the woman's head from time to time downward as she kneels.

8   Next follows the serving of drink. In the same manner, the Albatrossian woman first gives the cup to the Albatrossian man to drink from, then circles among the male participants (guests), then among the females, finally returning to her place and resuming the kneeling posture.

9   After another pause, the two Albatrossians rise and proceed around the circle of guests, communicating with each other through the customary clicking sounds. Without making clear indications to the participants, they select the female guest with the largest feet. That participant is then led over to the Albatrossian chair and she, like the Albatrossian woman, kneels next to this chair.

10 The last activity of the ceremony is a repeat of the greeting. The Albatrossian man rises and makes the round of the circle, greeting each male guest. He is followed by the Albatrossian woman greeting each woman in turn. The two Albatrossians indicate to the selected guest left kneeling by the chair that she should follow them and the three people leave the circle.

Cultural assumptions and rationale

Part of the point of the Albatross exercise is to provide an opportunity for people to learn by observation, to infer meaning from the totality of what has happened. Since this 'cultural observation' is important, it is best to conduct the exercise with as much consistency as possible, and within a frame of reference agreed on by the Albatrossian performers. The following are some of the 'standard' cultural assumptions that are usually in play, and that participants have the problem of figuring out as the exercise goes on.

•   Though the exercise is set up deliberately to indicate otherwise to the audience, in fact the Albatrossian society values women over men. The Earth is sacred; all fruitfulness is blessed; those who bring life into being are one with the Earth and only women are able by virtue of their inherent qualities to walk directly on the ground. Men must wear shoes, and thus their greeting does not deal with the Earth, whereas that of women emphasizes the ground and feet. Only women are able to prepare and offer the fruits of the Earth.

•   The roles of men and women in the society reflect this relationship to Earth, though to the new observer it may appear as if other meanings are present. The fact that the Albatrossian man pushes down the head of the kneeling Albatrossian woman is a pursuit of his obligations in the society. It is his duty to remind her of sacredness, to approach it through her, to protect her from forgetfulness. He drinks and eats first to protect her and all that she represents from harm or defilement.

•   Albatrossians have a language, though only some part of it is required or used in the greeting ceremony (the clicks, hums, hisses). It may be useful to approach the language question on another assumption: that Albatrossians communicate via mental telepathy and that the few sounds they use are mainly means of getting a person's attention.

- The society values calm, serenity, stateliness. The Albatrossians are peaceful, welcoming of strangers, generous, loving and tolerant. They eat and drink things they like. Their patterns of life and their ceremonies (such as the greeting cere-mony) are time-honoured and are considered to be self-evident and correct.
- It is *very* important for Albatrossians to bear in mind (and for participants to realize later in discussion) that what is, is – and that Albatrossians are no different from any other people in making the unconscious assumption that what they are is 'normal'. They assume that visitors want to be greeted, that the visitor knows as well as they what is correct (though they are tolerant and gently correcting of lapses), the woman with the largest feet among the participants is completely in accord with the necessity of her selection, etc.

The ceremony is a greeting one – it is not to be implied as the totality of the society. For example, a church service is a bona fide segment of cultural behaviour but not indicative of everything in that culture.

During the discussion following the exercise, any inconsistencies in performance or tricky questions can always be explained as 'tribal differences'. But it is important for those doing 'Albatross' to make the jump into a different culture, one that does not at all need to be explained or justified. An Albatrossian is as much of a whole, self-evident, implicitly assumed person as is a Welshman, an Englishwoman, a Swede, an Italian, etc.

The discussion

There are two broad levels attainable in the 'Albatross' exercise, the first being the 'cultural observation' level. The exercise enables participants to test their powers of observation, to infer correct behaviour from non-verbal or indirect clues and to get an idea of what the Albatross society is like. The second broad level is one of self-awareness – of participants being able to assess their own reactions and feelings, to add to their self-knowledge.

Participants after an Albatross are usually full of their own reactions. Therefore, it is best to structure the discussion on this pattern.

(1) Collect ideas from the group on what happened, what sort of activity it was, 'where they have been'. This will develop into some generally agreed understand-ing that they have had contact with a kind of 'culture'. Let the ideas arise without confirmation or denial, but rather as an introduction to the discussion. This will also tell you something about the group.

(2) The discussion should move on to what was objectively observed. Collect all impressions and ask the group to describe what they know about the Albatrossian culture, not at this point what they felt about what was happening to them. This part of the discussion will get into whether the culture was one that oppressed women, whether there was male superiority. Let contrary views arise from the group if at all possible.

In the area of cultural observation, the major points to be realized are:

- how well we observe even to begin with (do we really pay close attention, notice details?);
- how we can infer a lot of useful information and learn what is expected of us without being told in so many words;
- how things aren't always what they seem.

This part of the discussion is about sharing information and opportunities to think about the participant's own skills in observation. It may be useful to make the point that many if not most of the observations are value-laden. Whether a participant points this out or you do, it is important that this idea is heard and digested.

The participants will want answers: 'Why did they ..., do all Albatrossians ...?' The goal here will be to try to get responses from the group, which can be varied or contradictory and, at an appropriate moment, confirmed by the facilitator as probably right or as a hypothesis. The facilitator should help the group to understand that questions like 'Do all Albatrossians ...?' are inherently meaningless in the light of their own common sense and cultural experience. The leader should aim to create the awareness that the 'whys' of human behaviour do not usually lend themselves to simple, neat, concepts and answers.

(3) Move the discussion into the area of personal feelings and reactions. Help participants to see that their own reaction is relative: that sitting next to them is someone with quite a different response. Make the point that the exercise is not good or bad or boring but takes on this or that character through the experience of individuals, that each individual sees through a pair of personal glasses. Let any and all reactions be expressed but develop the awareness that what happened is the responsibility of each participant.

(4) As participants frequently do not like their own reactions and behaviours, there will inevitably be comments like 'if only the exercise were done differently' or 'had it not been artificial'. It must be made clear that the 'Albatross' exercise was artificial in that it was a simulation. But it was not artificial in what matters most: during the exercise in that room a group of participants did this and this and had real reactions. It is up to the participants to admit that, whatever those reactions and behaviours were, they happened and it is immaterial how 'well' or 'realistically' the exercise was run. This insight, if gained, is valuable. It will seem self-evident to some, meaningless or alien to others. It helps to point out that 'Albatross' is a way to look at ourselves, to realize that there is no right or wrong to the exercise but simply a means of increasing each person's inward awareness.

Reference
From D. Batchelder and E. Warner, *Beyond Experience* (Brattleboro, VT: The Experiment Press, 1977).

Humming Exercise   CO 2

Category
• Communication skills

Learning objectives
• To become aware of the possibilities of non-verbal communication and to realize the importance of patience in communication.
• To become aware of the importance of one's own initiative when trying to overcome communication problems.

Duration
Unpredictable: it can last between 5 and 30 minutes or even longer per round.

Group
Up to 30. If the group is larger, split it into smaller groups. Can be used with either monocultural or multicultural groups.

Description of exercise
Group exercise involving everyone in the action. Exercise gives exaggerated sense of what 'non-verbal' communication can mean.

Instructions
1   One or more volunteers leave the room after they have received the group leader's instruction: 'This is a serious communication exercise; you will not be fooled.'
2   The group thinks of simple actions that the volunteers have to perform after coming in again (drink a glass of water, write something on the chalkboard, etc.).
3   After the first volunteer has entered the room again, the group starts humming. The loudness of the humming should lead the volunteer to do the action he or she is expected to perform. If the volunteer gets closer to the action, the humming becomes louder. If the volunteer moves away from the expected action, the humming becomes lower. The group is not allowed to use any other non-verbal signs, such as nodding, laughing, other gestures or mimicry. It is essential to continue the exercise until the volunteer has done the expected activity.
4   When the first volunteer has done the expected action, and if there is a second volunteer waiting outside, the second volunteer may come in and the exercise is repeated with a different action.

Variations
It is possible to send the second volunteer out of the room *after* the first round, with the effect that he or she already knows the basic rules – only the action will be new.

Comments

It is important to reflect on the process of the exercise and on the feelings both of the volunteer(s) and of the whole group during the exercise. Discuss the following questions:

• What messages were conveyed among the volunteer(s) and the other pupils?
• What is the importance of language and of non-verbal communication? What possibilities exist to communicate with people who do not know your language?

Babel   CO 3

Category
• Communication

Learning objectives
• To experience how language barriers result in tension or fear and make communication difficult.
• To become aware of the usefulness of non-verbal communication in situations where verbal communication is difficult or impossible.
• To understand the communication problems of foreigners in one's country.

Duration
Sixty minutes.

Group
Unlimited, but would work well with a class size of between 28 and 32 pupils. Can be either monocultural or multicultural by composition.

Supplies/resources
Blindfolding scarves.

Description of exercise
A group exercise designed to emphasize the difficulties of language barriers and to give confidence and awareness of non-verbal communication. (This can be very reassuring for participants who have little aptitude for learning a spoken language.)

Instructions
1   Split up into small groups of four to eight participants each. Explain that each group must now make up a language of its own. These languages must be clearly different from any well-known language and should include the following vocabulary.
    • Greeting.
    • A scene from everyday life that demands help from and dialogue with a representative from another language group, i.e. shopping, ordering a meal, asking for information on time, direction, travel, etc.
    • Goodbye greeting.

2 The small groups go to separate rooms (or spaces) and take 15 minutes to prepare the scenes to be played twice in front of the others.

3 A representative from one small group must communicate with one or more representatives from another small group (number depending on selected scene) and try to fulfil his or her task. Only verbal communication is allowed. To ensure this, blindfold all 'actors' involved.

4 If verbal communication does not lead to the desired result, the scene should be played again – this time removing the blindfolds and allowing non-verbal communication, such as gestures or facial expressions.

5 The exercise can be repeated with different settings of small groups.

Variations
The requests concerning the language can be changed, making the task easier or more difficult.

It is possible to use correct words or sentences of languages not known to anyone in the group. The teacher or group leader could provide words or sentences from such languages.

Evaluation
Discuss the following questions.

• What feelings did pupils experience?
• What conclusions can be drawn after playing these scenes?
• What could one learn about oneself through an exercise like this?
• What problems do pupils think could arise for persons speaking more than one language – one at home, another at school?

Comments
Through this exercise, the pupils hopefully gain insight into the world of language problems – and get to experience that even big language barriers can be overcome through non-verbal communication.

Reference
Idea developed from H. Fennes *et al.*, *Projektunterricht 'Interkulturelles Lernen in der Schule'* (Vienna: Bundesministerium für Unterricht und Kunst, 1984). Used with permission.

Charades   CO 4

Category
• Communication

Learning objectives
• To become aware of the possibilities and limitations of non-verbal communication.
• To realize the importance of patience in non-verbal communication.

Duration
Minimum 1 hour. Can be done endlessly.

Group
From 12 to 30 participants. Can be multicultural or monocultural with these instructions.

Description/instructions of exercise
1 The group splits up into two groups of equal size (for the purpose of explanation let's call them group A and group B).
2 Each group decides secretly on one or more nouns.
3 Group B informs a delegate from group A of the noun chosen. This must be done in such a way that the rest of group A does not know this noun.
4 The delegate from group A has to convey the noun non-verbally to the rest of his or her group. The group A delegate is only allowed to give signs of approval (e.g. nodding) or signs of disapproval, depending on whether the group is guessing in the right direction or not. He or she is also allowed to indicate numbers with his or her fingers. This step is only finished when the group finds the noun chosen.
5 Repeat steps 3 and 4 with group B guessing a noun chosen by group A.
6 Continue the exercise with new nouns as long as wished and time allows.

Variations
Instead of nouns it is possible to use proverbs, titles of books or films, etc. There are numerous variations. The composition of the class may help to define the subject to be played or acted out (e.g. proverbs would be difficult with a group made up of hosted pupils from another country as well as the home group).

Evaluation
What are the feelings involved when trying to express something non-verbally and not being understood? What are the feelings if one does not understand what is being conveyed?

Comments
This exercise can be a lot of fun and is very useful to create excitement and enthusiasm. Sometimes groups very quickly develop their own patterns of communication.

Building a Tower   CO 5

Category
• Communication

Learning objectives
• To understand that people have different perceptions of the same thing.
• To understand that there are different interpretations of and meanings to the same – verbal or non-verbal – expressions.
• To experience misunderstanding of others and being misunderstood.

- To learn to communicate non-verbally.
- To learn to cooperate on a specific task across communication barriers.

Duration
One and a half to two hours.

Group
Can be used for a group/class of any size. The exercise is most useful for bicultural or multicultural groups or during a class exchange but it can also be used in a monocultural group preparing for a visit abroad.

Description of exercise
Teams of six to eight pupils each build a tower made of paper and, by doing this, experience working towards a common goal as a team.

Supplies/resources
For each team four pieces of flip-chart paper, a ruler, scissors, glue and/or sticky tape. Each team has to have exactly the same resources.

Instructions
1 Introduction into exercise; objectives, structure. (5 minutes)
2 Divide into small groups of six to eight pupils each. In a bicultural/multicultural group mix the groups culturally as much as possible. Give the groups the following instructions. Each group has to build a tower *without verbal communication* using the material it gets. The tower has to stand without any other support within the given time limit. Do not give any indication as to what the tower could look like – leave it completely up to the imagination of the pupils. (5 minutes)
3 Pupils work in small groups on their tower, if possible each team in a separate room. (45 to 60 minutes)
4 Pupils discuss their work within their small groups. What was their perception of 'a tower' before the exercise? How did that change during the exercise? How did the communication within the group work? Were there any major misunderstandings? What communication problems did they encounter? How did they solve them? How did the group organize itself? Was there a leader? If yes, how was he or she appointed? What was the role of the other group members? Were any group members overruled? How was the working atmosphere in the group? (15 to 20 minutes)
5 Meet in plenary and let groups present their towers as well as their experiences while building them. (5 minutes per small group)
6 Discuss in plenary the questions raised in step 4. Summarize and close session.

Variation
It is possible to assign small groups to build bridges. An additional variation would be that pairs of small groups construct one bridge each in such a way that each group builds one half of a bridge that has to meet half-way.

Of course, it is possible to do the exercise allowing verbal communication – in this case the emphasis of the exercise is more on developing teamwork and cooperation in general.

It is possible to conduct the exercise as a competition: advise pupils that the tower will be judged according to the following criteria: height, stability, originality.

Evaluation
See step 4.

Comments
The exercise is a typical example of a 'triangular didactic' in which people with different cultural backgrounds relate to each other with reference to a common work, project or theme.

The Yes/No Game   CO 6

Category
• Communication

Learning objectives
• To recognize that there can be different interpretations of language and gestures.
• To realize the importance of appropriate communication.

Duration
From 35 to 45 minutes.

Group
From 15 to 35 participants, can be either monocultural or multicultural.

Supplies/resources
Space for the participant group, such as a classroom.

Description of exercise
Stereotypes are clichés that almost automatically acknowledge a simple, agreed-upon picture of another culture group. Prejudices are also collective and reflect a judgement on another person or group based on that group's origin, be it cultural, ethnic, political or religious. Prejudices are learnt, not acquired through personal experience.

Prejudices need to be worked with, in groups, and it may be desirable to 'live' the correction of the previously held idea. 'The yes/no game' is a useful tool that allows participants to confront prejudice in an abstract manner, understand that 'our view of the world is limited and that appropriate means of communication are necessary.

Instructions

Ask for, or assign, two members of the group, one boy and one girl. Explain that the object is for them to guess what is happening in a 'situation' that will be communicated by the rest of the group.

Tell the volunteers that they will be able to ask questions of anyone in the group, but that all the questions must be answered with either 'yes' or 'no'. Then send the volunteers to another room briefly while you explain the situation to the rest of the group. No 'situation' will exist. In order to respond to the questions, members of the group will use the following method.

1 They will respond only if the person asking the question is of the same sex. They will not respond to someone of the opposite sex.
2 They will respond 'yes' if the person asking the question is smiling.
3 They will respond 'no' if the person asking the question is not smiling.

Now call the volunteers back into the room and allow them to begin questioning the group. The volunteers are not going to understand why some people do not answer. If the volunteers are irritated, they also will not understand why they never get a positive response. In principle, they will be able, after some time, to detect the rules, or at least the rule about the sex of those whom they are questioning. Allow the questioning to proceed for about 15 to 20 minutes, or until the volunteers become frustrated, whichever occurs first. Let some irritation and frustration happen.

Stop the questioning and lead the participants in a discussion about the game and their feelings about it. Point out that rules of communication are complex and vary from culture to culture; learning the rules when being with people from another culture can be a frustrating experience because members of the other culture are unlikely to be able to explain the rules in a concise, understandable fashion. Discuss possible aggression resulting from lack of understanding or communication.

Variation

Can also be used in a situation where a communication problem already exists (multicultural classes, class exchanges, etc.). Here the exercise would help pupils to become aware of prejudices and communication barriers in a different context.

Evaluation

What have participants learned from the exercise? Will it make a difference when they go on their exchange? When they encounter a different culture at a school function? When they work with a 'supervisor' who is from a different cultural background?

Comments

This exercise is most useful in a monocultural group and is an excellent preparation for a group anticipating a visit to another country.

Evaluation Questionnaire
E1

Category
- Evaluation

Learning objectives
- To reflect on the process and outcome of the project.
- To become aware of what has been learned and how one has developed during the project.
- To learn for future projects.

Duration
Sixty minutes or longer depending on the length and intensity of the total project.

Group
Everyone who in some way was involved in the project should participate in the evaluation.

Supplies/resources
Copies of questionnaire, one for each participant.

Description of exercise
An evaluation is essential for this project, to allow the participants to reflect on the process and outcome of the project, to link the various parts of the project, to become aware of what has been learned and how one has developed along the project, and to think about possible consequences in one's future behaviour. At the same time, it allows the teacher/facilitator to learn for future projects.

Instructions
There are three parts to the evaluation.

1 Filling out the questionnaires individually.
2 Closing discussion in groups and plenary session. This could include a final comment by each participant.
3 Evaluation of the questionnaires to learn for future projects.

Reference
Idea developed from H. Fennes *et al.*, *Projektunterricht 'Interkulturelles Lernen in der Schule'* (Vienna: Bundesministerium für Unterricht und Kunst, 1984). Used with permission.

Questionnaire

The questionnaire is to be completed individually. It will not be rated or graded. The objective is rather to evaluate the materials and methods used in order to develop future intercultural learning projects. Therefore we ask for your comments, criticism and suggestions.

1. Compared with the normal way of teaching, I think the way the project was structured was

+3	+2	+1	0	−1	−2	−3
very good						very bad

Why?

2. I think that this kind of 'hands-on' and project-orientated learning should happen more frequently.

☐ I agree   ☐ I disagree   ☐ I don't know

Why?

3. I found the content of the project to be

+3	+2	−1	0	−1	−2	−3
very interesting					very boring	

Why?

4. The project has stimulated me to

5. Of the various parts of the project, the one(s) I liked most was/were (multiple answers possible)

☐ getting acquainted/warm–up/initializing events
☐ stereotypes and prejudices
☐ cultural differences, cultural identity/own culture
☐ lifestyles and behaviour
☐ global perspectives
☐ values
☐ communication
Why?

6. Through this project I have learned much about ...

7. The exercises we did

+3	+2	+1	0	−1	−2	−3
I liked very much					I did not like at all	

What did you like? What didn't you like?

8. Working in small groups

+3	+2	+1	0	−1	−2	−3
I liked very much					I did not like at all	

9. I would have liked to learn more about

10. The weaknesses of the project were

11. The strengths of the project were

12. In future projects, one should avoid/improve

13. Compared with the normal teaching situation I found the teachers/facilitators to be

+3	+2	+1	0	−1	−2	−3
very good					very bad	

14. Altogether I found the project to be

+3	+2	+1	0	−1	−2	−3
very good					very bad	

15. Other comments:

Thank you for your cooperation.

Evaluation: Completing Sentences

Category
• Evaluation

Learning objectives
• To reflect on what has been learned.
• To become aware of how one has developed.
• To realize any change in attitudes and behaviour.

Duration
From 20 to 30 minutes.

Group
Everyone who took part in the project, exchange, activity, etc.

Supplies/resources
Copies of questionnaire, one for each participant.

Description of exercise
Evaluation is necessary for any project or activity, to enable participants to reflect on what has been learned, to link the various parts, to become aware of development and growth, to think about consequences for future behaviour, to bring closure to the activity. This questionnaire is completed individually, and can be used solely for personal reflection or can be 'turned in' on an anonymous basis for the group leader/teacher. The questionnaire can be used as part of an evaluation process, which would also include full group discussion.

Instructions
Distribute the questionnaires, asking participants to complete the sentences based on how they feel as individuals about the activity. This can be completed outside class time as homework.

   If the questionnaire is to be used as a basis for group discussion, it must be made clear that comments are voluntary. Once a couple of comments are volunteered, the group is usually stimulated to engage in a full participatory discussion. Leading this kind of discussion can be somewhat daunting as there can be elements of 'one-upmanship' with clever answers.

Variations
Completed questionnaires can be asked for on an anonymous basis, which should mean that pupils feel comfortable about answering honestly and you, the teacher, gain insight into what has been learned.

Reference
Based on model used at European Youth Centre for seminar activities, Strasbourg.

Questionnaire

1. I liked...

2. Now, I know...

3. What pleased me...

4. At the end of the 'activity', I would still like to know...

5. I realized...

6. Now I feel capable of ...

7. Intercultural learning is...

8. I would like...

9. I am more 'ready'...

10. I am certain...

11. What I will change in my work/activities is...

12. The best moment in the project was...

13. I feel like...

14. Now I need...

15. Intercultural means...

16. I would take the risk of...

17. What I feel better about is...

18. I could have...

19. I have learned...

    This means...

20. During the project, it would have been good to insist that...

21. In a future project, I would like...

22. My vision of another culture is...

Glossary

Definitions of terms used in social sciences are subject to ongoing discussions. Nevertheless, the authors have tried to give a rough description of some terms frequently used in this book, being aware that detailed definitions reaching the agreement of everybody would not be possible.

acculturation   Acculturation is a bilateral or multilateral process in which groups or individuals acquire elements of culture from each other. This process is usually not balanced.

adaptation   An individual's process or the result of such a process, establishing a balance between the capability, needs, expectations and objectives of the individual on the one hand and the demands of the social environment towards the individual as well as the possibilities of covering the individual's needs on the other hand.

assimilation   See *cultural assimilation*.

behaviour   Generally, all activities or reactions of an organism. More specifically, every activity or reaction – expression of thinking, feeling, etc. – whether or not it is related to an intention or objective of the individual concerned.

bicultural   The presence of two cultures within a specific group, environment or society. Special case of *multicultural*.

class   A social group defined by its relation to the means of production as one stratum of society in a hierarchical order. There will also be a certain degree of consciousness of belonging to a specific class.

country   A political and social entity defined by internationally acknowledged territorial borders.

cross-cultural   Concerning the interface between cultures or the comparison of traits of cultures. Also used as a rather vague term synonymous with *intercultural*, *multicultural*, *transcultural*, etc., especially before the term intercultural became popular.

cultural assimilation   The complete and totally new socialization of a person into a newly dominating social group with a different culture.

cultural group 'Any group of people who consciously or unconsciously share an identifiable complex of meanings, symbols, values, and norms' (Patterson, 1975, p. 309).

culturalism The notion that the behaviour of foreigners and immigrants can be explained in terms of culture only without requiring any other considerations. As A. N. Çağlar put it: 'It is as if Germans had a psyche whereas Turks have culture.'

culture Has many definitions for different purposes. It would be superficial to describe this term in a few sentences. See Chapter 3 for a more complete discussion.

curriculum A structured programme organizing educational processes.

didactic A system of methods of teaching establishing a relationship between the subject, the teacher and the learner.

education An individual pool of cognitive knowledge, social skills and technical skills. Also the process of acquiring knowledge and skills.

empathy The ability to have an understanding of and sensitivity towards someone else's thoughts and feelings by taking his or her view or position. A term coming from and used in psychology. Sometimes confused with sympathy.

enemy image A political and social prejudice. Enemy images are stereotyped negative notions about a political opponent. Enemy images are adopted and enforced in the socialization process, especially through media, opinion leaders, etc. Enemy images usually make use of existing stereotypes and prejudices.

ethnic group *See ethnicity.* Differs from a cultural group in three ways. First, a conscious awareness of belonging to a group is central; secondly, it does not need to be culturally homogeneous and, at least in an urban and/or migration context, will usually not be; thirdly, if conditions for ethnicity are met, segments of a cultural group may be transformed into an ethnic group, which does not mean that all members of a cultural group need to become part of the ethnic group (Patterson, 1975, pp. 309–10).

ethnicity 'That condition wherein certain members of a society, in a given social context, choose to emphasize as their most meaningful basis of primary, extrafamilial identity certain assumed cultural, national or somatic traits' (Patterson, 1975, p. 308).

ethnocentricity To measure other people's way of life by one's own standards, which are determined or at least influenced by the ethnic group one is part of or identifies with. In extreme cases, ignorance of cultural diversity.

ethnopluralism An ideology that tolerates the presence of cultural diversity under the condition of cultural segregation. It implies that there is minimal contact and interaction between the different cultural groups of a region or country. Frequently, ethnopluralism is linked to structural discrimination and to unequal access to education, work opportunities, housing and material resources. Sometimes the term 'multiculturalism' is used wrongly in actually describing ethnopluralism. This can happen on purpose to hide or disguise the real intention.

exoticism Idealistic adoration and glorification of the foreign. Usually this adoration is attached to the foreign far away, which has no consequences for one's own life. Exoticism can be interpreted as compensation for the fear caused by the foreign or social change in one's immediate environment and, thus, can be interpreted as escape from one's personal situation into idealism. Exoticism is a special case of *xenophilia*.

integration   The interactive process of ascribing and assuming positions and functions within a (newly formed) group or society.

intercultural   Concerning the relationship between cultures. More specifically, concerning the interaction of cultures on the basis of mutual respect.

intercultural learning   It would be superficial to describe this term in a few sentences. See Chapter 5 for a more complete discussion.

learning   'Learning is an intended activity demanding a certain effort to acquire knowledge and skills. Learning is in a larger sense the totality of hypothetical processes, which as a result of reacting to specific stimulating situations correspond with those changes in behaviour and experience, which have not appeared as a result of tiredness, maturing, drugs, exogenous interferences etc.' (Sturzebecher, 1973).

methodology   A system of methods, including reflection upon them.

methods   A structured and infinitely replicable way of doing something.

migrant   A person moving the centre of his or her activities from one place to another, either once or repeatedly, regardless of how far apart the places are and regardless of the nature of the difference between them. Migration can be international or internal, between societies or within them, between culture areas or within them. Rural–urban migration, for instance, will normally be intercultural regardless of whether international borders are being crossed in the process or not.

monocultural   Cultural homogeneity of a specific group, environment or society.

multicultural   The presence of more than one culture within a specific group, environment or society. The term does *not* apply to individuals.

nation   An 'imagined community' (Anderson, 1983) of people not bound together by face-to-face interaction but living together within a space of intensified and self-centred economic and political ties. A product of the development of industrial capitalism.

nationalism   An ideology or political theory requiring that cultural boundaries and the territorial boundaries of states should coincide. Also a sense of belonging to a nation and, further, the notion that that particular nation is or should be of more importance than all others.

norms   Rules of behaviour accepted within a specific social group or society; also expected regularities of social behaviour. Deviations from norms are sanctioned.

orientation   A learning process that is not only incidental but also structured. Thus exchange programmes include a number of events before, during and after the stay abroad to support and deepen the learning experience and to enable participants to reflect on their experience in a structured and cognitive way. This concept is referred to as orientation. Orientation activities are organized before the stay abroad (preparation), during the stay abroad (guidance) and after the return to the home country (assessment or reorientation).

pedagogy   Science concerned with the problems of teaching and learning processes.

prejudice A strong, preconceived opinion about persons or groups that is not easily changed or corrected. It has an emotional dimension and frequently includes a moral judgement: positively (especially about oneself and the group one is part of) and negatively (especially about others or another group). Usually the information prejudices are based on is superficial, incomplete, distorted or even wrong. Prejudices are adopted and enforced in the socialization process. Frequently prejudices are a result of experiences with individual members of another group, which are generalized and attributed to every member of the respective group. Prejudices also serve the positive valuing of oneself or the group one is part of.

race Groups of people distinguished by complexion and other genetically produced features of the body other than sexual or pathological ones. Biologically the distinction is irrelevant as only about 3.5 per cent of human genes are involved in producing phenotypical and racial distinctions.

racism First, an attitude seeking to justify social and economic differences by reference to race. Second, policies and actions maintaining or aiming to maintain social, economic and political differences along racial distinctions. Third, the explanation of cultural differences in terms of race, usually coupled with the assertion that such cultural differences cannot or should not be overcome. In this sense, racism is a special form of culturalism.

religion A concept of beliefs and rituals pertaining to communication with spiritual or supernatural entities. These beliefs are not to be questioned owing to their supernatural origin. A specific characteristic of a religion is that it is shared by a larger group.

ritual Formalized sequence of collectively performed activities according to accepted social rules.

social group At least two people form a social group if the contact between them has a degree of regularity and intensity going beyond mere coincidence. There will also be a certain degree of consciousness of being in a social group.

socialization The process by which an individual learns the relevant rules and roles of life in a given social group or society.

society The largest system of human cooperation, interaction and division of labour. Of necessity internally divided. A somewhat fuzzy term.

state Formal, political organization of people of a country, centralized to a certain degree. A state necessarily has the exclusive competence to set laws for all members of the state and enforce these laws. A further condition is sovereignty of a state towards other states.

stereotype A strong, constant notion of persons, groups, events or objects, frequently positively or negatively valued. Stereotypes usually contain only a few superficial characteristics of a specific situation. Stereotypes are adopted and enforced in the socialization process. It is difficult to change or correct a stereotype, even by experiences contradicting it. Stereotypes can be helpful for the individual for his or her orientation within and interaction with the environment.

transcultural Concerning the process of moving beyond culture or moving from one culture into another culture. Does not necessarily imply interaction between cultures. Sometimes erroneously used synonymously with *cross-cultural*.

values Conscious or subconscious ideas guiding the decisions people make.

xenophilia Love and adoration of the foreign.

xenophobia Aversion to foreigners. Sometimes also aversion to the foreign in general. The term has become quite fashionable and is frequently used and interpreted in an incorrect way for anything from fear of foreigners to hostility to foreigners (not to be confused with 'phobia' as used in medicine and psychology, where it means a pathological fear). Contrary to a widespread assumption, the authors believe that fear of foreigners and the foreign in general, as well as xenophobia, is not a natural phenomenon but is to a large degree learned through socialization.

Characteristics of School Links and Exchanges

Intercultural learning projects are frequently organized within the context of school links or exchanges. Therefore, special reference is made to the characteristics of such activities. Most of these characteristics can be used to analyse and describe intercultural learning projects not involving a school link or exchange.

The content and structure of school links and exchanges depend on a number of components, which are interlinked in a rather complex way. The following description of these components provides a thumbnail sketch of what is involved in international school links and exchanges.

INITIAL MOTIVATION

Any school link or exchange is strongly determined by the event or action through which it has been initiated. What was the initial stimulus, the initial reason for establishing contact with a school abroad? How was the contact established? Whose personal engagement did it result from? The initial stimulus is usually reflected in the objectives and the shape of a school link, even if the origin has long been forgotten.

OBJECTIVES

The content and structure of a school link are affected by the objectives pursued. There is a wide range of different objectives underlying school links, which can have very different effects on its content and structure. The following are some examples:

- expanding education in various subjects, such as history or geography;
- development of foreign language skills;

- development of communication competence in general;
- social learning and personal development of pupils;
- reducing prejudices and stereotypes;
- intercultural learning;
- development of international and global awareness;
- political education;
- development of a sense of solidarity;
- introduction of new educational methods;
- revival of school life.

Intercultural learning is only one of many objectives that can be pursued with a school link or an exchange. Chapter 6 outlines in detail the objectives of intercultural learning in general.

CONTENT AND STRUCTURE

The content and structure of a school link are closely interlinked with the objectives pursued. The following types of school links exist.

- Project-orientated school links where the pupils from different schools in different countries work on the same themes at the same time; this does not necessarily imply a personal encounter of the pupils involved in the project.
- School links including personal encounters of pupils from different countries, e.g. through exchanges, which aim at social and intercultural learning.
- School links that are mainly focused on foreign language learning.

Combinations of the above types are possible, especially when schools with different objectives link with each other. For example, a school from a German-, English- or French-speaking country linking with a school from a country with a less spoken/taught language might be interested in a project- or encounter-orientated approach, while the partner school might put the emphasis on foreign language learning. If the different intentions are clear, this does not necessarily have to be a problem as long as the two schools are able to design a content and structure that meet both interests.

AGE OF PUPILS

The influence of the age of the pupils on the content and structure of a school link is clear. School links between primary schools (age up to 10 to 12 years) refer to the affective rather than the cognitive learning process. They will include more playful elements, the presentation of each other's traditions, rituals, songs, etc. They will combine the exploration of their own environment with that of a foreign environment. Encounters will usually only last for one day; accordingly, the geographical distance between the partner schools will be small.

School links involving pupils aged 12 to 14 or older will have a stronger cognitive and intellectual aspect. The content will be more theme-orientated and foreign language skills will play a more important role. The duration of a visit abroad can be longer – up to a month or more – and, consequently, the geographical distance between the schools can be much greater.

TYPE OF SCHOOL

The type of schools involved in a school link normally has an effect on its content and the themes pursued. Schools with a special emphasis, such as technical or commercial, tend to strive for a corresponding type of school partner, while general schools tend to pursue a more general content.

DISTANCE BETWEEN PARTNER SCHOOLS

Since for most school links a personal encounter through an exchange is anticipated, the distance between the schools involved plays an important role. The following exchanges are possible.

Links between schools in neighbouring countries that are reasonably close to the border they have in common

Such school links allow frequent visits to work continuously on common projects and themes. The disadvantage is that there is practically no need to stay overnight in the community with families of the partner school. This takes away an important element of common social and intercultural experience.

School links over a distance that can be travelled both ways during a day or a weekend (up to 140 miles/200 kilometres)

This seems to be the limit for links for the age-group up to 12 years. Beyond that distance, a school link for this age group is usually limited to correspondence. This distance still allows the organization of common projects without great effort. For older pupils (age 13 or older), it is quite an attractive distance. It is far enough to be interesting (further than a regular excursion would go), far enough to require a stay overnight now and then, but close enough to follow up on relationships privately, e.g. during weekends.

School links over a larger distance, which cannot be travelled both ways during the course of the day

The effect of such a distance is that the link can only be realized through correspondence or through exchanges lasting for a few days or even longer. While the latter require more effort and reduce the frequency of personal encounters, they provide for much more intensive social and intercultural learning processes.

DURATION

There is a wide range of possibilities, from encounters between pupils of two schools taking place only once to long-term links, from visits lasting only a day to visits lasting some weeks. As intercultural learning implies a long-term pedagogy, personal encounters taking place only once and only for a short time will not allow for intensive intercultural experiences and learning processes. This requires a long-term relationship between pupils, parents and teachers of two schools in different countries, involving regular personal encounters, common activities and a continuous communication. Only then can it be considered a school link in its actual sense.

SCHOOL ENVIRONMENT

The environment of a school can have an effect on a school link, e.g. if the partner schools are in an urban or rural environment, in an agricultural or industrial environment.

There is no general rule that one should strive for similarities or contrasts in a school link. There will be contrasts in any case. It is even possible that the apparent contrasts caused by different environments will reduce the perception of the sometimes more subtle cultural contrasts. In a diverging environment, one has to be aware that not everything that is perceived to be different from one's own culture is culturally determined but that the same differences might also exist within one's own culture or country. A diverging environment will only mean an additional effort and challenge for pupils as well as for the teachers.

PARTICIPANTS

The following groups can be involved in a school link:

- a group of pupils (from one or more classes);
- a single class;
- a number of classes or the whole school;
- a part of or the whole community.

The participation of these groups in a link will also depend on the legal situation and specific regulations of school authorities in each country, which will affect the structural, organizational and methodological approaches.

The involvement of parents in a school link is both possible and to be encouraged. The involvement will range from a minimal role of receiving a pupil from abroad in the family to active engagement in preparing and organizing extra-curricular elements of the link.

ORGANIZERS

A school link is very much determined by those who organize it, who take responsibility for various tasks and functions, who take care of continuity. The style and atmosphere of a link can be very different depending on who organizes it. Organizers can be:

- the pupils themselves, which would demonstrate a high degree of participation;
- the parents or a parents' association, which would contribute to the strength of the school community;
- the teacher(s), who frequently organize a link on top of their regular work, to overcome the routine of the classroom;
- the headteachers, who, because of their position, can achieve much with respect to organizational aspects of a link but still largely depend on the active engagement of teachers.

Usually, the organizers will be a combination of the above groups. It can be very useful if all these groups are represented in the group of organizers.

Resolutions of the Standing Conference of European Ministers of Education

RESOLUTION NO. 1 ON 'THE EUROPEAN DIMENSION OF EDUCATION: TEACHING AND CURRICULUM CONTENT' (17TH SESSION, VIENNA, 16–17 OCTOBER 1991)

Introduction

1. The European Ministers of Education, meeting for the 17th Session of their Standing Conference in Vienna on 16–17 October 1991 to discuss 'The European dimension of education: teaching and curriculum content';

2. RECALLING a number of official political texts relevant to their discussions:

   • Recommendation 897 (1980) of the Council of Europe's Parliamentary Assembly on 'Educational visits and pupil exchanges between European countries';

   • Recommendation No. R (83) 4 of the Council of Europe's Committee of Ministers on 'The promotion of an awareness of Europe in secondary schools';

   • Resolution of the Council and the Ministers of Education meeting within the Council of the European Communities on the 'European dimension of education' of 24 May 1988;

   • Recommendation 1111 (1989) of the Council of Europe's Parliamentary Assembly on the 'European dimension of education';

   • Resolution 225 (1991) of the Council of Europe's Standing Conference of Local and Regional Authorities of Europe on 'The contribution of local and regional authorities to European education policy';

3. RECALLING also the political goals that underlie the overall objective of promoting European unity through closer cultural, economic and political ties between European nations, viz.,

- to establish lasting peace, cooperation and mutual understanding between the peoples of Europe;
- to safeguard what has already been achieved and to develop the common European heritage of political, cultural, moral and spiritual values which lie at the root of civilised society: human rights, pluralist democracy, tolerance, solidarity and the rule of law;
- to promote sustained economic and social progress, while reducing disparities and safeguarding the environment; and
- to give Europe sufficient weight to fulfil its responsibilities to the whole world;

4. CONSIDERING the changing situation in Europe, notably the accelerating movement towards European unity, the democratisation of countries in Central and Eastern Europe, the prospect of a European economic space and Europe's growing interdependence with the rest of the world;
5. RECOGNISING that these changes will greatly accelerate the trend towards a multi-cultural, multi-lingual European society requiring understanding, tolerance and solidarity between diverse national, ethnic and migrant communities and in which work, study and leisure are characterised by mobility, interchange and communication; in short, that the daily lives of Europeans will increasingly take on a 'living European dimension';
6. AWARE that these developments will not only bring opportunities and challenges but also create difficulties and tensions which education must help to meet and resolve through appropriate policies on school organisation, curriculum content and teaching methods;
7. WELCOMING the work of the international organisations and institutions to promote the European dimension of education, and in particular that of the Council for Cultural Cooperation (CDCC) whose new project 'A Secondary Education for Europe' covers both Western and Eastern Europe;
8. URGING the international organisations and institutions to work together as far as possible in the design and implementation of their programmes on the European dimension of education;
9. ADOPTED the following guidelines designed to further intensify the European dimension of school education:

Educational objectives

10. Education should increase awareness of the growing unity between European peoples and countries and of the establishment of their relations on a new basis. It should also help make the younger generation conscious of their common European identity without losing sight of their global responsibilities or their national, regional and local roots. It should foster understanding of the fact that, in many spheres of our lives, the European perspective applies and that European decisions are necessary. Young people should be inspired to take an active part in shaping Europe's future.

11. The basic values of political, social and individual life which underlie the educational process must be viewed in the framework of a wider European community of peoples and states. This involves:

- the willingness to reach understanding, to overcome prejudice and to be able to recognise mutual interests while at the same time affirming European diversity,
- receptiveness to different cultures while preserving individual cultural identity,
- respect for European legal commitments and the administration of justice within the framework of human rights recognised in Europe,
- the will to co-exist in harmony and to accept compromises in the reconciliation of different interests in Europe,
- concern for preservation of the European and world ecological balance,
- support for freedom, democracy, human rights, justice and economic security,
- the will to maintain peace in Europe and throughout the world.

12. In order to realise this European dimension in education, the school should encourage awareness of:

- the geographical diversity of the European region, with its natural, social and economic features,
- the political and social structures in Europe,
- the historical forces that shaped Europe, including the development of European thinking on law, the state and freedom,
- the patterns of development and characteristic features of European culture in its unity and diversity,
- the multi-lingual nature of Europe and the cultural wealth this represents,
- the history of the European idea and the movement towards integration since 1945,
- the tasks and working methods of the European institutions,
- the need for joint responses in Europe to economic, ecological, social and political challenges.

Implementation

13. In principle, all areas of the school curriculum can make a contribution to the European dimension in teaching and learning as a part of education for international understanding. For this purpose they should incorporate, albeit in distinct ways, concrete aims and themes as well as references to suitable material and methods.

14. In the elementary school, the European dimension should be grasped as far as possible through pupils' direct experience. As for secondary education, including vocational training, there are a number of points of contact in the range of compulsory and optional subjects offered which provide opportunities for specialist or multidisciplinary work.

15. The question of Europe and its development should be an integral part of all teaching in geography, history, social studies/civics as well as subjects incorporating elements of economics and law. In geography this primarily involves basic knowledge about the European region with its various types of landscape and its cultural, environmental and economic characteristics shaped by human activity over the centuries. In history it involves studying the origins of the European peoples and states and the social, political, ideological and religious movements, power struggles, ideas, cultural works, mobility and migrations which have shaped their development. In social studies/civics it involves study of political, social and economic developments and systems, their values, norms and realities. In subjects dealing with economics and law it involves understanding the economic and legal basis of a uniting Europe and the balancing of economic, ecological and social interests. Enabling people to participate in social and economic life in Europe is one of the top priority goals in the teaching of social studies/civics and in subjects dealing with economics and law. This subject matter should also allow pupils to appreciate Europe's role in the world through participation in such activities as the Council of Europe's 'One World' campaigns.

16. As many pupils as possible should be given the opportunity to learn foreign languages, the knowledge of which has a central role to play in opening up Europe's cultural world. In order to develop the ability to conduct a dialogue and communicate, special educational provisions, including bilingual classes at secondary schools and the appointment to schools of native speaker foreign language assistants can be encouraged. Foreign language teachers' initial and in-service training should take account of the communicative approach developed by the Council of Europe. Teaching of the mother tongue should demonstrate the links between that language and its literature, on the one hand, and neighbouring European languages and their respective literatures on the other.

17. Mathematics, natural sciences and technology, religion and philosophy, art and music as well as sport cannot be reduced to the level of national cultures, but, on the contrary, represent part of a common European heritage and part of a common educational tradition. These subjects also make a positive contribution to the process of promoting European awareness. The classical languages are also important for a deeper understanding of the common European heritage.

18. Above and beyond such subject teaching, other opportunities are available for the development of the European dimension. Here, projects on European topics and joint pedagogical projects with schools in neighbouring European countries, in which the exchange of pupils and teachers plays an important part, are recommended. These should involve as many European countries as possible, including partners in Central and Eastern Europe. Thus the environmental school network of the European Community has successfully worked towards cooperation in environmental matters and European environmental awareness. The European Schools Day Competition, with its annual activities and seminars for award-winners, is an important instrument for practical school work on European topics and for encounters between participants

from the countries involved in the educational work of the Council of Europe and the European Community. UNESCO's Associated Schools Project links European schools and those in other regions of the world.

19. The ethnic and cultural heterogeneity of school populations testifies both to Europe's common features and to its diversity. Their presence is an opportunity for intercultural learning in the classroom and for bringing out the wealth of Europe's culture. Learning together with young foreigners and migrants should be designed to strengthen mutual solidarity and the wish to live together peacefully, drawing on the results of the Council of Europe's work on intercultural education.

Recommendations

20. Ministers recommended that the Committee of Ministers of the Council of Europe should consider promoting the further development of the European dimension of education by inviting those responsible to implement the following measures:

   20.1 Full implementation of past resolutions on the European dimension of education and on intercultural and human rights education which should be taken into account in curriculum development.

   20.2 Pursuit of the work in progress within the Education Committee of the Council for Cultural Cooperation in the areas of modern languages, the European dimension of secondary education, adult education, the Teacher Bursaries Scheme, the European Schools Day, and educational documentation and research.

   20.3 Improvement throughout the curriculum of basic information on Europe, on European cooperation and integration and on changing European relationships, and development of educational material intended for both teachers and pupils.

   20.4 Enhancement of teachers' and pupils' motivation to deal with European questions through their own first-hand experience of Europe (increased participation in exchanges, encounters, the European Schools Day Competition, European Clubs, European Heritage Classes, the European Local and Regional History Project proposed by the Standing Conference of Local and Regional Authorities of Europe and foreign language practice) and through media education, making full use of the new information and communication technologies.

   20.5 Pilot projects to promote the subject of Europe in the classroom and European awareness in the school.

   20.6 Innovative forms of schooling such as bilingual classes, international sections, etc., designed to give pupils greater exposure to the European dimension.

   20.7 Development of methods for using school links and exchanges as part of teaching.

20.8   Encouragement of school partnerships, including with Central and Eastern Europe.

20.9   Encouragement of competence in foreign languages, including minority languages.

20.10 Consideration of bilingual teaching.

20.11 Incorporation of the European dimension and foreign language learning into initial teacher education.

20.12 Organisation of in-service education for teachers on the subject of Europe and the European dimension.

20.13 Mutual acceptance of school-leaving examinations and certificates.

20.14 Strengthening the European dimension of educational guidance and counselling services.

20.15 Strengthening contacts between the European region and the other regions of the world, notably the developing countries.

21. Ministers decided to examine the results of the CDCC's project 'A Secondary Education for Europe' at one of their future sessions.

III. RESOLUTION ON 'THE PROMOTION OF SCHOOL LINKS AND EXCHANGES IN EUROPE' (18TH SESSION, MADRID, 23–24 MARCH 1994)

The European Ministers of Education, meeting in Madrid at the 18th Session of their Standing Conference.

1   RECALL their Resolution on 'The European Dimension of Education' (Vienna, 1991) which noted that study, work and leisure in Europe are increasingly characterised by mobility, interchange and communication;

2   RE-AFFIRM that school links and exchanges are an essential element in preparing young people for life in a democratic, multilingual and multicultural Europe because they can:
(a) encourage understanding and friendship between young people from different linguistic, cultural and religious traditions;
(b) impart knowledge and experience of other regions and countries;
(c) develop open-mindedness, tolerance and respect for the culture, history and lifestyle of other peoples and nations;
(d) promote an awareness both of the common European heritage and of Europe's interdependence with other continents;

3   ARE CONVINCED that:
(a) as many young people as possible – in primary, secondary, vocational and special education – should be helped to participate in school links and exchanges.
(b) school links and exchanges are most effective when they receive strong political support, meet clear educational objectives and involve all educa-

tional partners: ministries of education, local authorities, parents, teachers, specialised agencies and non-governmental organisations;

(c) the success of school links and exchanges depends on thorough preparation, careful supervision and rigorous evaluation, as well as appropriate training and support for teachers and school principals;

(d) the development of school links and exchanges should not be hampered by legal and administrative problems, e.g. visas, the civil liability of accompanying teachers and the cost of insurance;

4　POINT OUT that such links and exchanges can involve most, if not all, subjects in the curriculum and that because of greater possibilities for international contacts, communication and travel, schools can now choose from a much wider range of forms of school links and exchanges than in the past, e.g.:

(a) the exchange of letters, photos, audio-cassettes, videos, computer disks and teaching material;

(b) school visits, field trips, and the short and long term exchange of pupils and teachers;

(c) fax, electronic mail, teleconferencing and satellite links;

(d) regional projects involving schools in neighbouring countries;

(e) bilateral and multilateral curriculum-based projects with schools in other countries and continents;

5　WELCOME the recent initiatives on school links and exchanges within the Council of Europe, in particular:

(a) the setting up, by the Council for Cultural Co-operation (the CDCC), of a European information network on school links and exchanges to promote the sharing of information, experience and good practice;

(b) the support given by the CDCC to the regular European Children's Theatre Encounters and activities on European Heritage Classes;

(c) the implementation, by the Standing Conference of Local and Regional Authorities of Europe (the CLRAE), of the twinning programme for Albanian schools, as well as the European Local and Regional History Project.

6　TAKE ACCOUNT of the fact that important activities on school links and exchanges are also under way in the other European Institutions and in international non-governmental organisations, e.g.:

(a) the pilot project on multilateral school partnerships of the Commission of the European Communities;

(b) the NORDPLUS Junior Project of the Nordic Council of Ministers;

(c) the Associated Schools Project of UNESCO;

7　CONGRATULATE the Europe at School/European Schools Day Competition on its 40th Anniversary and on its extension to countries in Central and Eastern Europe. This joint activity of the Council of Europe, the Commission of the European Communities, the European Parliament and the European Cultural Foundation has played a pioneering role in the promoting of the European dimension in schools, and, in the next phase of its activities, it should become the basis for new forms of school links and European projects;

8   RECOMMEND that member States should:
(a) acknowledge school links and exchanges as an integral part of education at all levels of schooling and support them with all appropriate means – political, legal, administrative and financial;
(b) favour measures to allow all young people, during their schooling and vocational education, to participate fully in international projects and exchanges;
(c) provide teachers, school principals and educational administrators with the training, support and legal advice necessary for the successful planning and implementation of school links and exchanges;
(d) recognise the periods of study of pupils who take part in long-term exchanges with schools in other countries;
(e) encourage schools to establish bilateral or multilateral links and exchanges with their counterparts in as many countries as possible, and not just to concentrate on the bigger countries or those whose languages are widely spoken;
(f) help teachers to take part in international exchanges which can broaden their professional experience and allow them to establish links of friendship with colleagues from other countries;

9   ASK the Council of Europe to:
(a) examine, in the Committee of Ministers, whether the European Agreement on Travel by young Persons on Collective Passports between member States could be updated to take account of the new pan-European dimension of school exchanges and the multicultural character of many schools in Europe;
(b) develop its Network on School Links and Exchanges as a service activity to:
   • organise the exchange and dissemination of information, experience and good practice, e.g. through a newsletter, publications and training seminars organised within the framework of the Teacher Bursaries Scheme;
   • prepare innovatory projects and studies on teacher training and the theory and practice of exchanges;
   • establish priorities for action at national and European level, in cooperation with the other European organisations (in particular the European Union, UNESCO and the Nordic Council of Ministers) and international non-governmental organisations;
(c) give high priority to the further development of the Teacher Bursaries Scheme, which should be expanded to cater for more teachers from Central and Eastern Europe;
(d) explore the educational potential of its European Cultural Routes Project, e.g. by encouraging links, field trips, exchanges and projects with an historical dimension between schools on the Routes.

SOCRATES: Promoting European Cooperation in Education

Education and training are of central importance to Europe's economic and social future. Through exchanges of people and ideas, European cooperation can contribute to raising the overall quality of teaching methods and materials and to developing more appropriate ways of meeting new learning challenges.

The European Community action programme for cooperation in the field of education, SOCRATES, was launched in 1995 and runs to the end of 1999. Spanning the 15 Member States of the European Union, as well as Norway, Iceland and Liechtenstein, it is the first European initiative covering education at all ages and forms part of a broader approach to the concept of lifelong learning.

Far from aiming at uniformity, the programme is designed to derive maximum benefit from the diversity of education systems in the different countries. It supports transnational cooperation as a means of searching out innovative solutions appropriate to particular circumstances.

Familiarity with other countries, languages and ways of life is an increasingly necessary educational and professional asset. Mobility and exchange schemes are therefore an important feature of SOCRATES. At the same time the programme aims to provide a European dimension to learning at home as well as abroad. Joint curricula development and school projects, exchange visits for teachers and university staff, the use of electronic distance learning methods and European networking between educational administrators are all part of the overall approach.

The programme gives particular consideration to making sure that poorer or more remote regions can participate fully. The educational needs of disabled or other disadvantaged people and equal opportunities are stressed in all aspects.

OBJECTIVES

Article 126 of the Maastricht Treaty on European Union, which came into force in November 1993, provides that the Community 'shall contribute to the development of quality education' by means of a range of actions, to be carried out in close cooperation with the Member States.

The specific objectives of the SOCRATES programme are:

- To develop the European dimension in education at all levels so as to strengthen the spirit of European citizenship, drawing on the cultural heritage of each Member State.
- To promote a quantitative and qualitative improvement of the knowledge of the languages of the European Union.
- To promote the intercultural dimension of education.
- To promote cooperation between institutions in the Member States at all levels of education, thereby enhancing their intellectual and teaching potential.
- To encourage the mobility of teachers, so as to promote a European dimension in studies and to contribute to the qualitative improvement of their skills.
- To encourage mobility for students, enabling them to complete part of their studies in another Member State.
- To encourage contacts among pupils at all types of schools.
- To encourage the academic recognition of diplomas, periods of study and other qualifications, with the aim of facilitating the development of an open European area for cooperation in education.
- To encourage open and distance education in the European context.
- To foster exchanges of information on education systems and promote exchange of experience among educational policy makers in the Member States.

WHO CAN PARTICIPATE?

SOCRATES applies to all types and levels of education, from kindergarten through to postgraduate courses. The programme encompasses:

- Educational institutions of all kinds, including all forms of general, technical and vocational schools, nursery schools, institutions providing initial and/or in-service teacher-training, universities and other higher education institutions, adult education establishments.
- Teaching staff of all categories.
- Learners of all ages, whether in formal schooling or adult education courses, studying on a full-time or part-time basis, at educational institutions or in open/distance learning contexts.
- Staff responsible for managing institutions.
- Educational counsellors and advisers.
- The educational inspectorate.
- Educational policy-makers at local, regional and national level.
- Associations and societies active in the educational field.
- Enterprises, organisations and agencies working with education or involved in the production and dissemination of educational materials and products.

In the European Union there are:

- 119 million young people (under 25), about one-third of the total population.
- 69 million pupils enrolled in 320,000 schools (35 million at secondary and 24 million at primary level); a further 10 million attend pre-school classes.
- Over 4 million teachers in primary and secondary education.
- 11 million students at more than 5,000 universities or other higher education institutions.
- Several million adult learners.

SOCRATES draws on the experience of European Community programmes launched in specific sectors of education in recent years.

These include the Erasmus programme in higher education and the Lingua programme for European language learning, which between them have offered study abroad opportunities to nearly 500,000 students since 1987.

There have also been smaller-scale actions, such as teacher exchanges and initiatives in intercultural education and for the children of migrant workers and occupational travellers.

SOCRATES extends these measures and incorporates them, together with other Community initiatives such as the European education information network Eurydice and the Arion study visits scheme for educational decision-makers, to form the first comprehensive and unified educational cooperation programme at European Union level.

The programme also interacts closely with other initiatives at EU level, notably the Leonardo da Vinci programme for vocational training, the Youth for Europe III programme and various parts of the 4th Framework Programme for research and technology development.

WHAT ACTIVITIES ARE INVOLVED?

SOCRATES has a budget of Ecu 850 million over the 1995–99 period, which is reviewable in 1997. The funding is designed to support a broad range of activities, including:

- The creation and promotion of transnational projects, networks, partnerships and associations.
- The development of curricula, modules, teaching materials and other educational products.
- Exchanges and mobility.
- Transnational training courses for educational staff.
- Visits to facilitate project preparation or sharing of experience.
- The preparation of studies, analyses, guides and data collection activities.
- Project evaluation.
- The dissemination of results.

The programme is structured to promote European cooperation in six areas:
- Higher education
- School education
- Learning of European languages
- Open and distance learning
- Adult education
- Exchange of information and experience on education systems and policy.

APPLICATION AND SELECTION PROCEDURES

Procedures for the submission and selection of applications for support within SOCRATES vary considerably, depending on whether the particular Action is managed centrally by the Commission or on a decentralised basis by the National Agencies designated by the participating countries. The National Agencies have specific responsibilities relating to the selection of projects under certain Actions, together with the monitoring and financial management duties which accompany this. In addition, the Agencies perform a number of important functions in the dissemination of information, channeling feedback on the way the programme is functioning, and ensuring operational complementarity with programmes and schemes operating at national level.

THE SOCRATES PROGRAMME AT A GLANCE

Chapter I Higher Education (Erasmus)

Action 1 **Grants to universities for European dimension activities**
Institutional contracts (for organizing student and teaching staff mobility, European Credit Transfer System, curriculum and course development, intensive programmes, study visits)
University cooperation projects on subjects of mutual interest ('Thematic Networks')

Action 2 **Student mobility grants**

Chapter II School Education (Comenius)

Action 1 **School partnerships** for European Education Projects, including teacher exchanges and visits

Action 2 **Education of the children of migrant workers, occupational travellers, travellers and gypsies/intercultural education**

Action 3 **In-service training, seminars and courses for teachers and educators**
3.1 grants for developing and organising courses
3.2 grants for participants

Chapter III Horizontal Measures

Action 1 Promotion of language learning (Lingua)
- A European Cooperation Programmes for language teacher training
- B In-service training in the field of language teaching
- C Assistantships for future language teachers
- D Development of instruments for language teaching and assessment of linguistic competence
- E Joint educational projects for language learning

Action 2 Open and distance learning (ODL)
- – European cooperation in Open and Distance learning
- – ODL activities related to other parts of SOCRATES

Action 3 Exchange of information and experience
- 3.1 Questions of common educational policy interest
- 3.2 European Information Network in the field of Education (EURYDICE)
- 3.3 Visits scheme for educational decision-makers (ARION)
- 3.4 Network of National Academic Recognition Information Centres (NARIC)
- 3.5 Other measures
- 3.5A Adult education
  - – promoting awareness of other European countries and the EU
  - – quality enhancement of adult education in Europe
- 3.5B Complementary measures
  - – European associations, publications on the European dimension
  - – awareness-raising activities to promote European cooperation
  - – monitoring and evaluation of SOCRATES actions
  - – information activities of SOCRATES National Agencies

For each part of the programme, Guidelines for Applicants are available, which contain all necessary details concerning the application procedures and the criteria taken into account during selection. This document and other information may be obtained on request from:

- the SOCRATES & Youth Technical Assistance Office, which provides the Commission with technical assistance in the implementation of the programme:

  SOCRATES & Youth Technical Assistance Office
  Rue Montoyerstraat 70
  B-1000 Bruxelles
  Tel: (32) 2 2330111
  Fax: (32) 2 2330150
- the SOCRATES National Agencies.

Addresses

INTERNATIONAL INSTITUTIONS AND ORGANIZATIONS

The European Commission
200 rue de la Loi
B-1049 Brussels
Belgium

The Nordic Council of Ministers
18, Store Strandstraede
DK-1255 Copenhagen K
Denmark

The Council of Europe
F-67075 Strasbourg Cedex
France

The Organisation for Economic Cooperation and Development (OECD)
2, rue André-Pascal
F-75775 Paris Cedex 16
France

The United Nations Educational,
Scientific and Cultural Organization
(UNESCO)
7, place de Fontenoy
F-75700 Paris
France

EUROPEAN AND INTERNATIONAL ASSOCIATIONS OF TEACHERS AND TEACHER TRAINERS

The Association for Teacher Education
in Europe (ATEE)
51, rue de la Concorde
B-1050 Brussels
Belgium

The European Association of Teachers
(EAT)
Koningsholster 64
NL-6573 VV Beck-Ubbergen
The Netherlands

The European Secondary Heads
  Association (ESHA)
p/a Ambtenarencentrum
Laan van Meerdervoort 48
NL-2517 AM The Hague
The Netherlands

The European Trade Union
  Committee on Education (ETUCE)
33, rue de Trèves
B-1040 Brussels
Belgium

The International Federation of Free
  Teachers' Unions (IFFTU)
NZ Voorburgwal 120–126
NL-1012 SH Amsterdam
The Netherlands

The International Federation of
  Teachers' Associations (IFTA)
3, rue de la Rochefoucauld
F-75009 Paris
France

The World Confederation of Teachers
  (WCT)
33, rue de Trèves
B-1040 Brussels
Belgium

The World Organisation for Early
  Childhood Education (OMEP)
Lille Frøens vei 10
N-0369 Oslo 3
Norway

The World Union of Catholic
  Teachers (UMEC)
General Secretariat
Piazza San Calisto 16
1-00153 Rome
Italy

COUNCIL OF EUROPE: NETWORK SCHOOL LINKS AND EXCHANGES

Albania/Albanie
Mr Vladimir Thanati
Ministry of Education
Department of International Relations
Tirana
Tel: 355-42-222-60
Fax: 355-42-320-02

Austria/Autriche
Mag. Dr Anna Steiner
Bundesministerium für Unterricht und
  Kunst
Minoritenplatz 5
A-1014 Wien
Tel: 43-1-53120-3511
Fax: 43-1-53120-3535

Belarus
Mr Iouri Beloussov
Senior Inspector
Foreign Relations Department
Ministry of Education
Sovetskaya 9
220010 Minsk
Tel: 7-0172–20-71-21/
    7-0172-26-44-84
Fax: 7-0172-27-17-36

Belgium/Belgique
French Community/Communauté
française
M. Georges Richelle
Ministère de l'Education de la
Communauté française Belgique
Agence intégrée des programmes
européens
Place Surlet de Chokier 15-17
B-1000 Bruxelles
Tel: 32-2-221-89-39
Fax: 32-2-221-89-23

Flemish Community/Communauté
flamande
Ms Annemie Dewael, Director of
Administration
Ministry of Education of the Flemish
Community
Koningsstraat 138, 5th Floor
B-1000 Brussels
Tel: 32-2-211-45-82
Fax: 32-2-211-45-35

Bulgaria/Bulgarie
Mme Ivanka Yordanova
Departement des relations internationales
Ministère de l'Education, de la Science
et des technologies
bd Dondoukov 2A
BG-1000 Sofia
Tel: 3592-88-49-74
Fax: 3592-88-49-74 (84-87-34)

Croatia/Croatie
Prof. Alida Matkovic
Ministry of Education and Sports
Trg Burze 6
HR–41000 Zagreb
Tel: 385-1-469-044 / 469-000
Fax: 385-1-410-492

Cyprus/Chypre
Dr Constantinos Yialoucas
Inspector of the Teaching of Classics in
Secondary Education
Ministry of Education
Nicosia
Tel: 357-2-443513
Fax: 357-2-443515

Czech Republic/Republique Tcheque
Ms Alena Bouskova
Department of International Relations
Ministry of Education, Youth and
Sports
Karmelitska 7
CZ-11812 Praha 1
Tel: 42-2-519-36-83/42-2-519-32-37
Fax: 42-2-519-37-94/42-2-519-37-90

Denmark/Danemark
Ms Annemarie Holm
ICU
Vandkunsten 3
DK-1467 Kobenhavn, K
Tel: 45-33-14-20-60
Fax: 45-33-14-36-40

Estonia/Estonie
Mrs Made Kirtsi
Department of Foreign Relations
Ministry of Culture and Education
11 Tonismägi Str
EE0106 Tallinn
Tel: 372-2-68-19-40
Fax: 372-2-31-12-13

Finland/Finlande
Ms Pirjo Immonen-Oikkonen, Senior
advisor
National Board of Education
PO Box 380
SF-00351 Helsinki
Tel: 358-0-77477038
Fax: 358-0-77477247

France
Mme Jenny Hall
Ministère de l'Education Nationale
Bureau DAGIC
173, Boulevard Saint-Germain
F-75006 Paris
Tel: 33-1-40-65-62-64
Fax: 33-1-45-44-00-24

Germany/Allemagne
Frau Ilse-Brigitte Eitze-Schütz
Pädagogischer Austauschdienst
    Sekretariat der Kultusministerkonferenz
Nassestrasse 8
D-53115 Bonn
Tel: 49-228-501-583
Fax: 49-228-501-500

Greece/Grece
Mme Roxani Elefteriadou
Ministère de l'Education Nationale
Chef de la Section 'Echanges Culturels'
15 rue Mitropoleos
GR 10185 Athens
Tel: 30-1-32-35-200
Fax: 30-1-32-21-521

Holy See/Saint-siége
Mgr Josef Benacek
Congrégation pour l'Education
    Catholique
Cité du Vatican
Tel: 39-6/698-84-165
Fax: 39-6/698-84-172

Hungary/Hongrie
Mr Zoltán Zarándy
Department of Public Educational
    Research and Development
Ministry of Culture and Education
Szalay u. 10-14
H-1055 Budapest
Tel: 36-1-153-06-00
Fax: 36-1-112-80-88

Iceland/Islande
Ms Erna Arnadottir, Educational
    consultant
Ministry of Culture and Education
Sölvholsgata 4
IS-150 Reykjavik
Tel: 354-1-609560
Fax: 354-1-623068

Ireland/Irlande
Ms Brídín Gilroy
LEARGAS
The Exchange Bureau
Avoca House
189/193 Parnell Street
Dublin 1
Tel: 353-1-873-1411
Fax: 353-1-873-1316

Italy/Italie
Mme Maria Elisabetta Sassi
Ministero Pubblica Istruzione
Direz. Gen. Scambi Culturali
Via I. Nievo 35
I-00153 Roma
Tel: 39-6-58495824
Fax: 39-6-58495835

Latvia/Lettonie
Mr Kalvis Salis, Vice Director
Youth and Environment Centre
'Saulesdarzs'
Ezermalas 24/26
LV-1014 Riga
Tel: 371-2-755-7998
Fax: 371-2-755-7687

Lithuania/Lituanie
Ms Rasa Snipiene
Foreign Relations Department
Ministry of Education and Science
A. Volano 2/7
2691 Vilnius
Tel: 370-2-62-2483/370-2-61-00-34
Fax: 370-2-61-20-77

Luxembourg
M. Edouard Schmitz, Professeur
  Chargé de mission
Service d'Innovation et de Recherches
  pédagogiques
Ministère de l'Education nationale
29 rue Aldringen
L-2926 Luxembourg
Tel: 353-478-5193
Fax: 353-478-51-30

Malta/Malte
Mr Charles Saliba/Mr Busuttil
Youth Service Organisation
Department of Education
M-Floriana, Malta CMR 02
Tel: 356-221-401/2/3
Fax: 356-240-898

Netherlands/Pays-Bas
Ms Anke Butteveld
European Platform for Dutch Education
Bexuidenhoutseweg 253
NL-2591-AM, The Hague
Tel: 31-70-381-4448
Fax: 31-70-383-1958

Norway/Norvege
Mr Lars E. Ulsnes
Norwegian Ministry of Education,
  Research and Church Affairs
P.O. Box 8119 Dep.
N-0032 Oslo
Tel: 47-22-34-76-63
Fax: 47-22-34-27-15

Portugal
Mme Margarida Belard
Coordinatrice nationale du Programme
  Dimension européenne dans
  l'Education
Av. 5 de Outubro 107/60
P 1000 Lisboa
Tel: 351-1-79-60-984
Fax: 351-1-79-60-984

Romania/Roumanie
Mme Viorica Tane
Ministère de l'Enseignement et de la
  Science
12, rue Spiru Haret
RO-70738 Bucarest
Tel: 40-1-613-9228/312-4753
Fax: 40-1-312-47-53

Russia/Russie
Mr Iourat Albetkov
Head, Division of International Exchanges
Department of International Cooperation
Russian Ministry of Education
6 Tchistoproudny Boulvar
101856 Moscow
Tel: 7-095-923-5002
Fax: 7-095-924-69-89

Slovak Republic
Dr Danica Bakassova
Ministry of Education
Hlboica 2
SK-81339 Bratislava
Tel: 42-7-39-77-02
Fax: 42-7-39-72-28

Slovenia/Slovenie
Ms Jelka Arh
Ministry of Education and Sport
Board of Education and Sport
Zupanciceva 6
61 000 Ljubljana
Tel: 386-61-322-776
Fax: 386-61-327-212

Spain/Espagne
Ms Lucia Gutierrez
Ministerio de Educacion y Ciencia
Servicio de Actividades de Alumnos
c/Torrelaguna no 58
E-28027 Madrid
Tel: 34-1-4082008 Ext. 239
Fax: 34-1-408-83763

Sweden/Suede
Mr Bertil Bucht
Deputy Assistant Under-Secretary
Swedish Ministry of Education and
  Science
S-10333 Stockholm
Tel: 46-8-763-17-91/17-82
Fax: 46-8-723-17-34

Switzerland/Suisse
Mme Silvia Mitteregger
Coordonnatrice d'Echanges de Jeunes
CH Jugendaustausch
Hauptbahnhofstr. 2
CH-4501 Solothurn
Tel: 41-65-625-2680
Fax: 41-65-625-2688

Turkey/Turquie
M. Ibrahim Demirel
Chef de la Section du Conseil de
  l'Europe au Ministère de l'Education
  Nationale
Milli Egitim Bakanligi
Disliskiler Genel Mudurlugu Bakaniklar
TR Ankara
Tel: 90-1-312-418-06-09/
  90-1-312-425-41-80
Fax: 90-1-312-418-82-89

United Kingdom/Royaume-Uni
Ms Elspeth Cardy
Central Bureau for Educational Visits
  and Exchanges
c/o The British Council
10 Spring Gardens
London SW1A 2BN
Tel: 44-171-389-4004/44-171-389-4733
Fax: 44-171-389-4426

EUROPEAN FEDERATION FOR INTERCULTURAL LEARNING (EFIL)

European Federation for Intercultural
  Learning (EFIL)
rue des colonies/Koloniënstraat 18–24
B-1000 Bruxelles/Brussel
Belgium

AFS Österreich
Austauschprogramme für
  Interkulturelles Lernen
Maria-TheresienStrasse 9
A-1090 Wien
Austria

AFS Interkulturele Programma's VZW
Brand Whitlocklaan 132
B-1200 Brussel
Belgium

AFS Programmes Interculturels ASBL
Boulevard Brand Whitlock 132
B-1200 Bruxelles
Belgium

AFS Ceska Republika
Zlatnicka 7
11000 Praha 1
Czech Republic

Dansk AFS
Nordre Fasanveg 111
DK-2000 Frederiksberg
Denmark

Suomen AFS r.y.
PO Box 47
SF-00131 Helsinki
Finland

AFS Vivre sans Frontière
46 rue du Commandant Duhail
F-94120 Fontenay-sous-Bois
France

AFS Interkulturelle Begegnungen e.V.
Postfach 50 01 42
D-22701 Hamburg
Germany

AFS Hungary
Alkotas u.37, 1/6
H-1123 Budapest
Hungary

AFS á Islandi
P.O. Box 753
IS-121 Reykjavik
Iceland

Interculture Ireland
10A Lower Camden Street
IRL-Dublin 2
Ireland

Intercultura Italy
Via Gracco del Secco 100
I-53034 Colle Val d'Elsa
Italy

AFS Scarptautiskas Apmainas
   Programmas Latvija
c/o Ministry of Education, Culture and
   Science
2 Valnu Street
1098 Riga
Latvia

AFS Interkulterele Programma's
Marnixkade 65A
NL-1015 XW Amsterdam
Netherlands

AFS Norge Internasjonal Utveksling
Akersgaten 18
N-0158 Oslo
Norway

Intercultura Portugal
Rua Joaquim Antonio de Aguiar 43,
   Cave Esq^a
P-1070 Lisboa
Portugal

National Intercultural Foundation
Building 6
2-A, Korolenko Street
Moscow 10714
Russia

AFS Slovakia
Ventúrska 4
811 01 Bratislava
Slovakia

Intercultura
C/Doctor Guiu 19B
E-28305 Madrid
Spain

AFS Interkulturell Utbildning
Box 45187
S-10430 Stockholm
Sweden

AFS Interkulturelle Programme
Löwenstrasse 16
CH 8001 Zürich
Switzerland

AFS Tunisia
61 rue de la Liberté
1002 Tunis
Tunisia

Türk Kültür Vakfi (TKV)
Valikonagi Cad.
Konak apt. 67/4
80220 Nisantasi, Istanbul
Turkey

AFS Intercultural Education
   Programmes
Arden House
Wellington Street
Bingley, West Yorkshire BD16 2NB
United Kingdom

Bibliography

AFS Intercultural Programs (1984), *Statement of AFS Educational Content and Learning Objectives*, Montreal: AFS Intercultural Programs.

Agnès, J. (1994), *The Fax! Programme*, Strasbourg: Council of Europe Press.

Albert, R. and Triandis, H. (1985), 'Intercultural education for multicultural societies', *International Journal of Intercultural Relations*, **9**.

Alix, C. and Kodron, C. (1988), *Zusammenarbeiten: Gemeinsam Lernen, Themenzentrierte Zusammenarbeit zwischen Schulen verschiedener Länder am Beispiel Deutschland-Frankreich*, Frankfurt: Deutsch-französisches Jugendwerk.

Alix, C. and Kodron, C. (1989), 'Schüleraustausch als Teil interkulturellen und themenzentrierten Zusammenarbeitens', in B. Müller (ed.), *Anders Lernen im Fremdsprachenunterricht. Experimente aus der Praxis*, Berlin/Munich: Langenscheidt.

Alix, C. (1990), *Pakt mit der Fremdheit. Interkulturelles Lernen als dialogisches Lernen im Kontext internationaler Schulkooperationen*, Frankfurt/Main: Verlag für interkulturelle Kommunikation.

Anderson, B. (1983), *Imagined Communities: Reflections on the Origin and Spread of Nationalism*, London: Verso.

Arbeitsgemeinschaft für Friedenspädagogik (1980), *Das Bild vom Feind*, Munich: Arbeitsgemeinschaft Friedenspädagogik eV.

Arbeitskreis deutscher Bildungsstätten eV (1990), *Außerschulische Bildung* 2/90, Bonn: Arbeitskreis deutscher Bildungsstätten eV.

Arora, R. and Duncan, C. (1987), *Multicultural Education: Towards Good Practice*, New York: Routledge & Kegan Paul.

Auernheimer, G. (1988), *Der sogenannte Kulturkonflikt. Orientierungsprobleme ausländischer Jugendlicher*, Frankfurt/Main, New York: Campus.

Auernheimer, G. (1990), *Einführung in die Interkulturelle Erziehung*, Darmstadt: Wissenschaftliche Buchgesellschaft.

Bachner, D.J., Zeutschel, U. and Shannon, D. (1993), 'Methodological issues in researching the effects of US/German educational youth exchange: a case study', *International Journal of Intercultural Relations*, **17** (1).

Barley, N. (1983), *The Innocent Anthropologist*, Harmondsworth: Penguin.

Barley, N. (1990), *Native Land*, Harmondsworth: Penguin.

Barres, E. (1978), *Vorurteil. Theorie. Forschungsergebnisse-Praxisrelevanz*, Opladen: Leske & Budrich.

Batchelder, D. and Warner, E. (1977), *Beyond Experience*, Brattleboro, VT: The Experiment in International Living.

Batelaan, P. (1983), *The Practice of Intercultural Education*, London: Commission for Racial Equality.

Belard, M. (1993), *European Clubs*, Strasbourg: Council of Europe Press.

Borelli, M. (ed.) (1986), *Interkulturelle Pädagogik. Positionen-Kontroversen-Perspektiven*, Baltmannsweiler: Pädagogischer Verlag Burgbücherei Schneider.

Borelli, M. and Hoff, G. (eds) (1987), *Interkulturelle Pädagogik im internationalen Vergleich*, Baltmannsweiler: Pädagogischer Verlag Burgbücherei Schneider.

Braham, P., Rattansi, A. and Skellington, R. (eds) (1992), *Racism and Antiracism: Inequalities, Opportunities and Policies*, London: Sage Publications in association with the Open University.

Bräuer, G. (1991), *Handreichung für den interkulturellen Schüleraustausch*, Bonn: Deutsche UNESCO-Kommission.

Breitenbach, D. (ed.) (1979), *Kommunikationsbarrieren in der internationalen Jugendarbeit*, Forschungsprojekt im Auftrag des Bundesministeriums für Jugend, Familie, Gesundheit, Band I-V, Saarbrücken/Fort Lauderdale, FL: Verlag Breitenbach.

Brislin, R. (1977), *Cultural Learning: Concepts, Applications and Research*, Honolulu: The East–West Center.

Brislin, R. (1981), *Cross-cultural Encounters: Face-to-Face Interaction*, New York: Pergamon Press.

Brislin, R. and Pederson, P. (1976), *Cross-cultural Orientation Programs*, New York: Gardner Press.

Byram, M. and Zarate, J. (1995), *Young People Facing Difference*, Strasbourg: Council of Europe Press.

Çağlar, A. (1990/1), 'Das Kultur-Konzept als Zwangsjacke in Studien zur Arbeitsmigration', *Zeitschrift für Türkeistudien*, no. 1, 93–105.

Central Bureau for Educational Visits and Exchanges (1991), *Making the Most of Your Partner School Abroad*, London: CBEVE.

Central Bureau for Educational Visits and Exchanges (1993), *The European Dimension in Education*, London: CBEVE.

Clark, J., Hall, S., Jefferson, T. and Roberts, B. (1976), 'Subcultures, cultures and class', in S. Hall and T. Jefferson (eds), *Resistance through Rituals. Youth Subcultures in Post-war Britain*, London: Hutchinson.

Calvino, I. *Time and the Hunter*, London: Picador.

Council for Cultural Co-operation (1989), *Experiments in Intercultural Education, Guides for Intercultural Teaching Activities*, Strasbourg: Council for Cultural Co-operation, School Education Division, Council of Europe.

Council for Cultural Co-operation (1989), *Using the New Technologies to Create Links between Schools Throughout the World*, Strasbourg: Council for Cultural Co-operation, School Education Division, Council of Europe.

Council for Cultural Co-operation (1991), *Council of Europe Action in the School Education*

Field, Strasbourg: Council for Cultural Co-operation, School Education Division, Council of Europe.

Council for Cultural Co-operation (1992), *School Links and Exchanges in Europe, a Practical Guide*, Strasbourg: Council for Cultural Co-operation, School Education Division, Council of Europe.

Council of Europe (1980–2), *Dossiers for the Intercultural Training of Teachers*, DECS/EGT (79) 103–125, Strasbourg: Council of Europe.

Council of Europe Network on School Links and Exchanges (1991–3), *Reports of Meetings*: First, Brighton, England, December 1991; Second, Colle Val d'Elsa, Italy, July 1992; Third, Stavanger, Norway, October 1992; Fourth, Stockholm, Sweden, October 1993; Fifth, Bialobrjegi, Poland, September 1994; Sixth, Solothurn, Switzerland, October 1995.

Craig, J. (1984), *Culture Shock. Singapore and Malaysia*, Singapore: Times Books International.

Cushner, K. (1990), *They Are Talking about Me!* New York: AFS Intercultural Programs.

Dankwortt, D. (1959), *Probleme der Anpassung an eine fremde Kultur*, Cologne: Carl-Duiserg Gesellschaft eV.

Dannemann, G. (1988), *Barriers to Youth Mobility*, Strasbourg: European Youth Centre, Council of Europe.

Devereux, G. (1976), *Angst und Methode in den Verhaltenswissenschaften*, Frankfurt/Berlin/Vienna: Ullstein.

Duroselle, J.-B. (1990), *Europe: A History of Its Peoples*, Harmondsworth: Penguin.

Erdheim, M. (1988), *Psychoanalyse und Unbewußtheit in der Kultur*, Frankfurt/Main: Suhrkamp.

Essinger, H. and Kula, O.B. (1987), *Pädagogik als interkultureller Prozeß*, Felsberg/Istanbul: Migro Verlag.

European Association for Teachers and European Research Group on Training for School Exchanges (1993), *Teaching for Exchanges – Aims and Ways of Teacher-training*, Strasbourg: Council of Europe Press.

European Federation for Intercultural Learning (1985), *Common Values for Humankind?*, Strasbourg: European Youth Centre.

European Federation for Intercultural Learning (1987), *Orientation*, Remich: European Youth Foundation, Council of Europe.

European Federation for Intercultural Learning (1989), *Understanding and Working with European Secondary School Systems*, Strasbourg: European Youth Centre, Council of Europe.

European Federation for Intercultural Learning (1991), *The Role and Implementation of Language Learning in EFIL Exchanges*, Strasbourg: European Youth Centre, Council of Europe.

European Federation for Intercultural Learning (1991), *The New Europe: Are We Ready?*, Strasbourg: European Youth Centre, Council of Europe.

European Youth Centre (1991), *Preparation and Programme,* Strasbourg: European Youth Centre, Training Courses Resource File, Council of Europe.

European Youth Centre (1991), *Introductory Approaches*, Strasbourg: European Youth Centre, Training Courses Resource File, Council of Europe.

European Youth Centre (1991), *Intercultural Learning – Basic Texts*, Strasbourg: European

Youth Centre, Training Courses Resource File, Council of Europe.

European Youth Centre (1991), *Intercultural Learning – Examples of Methods and Uses*. Strasbourg: European Youth Centre, Training Courses Resource File, Council of Europe.

European Youth Centre (1991), *Introduction to Simulation Games*, Strasbourg: European Youth Centre, Training Courses Resource File, Council of Europe.

European Youth Centre (1995a), *Domino*, Strasbourg: European Youth Centre, Council of Europe.

European Youth Centre (1995b), *Education Pack, for out of School and Informal Education Activities*, Strasbourg: European Youth Centre, Council of Europe.

Fantini, A., McCoy, M.V., Tannenbaum, E. and Wright, L. (1984), *Cross-cultural Orientation: A Guide for Leaders and Educators*, Brattleboro, VT: The Experiment in International Living.

Fennes, H. *et al.* (1984), *Projektunterricht 'Interkulturelles Lernen in der Schule'*, Vienna: Bundesministerium für Unterricht und Kunst/AFS Österreich.

Fennes, H. *et al.* (1993), *Grenzübergänge*, Vienna: Bundesministerium für Unterricht und Kunst.

Fennes, H. *et al.* (1996), *Internationale Schulpartnerschaften. Ein Leitfaden*, Vienna: Bundesministerium für Unterricht und kulturelle Angelegenheiten.

Freise, J. (1982), *Interkulturelles Lernen in Begegnungen*, Saarbrücken: Verlag Breitenbach.

Freud, S. (1974), *Kulturtheoretische Schriften*, Frankfurt: S. Fischer Verlag.

Grove, C.L. (1980), 'Using international experiences to build global perspectives: student exchanges', *Global Perspectives*, May/June.

Grove, C. (1989), *Orientation Handbook for Youth Exchange Programs*, New York: Intercultural Press.

Grove, C. (1991), *A Rose by Any Other Name and Other Stories about Host Families*, New York: AFS Intercultural Programs.

Grove, N. and Hansel, B. (eds) (1981–7), *AFS Orientation Handbook*, Vols I–VI, New York: AFS Intercultural Programs.

Gstettner, P. (1993), Die multikulturelle Gesellschaft – ein neues Feindbild?, *Klagenfurter Universitätsreden*, **24**.

Gudjons, H. (1986), *Handlungsorientiertes Lehren und Lernen. Projektunterricht und Schüleraktivität*, Bad Heilbrunn: Klinkhardtverlag.

Gudykunst, W., Hammer, M. and Wiseman, R. (1977), 'An analysis of an integrated approach to cross-cultural training', *International Journal of Intercultural Relations*, **1**(2).

Hall, E. T. (1969), *The Hidden Dimension*, New York: Anchor Press/Doubleday.

Hall, E. T. (1973), *The Silent Language*, New York: Anchor Press/Doubleday.

Hall, E.T. (1977), *Beyond Culture*, New York: Anchor Press/Doubleday.

Hall, S. and Jefferson, T. (eds) (1975), *Resistance through Rituals*, London: Harper Collins Academic.

Hapgood, K. and Fennes, H. (eds) (1987), *Intercultural Learning Materials – a Tool for School Curricula*, Brussels: European Federation for Intercultural Learning.

Hart, M. (1992), *The European Dimension in General Primary and Secondary Education*, Alkmaar: Centre for International Education.

Heinrichs, H.-J. (1985), *Das Fremde Verstehen*, Frankfurt: Fischer Taschenbuch Verlag GmbH.

Herber, H. (1985), *Motivationsanalyse. Theorie und Praxis*, Sindelfingen: Expertverlag.

Hernandez, H. (1989), *Multicultural Education, a Teacher's Guide to Content and Process*, Columbus, OH: Merrill Publishing Company.

Hofstede, G. (1991), *Cultures and Organisations: Software of the Mind*, Maidenhead: McGraw-Hill.

Hohmann, M. and Reich, H. (eds) (1989), *Ein Europa für Mehrheiten und Minderheiten. Diskussionen um interkulturelle Erziehung*, Münster/New York: Waxmann Wissenschaft.

Høeg, P. (1994) *Miss Smilla's Feeling for Snow*, London: HarperCollins.

Hoopes, D. (1972–6), *Reading in Intercultural Communication, Vols 1–5*, Pittsburgh: ICN.

Hoopes, D. (1980), 'The self in cross-cultural experience', *The Bridge*, **5**.

Höper, C.-J. *et al.* (1974), *Die spielende Gruppe: 115 Vorschläge für soziales Lernen in Gruppen*, Wuppertal: Jugenddienst-Verlag.

Huth, M. (1988), *77 Fragen und Antworten zum Projektunterricht*, Hamburg: Arbeitsgruppe Obkircher Lehrmittel.

Jansen, M.J. (1981), 'Personal/group identity and cultural literacy or roots for world citizens', Lecture at the Colloquium Cultural Literacy and Intercultural Communication, Strasbourg.

Jones, C. and Kimberley, K. (1986), *Intercultural Education: Concept, Context, Curriculum Practice*, Strasbourg: Council of Europe.

Kristeva, J. (1990), *Fremde sind wir uns selbst*, Frankfurt/Main: Suhrkamp,

Larcher, D. (1991), *Fremde in der Nähe*, Klagenfurt: Drava.

Larcher, D. (1992), 'Didaktische Ideenskizze zur Thematik', *Informationen zur politischen Bildung*, **3**.

Larcher, D. (1992), *Kulturschock*, Italy: Alpha & Beta Verlag.

Larcher, D. (1993), *Das Kulturschockkonzept. Ein Rehabilitierungsversuch*, Klagenfurt: Institut für Interdisziplinäre Forschung und Fortbildung der Universitäten Innsbruck, Klagenfurt.

Larcher, D. *et al.* (1988), *Zweisprachigkeit und Identität*, Klagenfurt: Drava.

Leggewie, C. (1990), *MultiKulti*, Germany: Rotbuch Verlag.

Lévi-Strauss, C. (1955), *Tristes Tropiques*, Paris: Librairie Plon (Harmondsworth: Penguin, 1976).

Marfeka, M. (1990), *Vorurteile–Minderheiten–Diskriminierung*, Neuwied: Luchterhand.

Michaud, G. (1978), *Identités collectives et relations interculturelles*, Brussels: Editions Complex.

Modgil, S. *et al.* (eds) (1986), *Multicultural Education*, London: Falmer Press,

Müller, W. and Kosmale, J.-D. (1991), 'Materialbox international', *Kleine Schriften*, **4**.

Neumann, K. and Ochel, H. (eds) (1989), *Europäische Dreiländerseminare. Grenzüberschreitende Zusammenarbeit von Schulen in Europa*, Heidelberg: Edition Schindele.

Oberste-Lehn, H. and Wende, W. (eds) (1990), *Handbuch Internationale Jugendarbeit. Interkulterelles Lernen*, Düsseldorf: Der Kleine Verlag.

OECD (1987), *Multicultural Education*, Paris: Centre for Educational Research and Innovation (CERI), Organisation for Economic Co-operation and Development.

OCED (1987), *The Future of Migration*, Paris: Organisation for Economic Co-operation and Development.

Ostermann, A. and Nicklas, H. (1982), *Vorurteile und Feindbilder*, Munich: Urban und Schwarzenberg-Verlag.

Österreichischer Informationsdienst für Entwicklungspolitik (1991), Schulpartnerschaften und Projektunterricht, in *Dritte Welt im Unterricht*, Vienna: ÖIE.

Otten, H. and Treuheit, W. (1994), *Interkulturelles Lernen in Theorie und Praxis. Ein Handbuch für Jugendarbeit und Weiterbildung*, Opladen: Leske u. Budrich.

Patterson, O. (1975), 'Context and choice in ethnic allegiance: a theoretical framework and Caribbean case study', in N. Glazer and D. P. Moynihan (eds), *Ethnicity: Theory and Experience*, Cambridge, MA: Harvard University Press.

Perotti, A. (1994), *The Case for Intercultural Education*, Strasbourg: Council of Europe.

Phillips, C. (1993), *The European Tribe*, London: Picador.

Pusch, M. (ed.) (1979), *Multicultural Education. A Cross-cultural Training Approach*, Yarmouth, ME: Intercultural Press.

Rabenstein, R. and Reichel, R. (eds) (1990), *Das Methodenset*, Münster: Ökotopia.

Rademacher, H. and Wilhelm, M. (1991), *Spiele zum interkulturellen Lernen*, Berlin: Verlag für Wissenschaft und Bildung.

Ruffino, R. (1981), *Fifteen Case Studies in Youth Mobility*, Brussels: Commission of the European Communities.

Ruffino, R. (1987), 'Culture: Human Life Seen as a Continuum', Lecture at a seminar held at the European Youth Centre, Strasbourg.

Ruffino, R. (1992), 'Ways of achieving the objectives of youth mobility in the fields of education, culture, environmental protection and sports', European Steering Committee for Intergovernmental Co-operation in the Youth Field, Council of Europe, Strasbourg.

Sayler, W. (ed.) (1987), *Bausteine zur interkulturellen Erziehung*, Saarbrücken/Fort Lauderdale, FL: Verlag Breitenbach.

Scheuermann, E. (ed.) (1977), *Der Papalagi. Die Reden des Südsee-Häuptlings Tuiavii aus Tiavea*, Zürich: Tanner + Staehelin Verlag.

Schmid, K.H. (1990), *Handbuch zur Internationalen Schulischen Telekommunikation*, Vienna: Interkulturelles Zentrum.

Schmölz, I. (ed.) (1992), *Lust auf Sprache*, Vienna: Verband Österreichischer Volkshochschulen.

Schwäbisch, L. and Siems, M. (1974), *Anleitung zum sozialen Lernen für Paare, Gruppen und Erzieher*, Reinbek bei Hamburg: Rowohlt.

Schwarz, G. (1991), 'In verschiedenen Logiken denken', *Hernsteiner*, **4**.

Seelye, H. N. (1993), *Teaching Culture, Strategies for Intercultural Communication*, 3rd edn, Lincolnwood, IL: National Textbook Company.

Shennan, M. (1991), *Teaching about Europe*, London: Cassell.

Simon, S. B., Howe, L. W. and Kirschenbaum, H. (1978), *Values Clarification, a Handbook of Practical Strategies for Teachers and Students*, revised edition, New York: Hart Publishing Company.

Sturzebecher, K. (1973), 'Lernen', in W. Fuchs *et al.* (eds), *Lexikon der Soziologie*, Opladen: Rowohlt.

The Experiment in International Living (1983), *Your Experiment in International Living: A Guide and Workbook to Field Language Acquisition and Cultural Exploration*, Brattleboro, VT: The Experiment Press.

Thomas, A. (ed.) (1983), *Erforschung interkultureller Beziehungen: Forschungsansätze und Perspektiven*, ssip bulletin 51, Saarbrücken: Verlag Breitenbach.

Thomas, A. (ed.) (1984), *Interkultureller Personenaustausch in Forschung und Praxis*, ssip bulletin 54, Saarbrücken: Verlag Breitenbach.

Thomas, A. (1985), *Interkultureller Austausch als interkulturelles Handeln*, Saarbrücken: Verlag Breitenbach.

Thomas, A. (ed.) (1988) *Interkulturelles Lernen im Schüleraustausch*, Saarbrücken/Fort Lauderdale, FL: Verlag Breitenbach.

Thomas, A. (1990), 'Interkulturelle Kommunikation und kulturelle Identität', *Außerschulische Bildung*, 2.

Treuheit, W., Janssen, B. and Otten, H. (1990), *Bildung für Europa. Interkulturelles Lernen in Jugendbegegnungen*, Opladen: Leske u. Budrich.

Trompenaars, F. (1993), *Riding the Waves of Culture*, London: Economist Books.

Ulich, M., Oberhuemer, P. and Reidelhuber, A. (1987), *Der Fuchs geht um ... auch anderswo: ein multikulturelles Spiel- und Arbeitsbuch*, Weinheim/Basel: Beltz Verlag.

UNESCO (1987), Report of the Meeting of Governmental and Non-Governmental Officials Responsible for Youth Exchange, Expert Meeting by Intercultura, the Italian Government and UNESCO in Rome, June 1987, UNESCO Youth Division, Paris.

Vopel, K. (1992), *Interaktionsspiele für Kinder und Jugendliche*, Hamburg: ISKO Press.

Watzlawick, P. *et al.* (1967), *Pragmatics of Human Communication. A Study of Interactional Patterns, Pathologies, and Paradoxes*, New York: W.W. Norton & Company.

Yebio, B. (1982), 'Intercultural education: What? Why? How?', *Educational and Psychological Interactions*, **78**.

Index